'*My Palestine* portrays, with profound sympathy and knowledge, the courage of the long-suffering Palestinian people as they cope with the catastrophe that has befallen them. It is, above all, an intimate and moving account of the resourcefulness of the human spirit to endure.'
Abdulrazak Gurnah

'This autobiography offers a gripping account of the trajectory – from destitute refugee to writer, scholar, banker and public advocate – of an extraordinary individual, while at the same time illustrating the story of the Palestinian people. Politically astute and sensitive to the nuances of the Western societies in which he was educated and worked, Mohammad Tarbush describes living in a world where Palestinians did not exist, or existed only as the nemesis of Israelis, and his efforts to remedy this erasure and bias.'
Rashid Khalidi

'Far more than a memoir, Mohammad Tarbush's remarkable and courageous life, which he narrates with great lyricism, offers readers a keyhole through which to see the immense forces that created one nation by stealing another. While insisting on justice for the crimes of the ongoing *Nakba*, Tarbush's vision for a shared future – rooted in true equality for all people, from the river to the sea – feels at once inevitable and irresistible.'
Naomi Klein

'With righteous indignation, his heart thumping, but a fair mind, his reasoning untainted by hate, Mohammad Tarbush delineates the catastrophe that has befallen his people, starting with his own family, and articulates how there can be no way forward in the Middle East but through truth-telling, good faith, justice, and co-existence. This book is a work of necessity and hope. Read it and be wiser.'
Yann Martel

‘A fascinating story about a boy who follows his dreams against all odds. About good people along the way. About help, compassion and friendship. And about the power of belonging to a landscape, to one’s family and to the family of man. This autobiography teaches us that nothing can destroy the human spirit and that there are no weapons that can kill hope.’
Nurit Peled-Elhanan

‘A poignant account of one Palestinian’s life journey, from the dispossession of the *Nakba* to international recognition in exile and a life of activism in pursuit of Palestinian national rights. An unforgettable book.’
Eugene Rogan

‘Here is a book with a big heart. A personal as well as political history of Palestine, poignantly written and closely argued. It’s impossible to read this and continue to argue for the status quo.’
Arundhati Roy

‘The interplay of optimism and sorrow in this memoir is extraordinary. The story of Mohammad Tarbush is a story of Palestine, but also the story of a singular, remarkable Palestinian.’
Kamila Shamsie

‘This is a tale of resilience and perseverance, of an extraordinary man, beautifully rendered and replete with joy and hope.’
Raja Shehadeh

MY PALESTINE

MY PALESTINE

An Impossible Exile

MOHAMMAD TARBUSH

SPEAKING
TIGER

SPEAKING TIGER BOOKS LLP
125A, Shahpur Jat,
New Delhi–110049, India

First published in the UK by Haus Publishing, 2024
First published in India by Speaking Tiger Books, 2024

This edition published in arrangement with Haus Publishing,
4 Cinnamon Row, London SW11 3TW

The publishers are grateful to Akiva Eldar, David Gilmour and the estate of Edward Said for their kind permission to reproduce the excerpts on, respectively, pages 258–260, 260–261

Heizhaus image on page 75 by Roberto Herrett, courtesy of SuperStock.

For sale in South Asia only

ISBN: 978-93-5447-810-9

10 9 8 7 6 5 4 3 2 1

Typeset by MacGuru Ltd
Printed in India by Chaman Enterprises, New Delhi

Foreword

Nada Tarbush

I grew up mesmerised by my father's story. My most vivid memory from childhood is tugging at the seams of my father's shirt, begging him to answer my question: '*w baaden shu sar* – and then what happened?' He used to recount his story to me with so many cliffhangers. At the same time tragic, dramatic, amusing and inspiring, it was the story of a Palestinian refugee who, at the age of sixteen, with broken English learned at a UN refugee school, a handful of dollars and a small duffel bag containing a single change of clothes, walked out of the West Bank city of Jericho without the knowledge of his parents and threw himself into the unknown, determined to make a different life for himself, his family and his people. I knew nothing of Palestine at that age, and I didn't understand what a refugee was. All I knew was that my father had survived an epic adventure, and that he was my hero.

His story shaped me and my life choices, and I felt privileged and grateful to have grown up hearing him tell it. I began asking him to write it down so that others outside of our family might read his story and be equally inspired. Asking turned into nagging, and I was so persistent during the Covid-19 lockdowns that he finally gave in to my demands. '*Amrek yaba* – at your command, my daughter,' he said, and started to write. The minute he sat down to write, words flooded out onto the page. He could not stop. I would find him typing away until the early hours of the morning, taking short breaks to eat. It was as though the act of looking back at his life had unearthed a wellspring of memories that came bubbling to the surface and that he could no longer contain.

To my satisfaction, by the end of the pandemic the first draft of the manuscript was ready. Yet as fate would have it, time was not on his side and my father very sadly passed away in January 2022 before the editing of his manuscript was complete, his heart weakened by old age. There are not enough pages to describe the immeasurable sense of loss and grief I felt at the passing of my father. My only consolation was that I held in my hands a manuscript that he cherished and on which he had worked during the final years and days of his life. In trying to dampen the feeling of his absence, I felt a certain solace in dedicating my time to bringing to fruition this project, and I was pleased when Haus Publishing expressed a desire to take over where my father had left off and publish the book that you now hold in your hands. I am grateful that my father's last words to the world have been eternalised in this memoir.

The theme of this book is Palestine and its history, and the displacement and exile of its people. But it is, above all, a human story. Personal tragedy and national tragedy cannot be decoupled. And no one can fully grasp the seismic events that have transformed the Middle East over the past hundred years, including the gradual erasure of Palestine – or begin to consider solutions to the ongoing injustice faced by the Palestinian people – without first understanding the very real and transformative consequences of these events for ordinary Palestinians and their lives, identities and culture. Many people know about Palestine, but fewer know about the Palestinians themselves, who continue to experience prejudice and dehumanising portrayals in the Western media. My father's story makes the basic point that, like all people, the Palestinians are made of flesh and blood and their children feel the agony of pain as strongly as they enjoy the warmth of happiness.

His personal odyssey, against all odds, is also an inspiring account of how determination, modesty, the kindness of strangers, intellectual curiosity and vision can help overcome seemingly insurmountable obstacles. His journey from Palestine to Europe was filled with bumpy roads and any external onlooker would have deemed his plan to hitchhike from Jericho to Switzerland, inspired by a Swiss postcard featuring the Alps, to be veering on fantasy. His personal success conveys the message that with resilience and hard work nothing is impossible. Despite that, his exile *was* impossible – to him – because he could never leave Palestine behind. His attachment to his homeland was too strong and his identity as a Palestinian too endangered to ever forget or move on.

Throughout his years of exile, including during his high-level career in banking, the former refugee kid could never set aside his childhood family experiences: their relative prosperity as successful small-holding farmers; their expulsion from their property; their languishing in poverty as refugees; the hopeless future facing all the victims of a defeated, deprived and powerless Palestine. His work allowed him to rub shoulders with important figures in the worlds of global economics, politics and international affairs. So he decided, from his perch in the world of finance, to capitalise on the wide network of friends, contacts and connections he had built up with diplomats, politicians and the media. He used every opportunity he had to start a conversation with the Western public and explain the justice of the Palestinian people's cause, using the most prestigious platforms he could to deliver his message.

Until his death, Palestine was his beacon of light. It defined and guided every aspect of his life: what he thought about, what he wrote about, what he ate for breakfast, what he grew in his garden, what he loved most. When I visited my father at home in the French countryside, I would almost always find him in the garden, tending to the olive, fig and pomegranate trees he had planted as if they were his children. He wanted to recreate a mini-Palestine in exile, he said. Our conversation would then shift to whether I had drunk *maramiyeh* (wild sage) tea that morning and to him reminding me that it, and olive oil, must always form part of my daily diet, these staples of Palestine having a multitude of health benefits.

If my father's story has taught me one lesson, it would be *do not despair*. He lived by and embodied that motto. Nothing was unattainable, no situation desperate enough to throw up hands and give up. There was always a solution, always ease to be found after hardship. Despite the tragic story of his family and his people, he maintained a relentless and stubborn hope. It is this attitude that led him to believe, with unwavering conviction, that the Israeli occupation of Palestinian land will come to an end, that the Palestinian refugees will realise their legitimate right of return and that Israelis and Palestinians will live together in peace and prosperity as equals in a single state.

Given the events of and since 7 October 2023 in Israel–Palestine, this book is more relevant than ever, and perhaps it is down to fate's wisdom that it is being published only now. These tragic developments cannot be isolated from their historical and political context; they are the culmination of more than seven decades of history, which are duly analysed in this memoir. They show that the status quo is untenable and that it is high time, for the sake of peace for Palestinians and Israelis alike, for action to be taken – not only to end the current tragedy but also to finally address and resolve the root causes of recurrent crises and suffering. Namely, seventy-six years of Palestinian dispossession and subjugation, fifty-seven years of military occupation of Palestinian land, seventeen years of illegal blockading of Gaza and chronic impunity for violations of international law.

And change is possible. As the International Court of Justice prepares its ruling in South Africa v. Israel, in which Israel stands accused of committing the crime of genocide against the Palestinian population in Gaza, and an advisory opinion on the legal status of Israel's occupation of Palestinian land and decades-long denial of the Palestinian people's right to self-determination, the next few months and years will be instrumental in shaping the future of Palestine and Israel. These days have also seen an unprecedented rise in awareness worldwide of the Palestinian cause, marking a generational shift. Despite decades of frustration and defeat, a fast-growing movement of people advocating for the respect of universal principles of international law, accountability, human rights and justice for Palestinians gives cause for hope that the future will be more grounded in these principles, more just and more peaceful.

With eternal gratitude to my unconditionally loving old man, as he called himself, who imbued me with a passion for justice and for the Palestinian cause, I send this book into the world in the hope that my father's story will inspire readers just as it has inspired me, and that brighter days will shine upon his Palestine.

Geneva, March 2024

Acknowledgements

Nada Tarbush

When he finished the first draft of his manuscript my father approached Iradj Bagherzade, the founder of I.B. Tauris, a leading international publisher of books on the politics and history of the Middle East. Iradj had recently established a new publishing house, and felt that my father's book would make a big splash; he quickly agreed to be its editor and publisher.

After my father passed away, Iradj and I continued to work on his memoir. Propelled into the world of publishing for the very first time, I felt lost. Yet Iradj listened patiently and I was impressed by his warmth, generosity of spirit and incredible wit. He became a grandfather figure of sorts to me. In January 2023, one year after losing my father, Iradj too very sadly passed away, but his mark on my heart and the hearts of all who knew him lives on. He has left a legacy in the publishing world that will be remembered for many generations to come.

With heartfelt thanks to the publishing team at Haus, foremost Barbara Schwepcke and Harry Hall, to all the editors who worked on the book and contributed to making it a reality – Iradj Bagherzade, Elizabeth Stone, Stephanie Hale, Simon Smith and Ed Doxey – and to Cameron Ott. I am grateful for your immense talents and for your patience, support and kindness throughout.

Contents

Preface

This book is my story as a Palestinian refugee who has had to struggle for things most people take for granted, who did not accept that as a preordained destiny and who, through resilience, hard work and faith decided to do something about it. Already, as a teenage refugee in Jericho, I had dreamt about and aspired to a university education in Europe. That propelled me to plunge into a dark unknown with a handful of dollars and hitchhike to Europe to seek out a Swiss couple I had met in Jericho several years earlier for only a few hours as a twelve-year-old. With a mixture of providence and determination, I survived the journey, found my Swiss couple and later, against all odds, realised my ambition to pursue my education in Britain.

Subsequently, opportunities arose for me to work and lead as normal a life as most people in the developed world. But no university education nor all the trappings that came with lucrative jobs and a matching lifestyle could take away the grief related to my national identity.

*

I was born to Palestinian parents. Our way of life was steeped in Palestinian traditions. We ate Palestinian food, we spoke Arabic with a Palestinian accent, and the name of our village appears on very ancient maps of Palestine. Yet, during my travels in Europe as a teenager, I realised that Palestine had vanished from the map of the world, and my identity meant nothing to many of my European friends, acquaintances and colleagues.

Since my departure from the world of Palestine I have looked forward to writing my life story. When I finally sat down to write this book I found myself shifting between, of all things, pronouns – *I*, *we*, *our* and *they*. My efforts to avoid alternating from the first to the third person were futile. The personal narrative merged with the national history of the Palestinian people and at times the two became indistinguishable. Striking a balance between the two required discipline to prevent the narrative from being too autobiographical or veering too far towards history and politics.

Another challenge was finding an appropriate title, one that would capture my feelings and at the same time provide a framework to the narrative. Experiencing my life while Palestinian society was being torn apart, I needed a fitting title that would weave my story into the cataclysm that occurred for Palestinians in the 1940s and thereafter. That is why, together with my editors, I finally settled on the present title. This is indeed my story within the framework of my Palestine.

Painting by Monica Merlitti inspired by my life story

Introduction

This book starts with a vivid description of my family's exodus from Beit Nattif in 1948 and their lives as refugees, first in Bethlehem then Jericho, where I grew up and eventually went to school. Intuitively, from an early age, my motto in life was '*la tai'as*' (do not despair). With that mindset, as a child I started dreaming about going to Europe, where I could work and study at the same time.

The narrative then continues to describe my hitchhiking journey to Europe and my sojourn for about a year as a foreign worker in Italy and Switzerland, before saving enough money to make it to Britain where I started studying for my A levels with the aim of eventually going to university. Transforming that unrealistic ambition into reality entailed undertaking all kinds of manual jobs supplemented by imaginative schemes that enabled me to meet a king and a president and persuade them to subsidise the cost of my education.

But that was also the time when I felt overwhelmed by a rare sense of helplessness, even despair, at realising how little the British public and other Europeans knew or cared about the Palestinian people's plight. What was perhaps unique about the Palestinian tragedy was that we were not only expelled from our homeland under all sorts of pretexts – that went as far as divine postulations – but that the onus was on us to explain and prove our victimhood. More often than not, I was faced with the harsh reality in which we were viewed as villains out to undermine Israel's security. Discussions would then swiftly switch to the atrocities committed against European Jews, while the human catastrophe that was meted out to the Palestinians was nonchalantly dismissed and swept aside.

Naively, I assumed that the extent and severity of the Palestinian story would guarantee a measure of understanding, even empathy, for our plight. Alas, that was rarely the case. At times I felt choked, like someone being assaulted in his home who, when he manages to escape and run into the street, finds himself surrounded by a crowd gathered in response to the assailant's yelling and pleas for help who then beat and bind the real victim, denying him the chance to speak.

By a stroke of genius, the Zionist movement succeeded in conflating its modernist political ideology with ancient Judaism. (Imagine the power and outreach of a political movement that claimed to represent all Muslims or all Christians – and was recognised as doing so!) Given the tragic history of European Jewry, how could any sane person not sympathise with the Jews or with a movement that promised to build them a safe haven? Viewed from that prism, and notwithstanding the irony that nowadays Jews are safer anywhere in the world than in Israel, the Palestinian experience was blurred and could only be recognised and criticised by a small (now growing) informed minority.

While, through coercion, the Zionist movement set out to transform its settler-colonial ambitions into concrete reality, it simultaneously embarked on spinning the geographical reality of Palestine and its Palestinian population, their culture and traditions, into fiction, that they were interlopers and had no right to own or even inhabit the lands that had been theirs for centuries, if not millennia.

Very quickly the nascent Israeli state developed a formidable PR machine that systematically disseminated disinformation claiming the non-existence of the Palestinian people and the barrenness of historic Palestine. Modest attempts to nuance Israel's alleged miracles – for example, by showing that the flood of financial, economic, diplomatic and military aid it received, mostly from the USA, followed by Western Europe, would have been enough to elevate even a failed state to the top league of developing countries – were mocked or shouted down.

It was during the weeks preceding the June 1967 war that Israel's PR potency became clear to me. The widespread propaganda portraying brave little Israel about to be annihilated by a sea of Arabs was omnipresent and highly convincing. I did not escape being conditioned by all the hype claiming Israel's vulnerability, so much so that when the war actually broke out on 5 June and on that first day Israel incapacitated the air forces of its three surrounding Arab neighbours, I met the news with utter scepticism and needed a couple of days to digest its veracity.

Feeling barraged with, and oppressed by, the endless repetition of the brave-little-Israel message, I made strenuous efforts to explain and defend the Palestinian cause as soon as I could express myself in reasonable English. To be heard over the din of that orchestrated chorus was arduous and exhausting. When I succeeded in getting a word in edgeways, my humble efforts drew exaggerated applause. My first published letter in *The Times* (1972) asking those who were calling on the Soviet Union to allow Soviet Jews to emigrate to Israel to spare a thought for Palestinian refugees longing to return to their homes, was hailed by many readers, more for actually getting published than for its content.

Over the years the general apathy in the West towards the plight of the Palestinians finally began to change and a greater level of concern started to surface, but what has not been assimilated enough into the Western public psyche is the fundamental fact that, before the advent of Zionism, peaceful coexistence between Jews, Muslims and Christians had been the hallmark of life in historic Palestine, and, more generally, harmony prevailed between Jews and Muslims, be it in Arab-ruled Spain, North Africa or the Middle East. I strongly believe this attitude towards Judaism and the Jews in general to have remained largely intact, despite the propaganda campaigns which routinely shove Arabs in general, and Palestinians in particular, into the imbroglio of anti-Semitism.

Israel's relationship with Palestine should be seen in terms of occupier/occupied. Full stop. The same goes for criticism of the inconsistent application of international law and human-rights norms when it comes to Israel. It is a calling out of the policies of the Israeli state, nothing more. When Arab and predominantly Muslim Kuwait was invaded and occupied by neighbouring Arab and predominantly Muslim Iraq, a principled stance was taken against the occupation, and within less than five months an international military force, not seen since the Second World War, was mobilised to end that occupation. Yet the international community has never been as conscientious about Israel's decades-long occupation of the West Bank, including East Jerusalem, and Gaza.

Because Israel, the occupying power, was Jewish, Western media and public opinion, conditioned by a sense of guilt at the anti-Semitism which had produced such catastrophic consequences for the Jews in the West, were on the whole unable to look at Israel's actions with the degree of objectivity they readily applied when analysing other states' actions. So they found it difficult to regard Palestinians resisting a harsh military occupation, which denied them their basic human rights, as people attempting to preserve their rights, their property, their identity and their very existence as a people.

In my reflective moods I sometimes wonder what rationale, if any, lies behind the indifference and ease with which world powers, the supposed custodians of international and human-rights laws, discarded the Palestinian people and left them to perish by the wayside. For us, the Palestinians, what had befallen the Holy Land and its people was not a natural disaster. It was a manmade catastrophe – the *Nakba* – permitted and enabled by external powers.[1] Against their will the Palestinian people became a factor in US legislative, presidential and sometimes local elections. It is strange to see candidates one-upping one another in promising unconditional support to guarantee Israel's hegemony and security without a thought for the dispossessed natives and the region's ensuing insecurity. I also wonder why Britain never spent any time probing what had befallen the Palestinian people. For over a century now Palestinians have waited for successive British governments to indulge in some introspection and endeavour to confront the misery its policies unlocked in Palestine, leaving its people forlorn and defenceless. But my deepest thoughts go to Germany, which, in its desperate search for redemption after the near-permanent blackening of the word Germany by the Nazi experience, has for seven decades provided state-of-the-art armament and granted billions of dollars towards the construction of Israel with hardly a thought for the subsequent destruction of Palestine or its people, the accidental victims of Germany's crimes against the Jews. It's all very confusing, as Alice says in her Wonderland!

I have Ottoman deeds testifying my family's ownership of land with olive groves in Palestine dating back to 1802. We never sold that land, Britain had no right whatsoever to pass it on to anyone, and the Zionist movement had no right to claim it let alone to acquire it. This is a statement of law. It is no more anti-Israeli than anti-British, let alone anti-Jewish. We will continue revendicating those rights irrespective of the religious affiliation or ethnic origins of those negating them and regardless of what government there is in Tel Aviv, London, Washington, DC, Berlin or Brussels. To informed Israelis, and indeed Jews wherever they may live, the quest of Palestinians for equality and dignity will have a familiar ring.

☀

Finally, this book – for all its switching between first-person and third-person pronouns and its intimate interlacing between the personal and the national – is divided into three parts.

The first is about Beit Nattif, my birthplace, my childhood and schooling and my adventure travelling from Jericho to Europe. The second is about living and studying in the UK, where my identity as a Palestinian came to the fore and my conversation with the British public began through writing. The final part is about my professional life and freelance writings – mainly in *Le Monde*, the *International Herald Tribune* and the *Los Angeles Times*, commenting on major international events with a bearing on Palestine and the whole Middle East – in the context of attempts at peacemaking and the wars that ravaged the Middle East between 1990 and 2021.

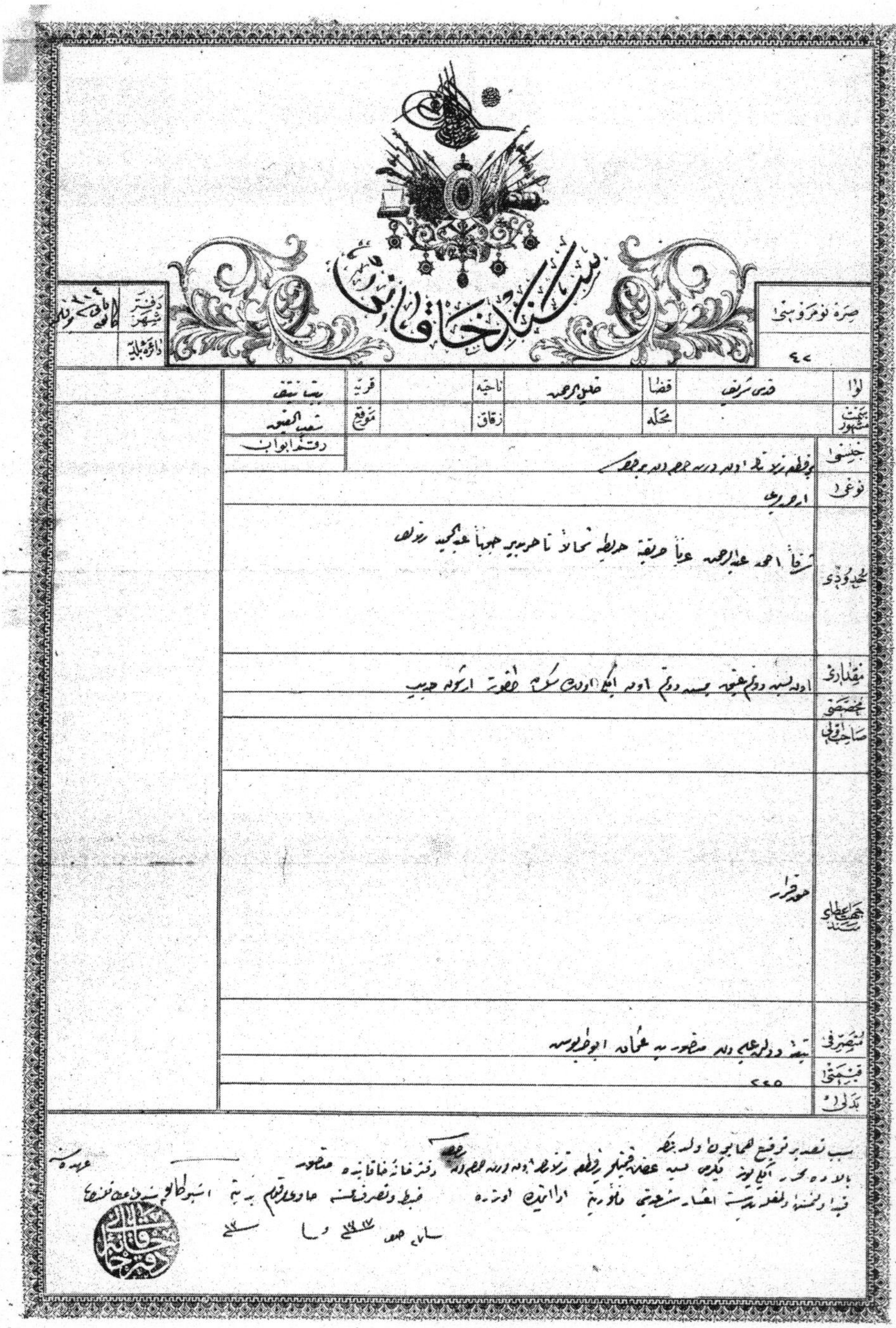

Ottoman land deeds belonging to my family dated 1802

I

Leaving Home: From Palestine to Europe

Beit Nattif from the ruins, 1999

1

The village where we come from in Palestine, Beit Nattif, was large enough to appear on maps of the country. I have often wondered what it is like for those Palestinians from a village so small that they do not even have the comfort of pointing a finger at it on a map, for whom the memory of it becomes a fading dream of a place that might never have existed.

Beit Nattif is derived from the Roman name Betholetepha. It lay on the north-western Hebron Hills about twenty kilometres west of Bethlehem, right in the heart of Palestine, exactly halfway between the Mediterranean coast and the Dead Sea, where the hills start to trail off into the rich plains that stretch out west to the Mediterranean. In 1596 it was part of the Jerusalem *liwā'* (district), with 572 inhabitants who cultivated wheat, barley, olives and a variety of fruit, reared goats and managed beehives. In Roman times Beit Nattif was the capital of a province. Ancient documents place it midway along the ancient road between Eleutheropolis (Beit Jibrin[1]) and Jerusalem.

The route to Beit Nattif from Bethlehem was a narrow road that twisted its way through the quiet cone-shaped hills encircled with terraces of white stone, where the vines clawed up through the dark, rust-red earth. Gradually the road started to descend into a wide valley filled with a lush greenness that included the 44,587 dunums (44.5 square kilometres) of land belonging to the village.

To reach the village the route continued up a twisting dirt road. From the hilltop the star-shaped village – with its scattered houses, school, mosque, some shops and wide streets – was clearly visible. In 1944 2,150 people lived there. Our house was on the north side, near a great mulberry tree, where our family lived with my grandparents. I myself would not appear until early 1948.[2] These descriptions and the events leading up to my family's exodus from Beit Nattif were recounted to me in meticulous detail by my brother Yousef as I became older, which is how I have managed to recollect them here.

Our house looked onto the farmyard where the chickens strutted and pecked ceaselessly and around which lived the sheep and goats in their pens and stables. Our relatives occupied the neighbouring houses, and the children were surrounded by affection and spoilt by many aunts. The houses were simple in design, cube-shaped, with shallow, domed roofs and arched doors and windows. They were ideally suited to the extremes of weather. To enter our house in summer was like plunging into a shaded well, so cool was the interior. Yet these houses were sturdy enough to withstand the worst batterings of winter, when raw winds often blew for days at a time, whistling through and fighting with the trees.

Winter was the time of storms, when the sky would suddenly darken and the animals became uneasy before a savage onslaught that might last for hours, thunder crashing through the hills and rattling the doors like loose teeth, while the whole sky lit up in spasms of naked pink. The children's mounting curiosity to rush out, dash up the hills and see what was rolling down from the sky onto the other side was always checked by flashes of lightning and by the roaring thunder that followed.

After the rain a gentle sky would emerge and the land looked as if it had been freshly painted, with everything glowing, and a lovely aroma would rise from the steaming earth. Snow often came in the winter, and it was not uncommon for us to be confined to the house for days on end. We welcomed the winter, for the rains and melting snow filled the wells with fresh supplies of water, and we kept warm enough in our snug house with olive branches crackling in the hearth, warming the house and enveloping it in a spicy perfume. Everybody would roast nuts, and the children would eat them still hot, singeing their impatient fingers.

The window of the room the boys shared with our grandfather looked down into the courtyard with its whitewashed walls and tiled floor. In one corner of the yard was the gate into the street; in the other was a specially built small shed where my older brother Yousef's goat was kept.

Yousef would go out early in the morning, the air still damp with the night, to rummage in the straw for eggs. The chickens would squawk, objecting to the intrusion as they squatted. He would then carefully place the warm, heavy eggs in a basket, feathers and straw still sticking to them, and run back to the house.

Everybody would wake before sunrise to the call of the imam. His voice swam into the house while my mother gently shook the children out of their dreams. They would eventually stumble out of their bedding on the floor, while the adults of the family were already at prayer, kneeling and performing the ritual movements on their prayer mats.

After prayers came milking. One or other of the children usually helped, lifting the latch to open the door for the others and running over the farmyard to the stables. Only after the animals had been cleaned out, the milking completed and the eggs gathered in, did everybody sit down to breakfast. The diet was simple and organic, and all food was home-produced: there was yoghurt and soft cheese, thyme, olive oil, plump olives and various kinds of vegetables and fruit.

Anything that needed baking was cooked in the *taboun*, a small outhouse where much of the floor consisted of a circular cover concealing a pebble-lined chamber where flattened dough or earthenware pots of food were laid. The cover was then replaced and a fire lit over it. Bread from the *taboun* was always dimpled from lying on pebbles and had an especially delicious taste, aroma and texture. My mother and grandmother used to gossip away happily as they baked the bread, shooing the children out of the way when they tried to snatch chunks off those crisp loaves as they emerged, hot and golden. The floor of the *taboun* became covered with powdery white ash and had to be swept out frequently. By the time breakfast was finished the village would be coming to life, and the hubbub of movement and voices would start to echo in the streets.

The village was an integrated place. Our ancestors had lived there for centuries. Beit Nattif is identified with Tappauch in the Old Testament, Joshua 15:34.[3] Marriages from within the village were the unwritten rule. The village functioned as if it were one big family, with all that entails: a cocktail of love, affection, solidarity, rivalry and jealousy.

As they grew older the children's interests started to extend outside the home, and the age of friendships began, at first with single acquaintances and later in groups of children of similar ages. They would race through the winding streets, up the narrow flights of steps that in places formed the pathway between houses, playing hide-and-seek, picking and gobbling up figs and green almonds as they moved.

Amid all the enjoyment of these games, there was, of course, school. Under the late period of Ottoman rule, education had been neglected. Learning Turkish at school instead of Arabic became compulsory, and people living within the Arab provinces of the empire – where literacy was already low – became less inclined to send their children to school.

Grandfather was much in demand to read out loud from the newspapers people brought back from Jerusalem, and men used to sit around him cross-legged and hushed while he read. On other occasions he would recite classical poetry, and the sound of the words in his deep, resonant voice would send many a shiver through some of the listeners. There was a poem about a blind boy that he recited regularly:

O, My Mother!
What is the shape of the sky?
And, what is light?
And, what is the moon?
You people talk about its beauty
Yet I see no trace of it
Is this world filled with never-ending darkness?[4]

Members of the audience would often be reduced to tears by his recitation. Some would close their eyes and sway gently in their places, softly chorusing '*Ya salam*. How beautiful.'

As late as 1940 there was no paved road connecting Beit Nattif with the neighbouring towns. The villagers were keen to expand their markets to Jerusalem, Bethlehem, Hebron and Jaffa. Beit Nattif was only a kilometre away from the main Bethlehem–Jaffa road, so creating a link with the outside world was no great problem once the benefits became clear. Work started in the summer of 1940 to pave the stretch of bumpy road connecting the village to that highway.

The months of labour to realise these projects were rewarded the day the first bus made its way cautiously up the slope to Beit Nattif, with people lining the route and running alongside. The vehicle snorted to a halt outside the school and stood there, throbbing. The noise and the big wheels were alarming to some, but everyone was swept away by the event. The first bus trip to Jerusalem followed soon thereafter. People scrambled to find seats. The bus was completely full that day, and many had to be turned away disappointed. The bus started to roar to life, and a shower of dust sprinkled against the windows as it moved off, its creaky body jolting from side to side. Villagers ran behind the roaring beast, then fell back waving vigorously. Mothers held their children tight as they wriggled and writhed, trying to stare out of the dusty windows. The countryside fell away so fast it seemed the bus was out of control. Then it would slow gradually to turn corners and speed up again down the next smooth stretch. The eager passengers craned to identify their homes, fast receding behind them, while children switched their gaze from one side of the bus to the other in order not to miss anything. We pounded around bends and swept up slopes, past dwellings from which people would rush out onto the road to wave. All too soon Jerusalem appeared in the distance. The children wished that bus journey could go on forever. Once in the city the bus disgorged its passengers, many of whom were going to see relatives. They carried with them baskets filled with fruit, eggs, olives and vegetables, even live chickens.

Jerusalem was a place of endless excitement. There, in the old city enclosed by those magnificent pale golden walls, life was concentrated, bursting through the narrow streets, a ceaseless throbbing as people yelled, sang, moaned, laughed. The streets were lined with small, mysterious shops and workshops, each with its own characteristic smell. The whole range of traditional crafts was on offer and men could be seen beating metal, sawing wood among shavings piled thickly on the floor, stitching leather, working at the looms, and repairing shoes while customers sat on stools, sipping tea or coffee. The city was a maze of narrow, bewilderingly similar pedestrian-only streets and alleyways. All humanity was represented in Jerusalem. Among the crowd were *fellahin* in their Turkish *gumbaz* caps; Bedouins in robes, some wearing the abaya; townspeople in suits and red fezzes, looking staid; villagers, who, like the Beit Nattif group, had come in from the surrounding settlements, the embroidery of the women's dresses proclaiming their origins; Greek Orthodox priests with wonderful beards and tall hats, who looked so solemn.

And, of course, there were the British soldiers dressed in khaki shorts and shirts, with officers in peaked caps and the rest in berets. Their faces were often red and peeling, their noses in tatters. Sometimes one or two would venture to be friendly with the Arab shopkeepers, speaking the standard Arabic phrases with a stiff accent, appearing to be self-conscious. Although the shopkeepers might invite them to sit and drink coffee with them, people generally talked about the British with resentment. In the late 1940s an increasing number of stern-looking British soldiers in helmets would be seen patrolling Jerusalem's alleyways. My brother Yousef, who was about eight years old then, described later in life the atmosphere and feel of Jerusalem at that time. During the British Mandate he did not have the slightest interest in the reasons for the resentment the grown-ups felt or even any understanding of what they were talking about. He was occupied with playing and the excitement of day-to-day living.

My father had many friends in Jerusalem. It would have been quite possible for him to spend all day going from one shop to another with different shopkeepers insisting that he sit with them. Some would draw out a stool while a runner was sent to a nearby café with a brass tray to bring back steaming little cups of thick, black coffee.

For Yousef and his friends there was a secret Jerusalem, too. Slipping through a narrow door they would enter a low, dark passage and suddenly find themselves in a quiet courtyard away from all the noise of the souk. Steps led from the courtyard to the houses on the upper level. They would walk to the edge of their arched roofs and look onto the street below, feeling pleasantly giddy, the rooftops, domes and minarets of Jerusalem suddenly thrust close. And, inevitably, this would be followed by shrieks from their mothers, 'Come down. *Yalla*! Let's go!'

Then there were the spice shops with the coloured powders spilling out from gaping sacks, discharging a mixture of sharp and musty aromas, which, when breathed deeply, could cause fits of violent sneezing.

No visit to Jerusalem would be complete without praying at one of the great mosques. During Eid, prayer was the main purpose of making the journey to Jerusalem. The holy places were in spacious surroundings with trees and people strolling around in a solemn manner. The slow walk up the steps towards the Dome of the Rock and Haram al-Sharif felt timeless and created a sense of serenity for young and old. The complexity and colour of it all, and the immense golden dome shining brilliantly in the sunlight, produced a dream-like atmosphere. In the middle was the sacred rock itself, its surface rough and undulating, contrasting with the precision of the design and decoration of the ceiling, and reputed to be the stone on which Abraham was about to sacrifice his son Isaac to demonstrate his commitment to God before God intervened to stop him.

Once inside the Haram al-Sharif, cool air would envelop worshippers as they padded in noiselessly and barefoot over those endless overlapping carpets, each one of a slightly different design or colour. The mosque was a world of dignity and reverence that managed to silence even the most boisterous of children. The one visit to Jerusalem that stood out for Yousef was the last visit of that carefree period in his life – in April 1948, when he was about nine years old. On that visit, the old city's noise and activity had vanished, many shops were closed and the few shopkeepers who were still around talked to our father in whispers. The visit was cut short, and my family and the other villagers made a silent journey back home with the parents looking dejected and withdrawn, talking to one another in hushed tones. When they looked at the children they managed to force smiles, which even to the children's young eyes seemed false.

The following day the downcast looks and the doleful expressions continued. A sullen atmosphere hung heavily at home. The children could not understand why they could no longer play hide-and-seek with the others. They too suddenly vanished from the orchards where everyone used to play. Beit Nattif's hustle and bustle was replaced by an ominous silence, and bus journeys to Jerusalem came to a standstill. The grown-ups' answer to any question about the next trip they'd be taking to Jerusalem had become a vacant gaze, followed by '*Inshallah*, God willing, soon, *habibi*.' Years later they explained that on that last trip they had learnt about a massacre at Deir Yassin that had wiped out a third of the village's population. The words Deir Yassin became the key to a nightmare, the pivot around which my family's life would thereafter revolve. Those two words came to be wept over, whispered fearfully and shrouded people's faces with grief. The whole village reeled with shock and fear.

Up to this point the children had no knowledge and paid little attention to all the grown-up talk of getting rid of the British, the Jewish migrations to Palestine, a Zionist movement that wanted the creation of a Jewish state in Palestine or the United Nations (UN) Partition Plan for Palestine. But now things seemed to have changed. Zionists were fighting Palestinians, Palestinians were fighting Zionists, neighbouring Arab countries were sending troops to help the Palestinians, but those troops weren't actually doing much. Meanwhile, more and more Palestinians were having to flee their homes and their lands and become refugees. Eventually, to stop the fighting and the killings (most fatalities were Palestinians) and arrive at some sort of compromise solution, the

UN voted for the Partition Plan in November 1947, which divided Palestine between Jews and Palestinians, giving the Jewish population – who comprised less than a third of the total population and owned less than 7 per cent of the land – 55.5 per cent of the country,[5] including large swathes of the choice agricultural areas and practically exclusive access to the Mediterranean Sea and the two ports of Jaffa and Haifa. This 'compromise' was deemed by the Palestinians to be unjust, and the fighting continued, with the Zionists taking over even more Palestinian property. In the original 1947 UN Partition Plan our village, Beit Nattif, was in an area allocated to the Palestinians, but a few months later it was captured by the Zionist Harel Brigade.

Because of its strategic location on the highway linking Bethlehem to the Mediterranean coast, the area of Beit Nattif was the scene of fierce fighting until the signing of the Armistice Agreements in April 1949. Israel refused to sign those agreements unless it could keep half of the areas allocated by the 1947 Partition Plan to the Palestinians on top of the 55.5 per cent of Palestine already allocated to the Jewish population.[6] This, broadly speaking, meant the Zionists insisted on keeping whatever they had captured between the November 1947 UN Partition Plan and the April 1949 armistice, so Israel would control over 78 per cent of Palestine.

In *The History of the Haganah* – the Haganah were the Zionist paramilitary force that took on the British and fought against the Palestinians and eventually morphed into the Israeli Defense Forces (IDF) – Beit Nattif is referred to as 'the village of the murderers of the thirty-five', in reference to the thirty-five Israeli soldiers who were killed there.[7] They were later honoured by naming one of the four kibbutzim Israel built there after them: Netiv ha-Lamed-He.

As the war raged on and news of more massacres were circulated, families were panic-stricken. Impulsively, they grabbed a few things and started to leave the village in fear, walking in the direction of Bethlehem. Hastily, my family, too, gathered together a few blankets, a little food, and were then swept up in the mass of people marching quietly down the hill.

Road sign to Netiv ha-Lamed-He

A few of the men refused to leave, insisting on staying to look after the houses and the cattle. Some of them were armed with a few antiquated rifles dating back to the First World War. 'Arab armies are coming in to protect us,' they kept repeating. 'Stay safe in Bethlehem, and in a week or two we will be reunited again.' Some were later reunited – in refugee camps.

The landmarks where the children had played with friends had lost their significance, standing drab and dead. The slopes that had formed slides, where the clattering of the loose pebbles used to mingle with their shrieks of delight, had fallen silent, and the path they would scramble up breathless with laughter, racing one another, was now an impediment.

Before, fear, for the children, had been something they would relish – a thrill of excitement listening to some of Grandfather's outlandish stories, a groping in the dark that was almost an indulgence – but this present incapacitating fright was no child's fear to be dispelled by a mother's soothing, reassuring smiles. This was now the painful knot of a stomach contracting, which signalled the recognition of an existential threat.

'We must go on as quickly as we can,' was the mantra for

young and old. Goats clambered across the rocks beside the silent moving mass until they realised they were no longer needed and were left staring after the departing crowd like bored elderly people. Grandfather's breathing was laboured, his soft old face contorted with exertion. It seemed impossible that he would be able to make it up the slope.

The village lingered beneath them as they followed the winding upward path. Then it was swallowed up behind them, and they were alone up the hillside. For such a large crowd they were notably silent. The only sound was that of crying babies and the elderly ladies rapidly murmuring prayers. Grandmother was shaking violently, her hands stiff like big claws as she held onto one of the younger children. Yousef hugged the bundle of rugs that had been assigned to him, as much to comfort himself as to carry some useful items.

Night was creeping up on the evening. It would soon be dark with that very sudden disappearance of the sun that signifies day's end in Palestine. And the crowd went on, clutching their meagre bundles of belongings. Perhaps 'they' were after us now, everybody was silently thinking; maybe lying in wait among the hills stretching ahead. Who were they, these people who wanted to take the land? All who were on that journey that evening were filled with dread and confusion. The path became indistinct, but soon they could hear the tinkle of the spring that gushed from its hiding places between the rocks. Here, they paused, then some picked their way carefully over the boulders, kneeling at the gurgling source and refilling their flasks.

There was a half-moon that night, and they continued through the darkness on the hillside track to Bethlehem. Young children fell asleep and were carried. Each person in the group was fearful of every noise. Were they the movements of invisible hands clutching their daggers and poised to strike, have they surrounded us?

Grandmother kept stopping and whispering in a quavering voice, 'What's that?' But all that could be heard was the shuffle of the others' footsteps. Some distance away a fire could be seen, its size impossible to estimate. Tongues of orange flame leapt into the darkness, but their source could not be known.

The dense crowd of villagers had thinned out along the path, and our family was now at the end of the procession because Grandfather's progress was so painfully slow. He kept pausing for breath and frequently had to be helped over the numerous small obstacles. His breathing was growing fainter and shallower. There was a sound as Mother opened the flask, and he jerked as she splashed his face with water.

In agony from his swollen joints, he begged, 'You must leave me here. I am only holding you back.' It was not for another two hours that we could get him up to carry on.

Later, as we carried Grandfather along he moaned, 'Oh, I should have stayed in Beit Nattif.'

'We are nearly in Bethlehem now,' said Mother, trying to encourage him.

Nobody had given any thought to the state in which they would find Bethlehem. Their only concern had been to escape, and they were not prepared for the chaos that had swamped the formerly quiet town. The streets were spilling over with others who had been forced to abandon their villages and flee to safety. In this press of unkempt and weary-looking people, our family was swallowed up and jostled by the surging crowd from all directions. Two men were arguing in loud voices about what should be done now, and others gathered around and joined in. From all around came shouting, names were urgently called – it was easy to get lost in the mass of people thronging the streets.

Our family struggled through the crowd to join others from Beit Nattif, who were standing around looking confused. In normal times, as a village elder, Grandfather's advice and help would have been sought, but now he had collapsed on the pavement after swaying slowly back and forth while Grandmother peeled a discarded newspaper from the gutter and tried desperately to fan his face. His eyes screwed up, he raised his head, barely seeming to recognise us, gaping around him in bewilderment. Then his eyes closed and he sank into a heap, a film of sweat glistening on his face. People gathered around staring as Grandmother pinched his cheek, and we tried to lift his sagging body.

My brother Yousef kept reciting:

O, My Mother!
What is the shape of the sky?
And, what is light?
And, what is the moon?
You people talk about its beauty
Yet I see no trace of it
Is this world filled with never-ending darkness?

Then suddenly the voice of a man rang out. 'Quick, bring him to my house!' he shouted, then helped us carry Grandfather's alarmingly dead weight to his home nearby. The dark interior seemed to be as full of people as the street outside. Those sitting and standing stared as Grandfather was laid on the floor. Grandmother crouched beside him whispering his name repeatedly, shaking him gently.

'Is the man dead?' a little boy asked, wide-eyed. Slowly Grandfather came round, but could only lie there, his eyes expressionless.

The man started to talk about where we could stay. He had taken in many relatives and friends and had no more room himself. All the mosques, churches and schools had opened their doors to those who had fled and had long been full, but he said he had a friend, a schoolmaster, who, because of Grandfather's condition, might be able to make some space.

Our family traipsed over to the school hall to squeeze into the crowd already occupying the place. The schoolroom was choked with refugees surrounded by the few possessions they had managed to salvage. As they entered, the smell and heat of the room was overwhelming. It was the smell of people thrust together in a small space day after day with no proper washing or toilet facilities; it was a smell with which they all had to live. Several people fell sick. All were suffering from physical conditions. No one could keep clean with the shortage of water, and this, combined with the meagre diet, caused rashes and sores that refused to heal.

Our family huddled together in a corner and it was then, Yousef remembers, that the nightmare began to envelop him. 'As I gazed, stunned, around the room,' he recalls, 'I could only think, "What's happened to Father?" I remember Mother placing a piece of bread she had brought from home into my hand. I forced myself to eat, but the bread stuck in my throat, and I could hardly swallow. How long would we have to stay in this place? I wanted to stand up, to shout, "I want to go home. Now!" Grandmother was sitting with her hand shielding her eyes, weeping quietly, and tears caught at my throat, too.'

That night the schoolroom was noisy with the crying of babies and the constant sounds of people whispering and moving. 'My eyes were open wide in the dark,' recalls Yousef, 'and warm tears flowed across my face, trickling down around my ears. The familiarity of the blankets from home increased my sadness, and I buried my face in them. Dear God, please let Father arrive tomorrow to take us back home. But my stomach lurched when I thought of home, of what might have happened to Father.'

The next day was spent sitting, waiting, in the schoolroom. Many had slept overnight in the open or sheltered in caves. At one point during the day, word went around that food would be arriving shortly. By the time the food arrived, there was already a jostling, shouting mass of people, alarmingly rough in their desperation for food. Previously people in the village had entertained one another with graciousness and hospitality as they followed their traditional customs. Now, as they stood in line, they became ferocious in their pursuit of some dry bread and a little boiled wheat. Water was scarce, and its supply was unpredictable. The days that followed were much like the first, except that sometimes food supplies ran out altogether. Most of the time people just sat. Among our family members, hope for Father's return gradually began to evaporate. Many families had been split up by the fighting and faced the same uncertain wait as ourselves.

Mother became obsessed with the idea that Father might arrive in town and not be able to locate us. Each day she paced the streets with Yousef, searching the crowd. There were many false alarms. Yousef would approach many men who resembled Father with quickening steps only to find it was another cruel deception.

And still, no one knew for sure what had become of Beit Nattif and the men left behind there. Everyone hoped that they had either managed to hold out or that their deep knowledge of the countryside, its hidden trails and lairs, had allowed them to escape. And the days dragged through a tunnel of despair. Mother was seized with restless anxiety, unable to sleep at night, her eyes oddly transfixed in the daytime, constantly peering into the distance.

After the ordeal of the journey to Bethlehem Grandfather recovered a kind of determined energy that would flare up at times. Almost recovering his old spirit, he would wander off, confident that this time he would get to the truth, would find out for sure when we would be allowed back to Beit Nattif. A figure of nobility back home, here he was merely another shuffling old man, liable to be knocked and jostled in the crush.

'Let's go back, Granddad,' Yousef would whisper when he took him along.

'No, I am going to find out what's happening,' he would reply before stubbornly advancing on those trying desperately to bring some relief and order to the refugees, like someone expecting to be revered. Yousef could see that they saw him as a nuisance, constantly demanding they give him answers they did not have. '*Inshallah*, you will return home soon, haji,' was the stock answer. Back at the school, it was then everyone else's turn to ask him for answers *he* did not have.

Grandfather could not bear our existence in Bethlehem. He was not able merely to sit and brood. He was convinced there must be something he could do to change the situation. And he fell ill again, suffering a chronic weariness and succumbing to frequent shivering fits. Many were ill like this, not seeking medical help, for there was none, and, besides, what medicine could heal the trauma they were suffering?

This state of limbo was broken abruptly by the arrival of survivors from the village. The men were hardly recognisable. Now they had become strange, gaunt figures who appeared distracted. People from Beit Nattif swarmed around them clamouring to know what had happened, frantic for news. Quietly and grimly they spoke. They said that some villagers had been killed in the fighting when the Zionists attacked the village. Women became hysterical, tearing at their clothes as they heard that their husbands or sons had been among those who had fallen. But, as to what had happened to Father, they had no news. They had run out of ammunition and had to flee the village. They tried to encourage Mother, but their eyes betrayed their doubts that Father was still alive.

Grandmother took one of them aside and appealed to him, her aged hands rapidly clenching and unclenching. 'May God bless you, for your children's sake, tell us the truth,' she pleaded, staring into the man's eyes. 'Where is my son? Is he still alive?' she continued, whispering. She peered into his face as if trying to penetrate something concealed there. And helplessly he looked down at her, placing a hand gently on her shoulder.

Back in the schoolroom, my family flopped listlessly in their corner, drained of the hope that had somehow kept them uplifted ever since they had arrived in Bethlehem. A half-naked child tottered among the people in the room, perhaps an orphan, maybe the child of one of the sick mothers. Some women lay with their faces constantly covered, barely stirring, too tired even to cry any more.

Slowly it was dawning on people that they would have to move elsewhere to look for less crowded places in which to hold out until they were able to return home. The facilities in Bethlehem had been dwindling even before they had arrived. The first wave of refugees following the Deir Yassin massacre had already filled all the emergency shelters. But people showed great reluctance to move further from their villages. To move on would be to acknowledge a psychological defeat, would be an admission that the wait to go home was suspended or would be seen as an acceptance that they would have to settle somewhere that was not their home.

There were rumours about people, unable to stand the waiting and the uncertainty any longer, who had taken their destiny into their own hands and had risked returning, only to be killed or wounded by the Zionist forces occupying their villages. A handful of those making such a trip had returned to safety afterwards. They spoke of their village turned to rubble, with only a few shattered walls still standing and door and window frames protruding from the heaps of rubble, with goats running wild. Others who survived the venture of returning, particularly to bigger towns, spoke of deserted houses, some perhaps with a half-finished meal on the table, and the disorder of a hasty escape apparent.

News of Zionist victories became widespread, quashing any hope for a quick return. They were accompanied by talk of better shelter elsewhere. Mother sighed deeply and looked into the distance when two volunteers tried to convince her to move to Jericho, thirty kilometres east of Bethlehem. Jericho was only seven kilometres from the border with Jordan. After the 1949 armistice and Israel's imposed sovereignty over 78 per cent of Palestine, the Gaza Strip (1.3 per cent of Palestine's area) fell under Egyptian sovereignty, and the remaining 20.73 per cent – including Jericho, East Jerusalem, Hebron, Nablus, Ramallah and Bethlehem – fell under Jordanian sovereignty, becoming known as the West Bank.

The volunteers' efforts to persuade my family to leave Bethlehem were met with hesitation. 'What if Father were to arrive and was unable to find us here?'

They looked embarrassed. Maybe they knew he was dead. Trying to comfort Mother, they added that there would be a register soon. 'He will be able to trace you.'

Mother stared ahead. She felt trapped. Grandfather was confused when our family started to pack up its few possessions, then his face lit up. 'Are we going back to Beit Nattif?' he asked like a child. And Mother turned away, laughing nervously.

2

If my family had thought that by moving away we would be able to shake off the hardship that had beset us since leaving Beit Nattif, we were mistaken. The overcrowding and misery were not confined to that sojourn in Bethlehem.

We were lucky to get a lift in a truck to Jericho. The sight of families trudging slowly along the roadside, carrying a few bundles, was by now all too familiar. Sometimes a figure could be seen prone in the dust – it was impossible to tell whether it was death or exhaustion that had won. Whole families crouched despairingly by the roadside. The truck was overloaded with people all trying to escape the same hardship our family had endured in the two years since leaving Beit Nattif. We were all hopeful that by the time the truck came to a halt we would be in a place where fate would treat us a little more kindly. But, on reaching Jericho, we found more of the same.

Arriving there in summer 1950, we found ourselves transplanted into overcrowded streets. Peoples' faces bore the same sad and resigned expressions, and it quickly became obvious that there was nowhere to stay. The stories of accommodation that had drawn people here must have been out of date or vastly exaggerated. People said it was pointless to search for rooms and that it was best to join a queue for tents. Most of the day was spent waiting under the scorching sun. Only by nightfall was a tent finally erected on the stony soil where my family sat waiting.

Although not far from Beit Nattif and neighbouring villages, Jericho lay 240 metres below sea level, a sudden oasis in the flat brown plain of the Jordan Valley just before the river meets the Dead Sea. On that naked plain the sun beat mercilessly, making the temperature far higher than that to which the people from our part of Palestine were accustomed. During the summer days in Jericho, the swollen sun seemed to hover just overhead, hunting us and the new arrivals relentlessly, pounding the earth with intense heat. The sky became a vast reflector: it was impossible to look upwards into the blinding air. The trees stood upright and immobile; nothing stirred day after day. In that heat, Grandfather's health deteriorated. He would complain how cold he was, shivering while others tried to warm him. His eyes were glazed over and he mumbled, worrying about the jobs that must be done in Beit Nattif.

After a few days in the camp he fell into a delirium, tossing from side to side, his teeth chattering. Fearfully, all the family watched – Grandmother sat beside him, cradling his head and holding his hand, breathing words of comfort. Suddenly he sat upright, his eyes opened wide, and said in a hoarse but steady voice, 'Do you remember that olive tree, the one in the west corner of our orchard? I want to be buried there.' Groaning, he lay back once more and became calmer, his bloodshot eyes ceasing to roll and now closing. Grandmother kept calling his name, but his eyelids only flickered momentarily. Then she drew her headdress over her face and sobbed into it noiselessly to the faint background sounds of Grandfather's soft, rasping breaths.

My mother poured a little precious water into a glass, and they sprinkled it sparingly on his face at intervals when he might murmur gently. Grandfather's breathing became shallower, noiseless, and Grandmother suddenly raised her frightened face to Mother, whispering, 'Feel.' Mother's face trembled and split into a gasping cry. Tears erupted from her shaking body. Grandmother looked at her, pale.

'Call the neighbours, call anybody!' Grandmother cried, before collapsing in tears over Grandfather's body. They wept and howled, then Yousef threw himself at Mother, sobbing. He started to shake Grandfather, calling out his name. His waxy face lay limp at an odd angle, cold under Yousef's frantic embrace.

They came to take him away – kind but detached. They lifted his body onto a stretcher, struggling with it a bit. Grandmother wept quietly, repeating over and over that he wanted to be buried in Beit Nattif. Outside an anxious crowd peered in through the narrow opening of the tent. 'It was like being lost in the ocean,' said Yousef many years later. 'At any moment we could be swept under, and who would know or care?' My family huddled in the tent with our grief, cut adrift from home and rootless. We knew that no prayer would bring Grandfather back to life.

Nevertheless, my family was determined to keep the door to our past life open. This was the only way to cope with the misery, with the human wasteland spreading around. Every day new people arrived, stunned as my family had been, incredulously asking the same questions about work, shelter and when they would be allowed to return. My family clung to the hope that Father might still be alive. Each day they scoured the trucks arriving with new refugees, hoping that he would be among the travellers.

The air rose hazily from the scorching earth that was Jericho. Persistently, the sun rose all too early, demanding attention for another day. The tent became an oven, the air within static and solidly hot. And the insects! The children's legs were covered in red sores that festered and oozed, causing thick crusts to form. As soon as one batch was recovering, a fresh set of bites arrived as vicious replacements. 'Stop scratching!' Mother would yell at Yousef and the other children. Yousef went behind the tent so she could not see him and scratched and scratched until he drew blood. He and everybody else lived in perpetual fear of the scorpions and snakes that inhabited these parts. He lay awake at night listening for the tell-tale rustle and started to have nightmares, waking to find he was screaming. Grandmother often cried out in her sleep, waking the others.

'Yousef, Yousef! Look – there. Can you see?' my mother was yelling at my brother one day. Lazily he followed her pointing finger. There, engaged in conversation, was a figure wearing a *kufiyah*, the traditional Palestinian headdress, a figure resembling Father in height and profile. Hesitantly mother and son approached, gripping each other's hands, prepared for yet another disappointment. The man caught sight of the advancing pair, broke through the crowd around him and with a frozen expression stared motionlessly in their direction. Suddenly they were running into his arms. Tears shone in his eyes, and his voice was hoarse as one by one he embraced us. Mother raised her face to him, tears running down her cheeks. 'He wanted to be buried in Beit Nattif,' was all she could say. He said nothing. Suddenly, silence became the most powerful expression. My family was alarmed by his appearance: his lean face, bearded and burnt dark, seemed to be all sinew with an almost wild look. It was Father, yet much changed. When he walked, it was with a heavy limp. After the fighting he had escaped with our neighbour who had been wounded. Somehow they had reached a cave, and there his friend had sunk into delirium as Father watched helplessly. Soon he died. Father's leg wound had become infected and he lay in a fever for days before managing to drag himself through the occupied countryside like a wounded animal, walking at night.

Yousef in particular had imagined that if they found Father again normal family life would magically be restored. He, like everyone else, now saw that Father was in the same desperate situation as all of us. Father, too, looked distant and seemed to harbour a sense of defeat and shame. What could he do? He pinched the children's cheeks, including mine – his now two-or-three-year-old Mohammad – trying to make us laugh, but Yousef could only raise a weak smile. Grimly Father described the fighting in the village in a flat, tired voice. He told of those who had been killed, how they were outnumbered, of the faulty old rifles. In a voice thick with emotion, and with tears in his eyes, he spoke of the death of our Beit Nattif neighbour.

That afternoon he hobbled to the relief centre with Yousef, who could not get used to his limp and watched horrified out of the corner of his eye as he swung from side to side. They issued him with a United Nations Relief and Works Agency for Palestine Refugees in the Near East (UNRWA) ration card. 'Was our dispossession preplanned?' my father asked the man behind the desk. 'I came to ask when we can go back home.' This was the question every refugee raised at any encounter with officials.

'I will pass your message to God,' the tired-looking officer answered in a matter-of-fact tone.

Long summer days and weeks followed under the sun's fierce gaze. Autumn came, followed by winter's chill. When it rained, my family's tent would flood, sometimes collapsing altogether. We would crouch together for warmth while the tent flapped in the wind. We prayed that it would not break loose from its moorings yet again. Simple as our home at Beit Nattif had been, my family recognised how much for granted they had taken the protection of its solid stone walls.

Father tried to find work in Jericho. He would return downcast, retreating into silence. Life became dominated by a few crude necessities: attempting to keep warm, queuing for rations of food and, most humiliating of all, lining up for old clothes. The few clothes we had brought with us when we left home were inadequate protection from the weather. The children's clothes were becoming too small and worn out. Occasionally, the welfare centre received sacks of clothes that it distributed to hesitant refugees. Eventually my parents joined the growing lines of people queuing for other people's cast-offs.

In Beit Nattif Mother and Grandmother used to wear the elaborately embroidered traditional dress of the village; in Jericho the refugees were dressed in an odd array of clothing. Yousef remembers he was given shoes that were not even a pair and a shrunken jumper that needed darning. Grandmother was offered a baggy old crumpled coat that she accepted despite the cigarette burns. The clothes felt greasy and had a stale smell about them. They picked their way back through mud and stones to the gloom of the tent where Father sat staring at nothing in particular. All heads were lowered, loathing these garments. And so we survived, although life felt devoid of purpose. Yet, through all the degradation, Father never gave up. He would set out, again and again, to look for work, now more proficient in steering his damaged leg. He kept his ears open, trying to keep abreast of the latest developments regarding the fate of Palestine.

As spring arrived Father reached a decision. He planned to go to Syria to visit an old friend, Uncle Rushdie, as we called him. He was a Syrian doctor who used to practise in Jerusalem, sometimes visiting Beit Nattif. On retirement he had returned to Syria but visited our family whenever he was back in the area. Father managed to beg a lift on a lorry as far as Amman, from where he would try to get to Syria. That morning, as my mother and Yousef went into town with him, dawn had just broken and the silent camp was peaceful under a rose-pink sky. But in another hour or so the place would be teeming with people rushing to join the queues for food and water. Both Mother and Yousef longed to go with him, to be transported from that place. Instead, they had to wave him goodbye. They stood until the truck was a speck surrounded by clouds of dust.

'Please God, take care of him,' Mother said quietly as they turned back to the camp.

After a few days in Damascus Father returned looking worn out but holding with a firm grip the small bundle of banknotes he had managed to borrow from Uncle Rushdie. '*Inshallah*, we shall soon be out of this place,' he said. He had brought nuts and sweets from Damascus that we hoarded as reminders of the past. Rushdie had tried to persuade Father to take the family to live in Syria, but Father was adamant. 'We must stay as close as possible to home.'

And so, after about a year and a half living in the tent, early in 1952, my family finally succeeded in finding a small room in a dilapidated house in the poorest part of Jericho. Broken shutters hung from the window, but by comparison with the tent it was a palace: it had a roof and solid floor and walls. We could now escape the demands of the weather and no longer breathed in choking dust or sat and shivered as the rain dripped through the canvas. But, if some of the more acute physical discomforts had been reduced, after the initial excitement of moving, my family and our fellow refugees – grown-ups and children alike – became gradually more conscious of the destruction of our way of life as it had been before the war. It was also during that period that the children became aware of the pall hanging over their lives.

My family's attempts to keep out of the camp created a continual struggle. To keep the room we needed a regular influx of money, and Father would certainly have played down the severity of our plight when he went to Syria. Unemployment in the Jericho area was very high. Men would queue for hours at the local farms, only to be turned away more often than not. Father would get up early in the morning to arrive near the beginning of the line and did sometimes succeed in landing a job. The work brought him a little money but filled him with bitterness – that he who had his own land, grew his own wheat, figs and olives, who had people working for him, was now someone else's hired hand.

Employment was erratic. Often my family was penniless. Mother earned a little at dressmaking since she was skilled at the intricate design embroidered on traditional Palestinian costumes. Dressed shabbily herself, she sewed garments that should have been her everyday wear, squinting by a little lamp, stitching hour after hour. The landlord was impressed by my parents' hard work and was not too harsh if the rent was late, but we lived in constant dread of the knock on the door and the demand that we leave.

Anything that would have been taken for granted in Beit Nattif now had to be fought for. There was a chronic shortage of food in the shops, and even when it was there it was too expensive to buy. My parents were always in debt. Father was forced to find new ways to feed the family. Later in life, I discovered that, in addition to his farming activities, father had had a grocery shop in Beit Nattif and had co-owned, with a friend from the nearby village of Husan, the company that ran the Beit Nattif–Jerusalem bus. The contrast between his once comfortable and dignified life and later demeaning existence in Jericho was clearly unbearable. He would sink into moments of silence and be short-tempered when disturbed. Somehow that ramshackle life drifted on and seemed to stretch inexorably into the future. There was still the desperate hope that any day we would be allowed home. '*Inshallah*, this will be our last summer in Jericho,' was my family's mantra as our fourth summer of exile passed and that decaying room, where we slept and ate, was still home.

Around Jericho the camps had rapidly expanded, sprawling tent-and-shack slums. With the three surrounding refugee camps, a town of 3,000 inhabitants before the war suddenly became home to 100,000 people. The relief organisations did their best but could do no more than stave off famine and epidemics. My parents kept in contact with other refugees from Beit Nattif in the camps. The spirit of camaraderie and shared memories kept them close together and restored some meaning to their lives.

The only halfway-good thing about our room was that the window looked out onto a big fig tree. However, sometimes one of the local children would climb up and peep inside. Enraged at this intrusion, Father would shout through the window, which might send the child scampering down the tree or keep him sitting there just out of reach, pulling faces.

Our fortunes improved when a combination of perseverance and luck enabled the family to move to Khedive Hill, or Tal al-Kidaiwi.

*

Towards the end of the nineteenth century, Ismail Pasha, the former Khedive of Egypt and Sudan, ordered a winter retreat for his family to be built in Jericho. Only the foundations and ground floor had been completed before he fell ill and died in 1895. After many years, as stipulated in Shari'a (Islamic) law, with no claimants to that abandoned property, it became a religious endowment, or *waqf*. It could not be bought or sold but used only for community purposes or leased at a token rent to needy families. Our family was allocated one of these houses against a small rent. It took Father a few months to pay for the works necessary to add a roof, windows and some interior installations before we were able to move in, but we ended up living in a two-bedroom concrete house with a little garden. During summer nights the roof became a terrace with a panoramic view of the surrounding orange and banana groves.

I must have been five years old when in 1953 we moved to

Tal al-Kidaiwi on the edge of an overcrowded area a kilometre north-west of Jericho's city centre. Soon after my family moved in I was enrolled at a kindergarten with the promising title Hadanat al-Jeel al-Jadid (the New Generation Kindergarten). It was owned and run by a single teacher called Madiha. In line with the traditional way of addressing a female teacher at a daycare preschool, we called her Abla Madiha – *abla* being a prefix that translates as something like auntie, but usually given to a younger woman. I have only vague memories of sitting on benches in a spacious room together with other children around a table – or perhaps several tables placed together – in the care of a well-built, round-faced lady with a milk-white complexion and shoulder-length black braids. She taught us how to count, read, write and draw. For drawing I remember her distributing small potatoes cut in half on which she asked us to engrave the shapes that crossed our mind using a small cutting tool. Then each one of us had to dip our potatoes into a bowl filled with tinted water and use them as stamps to print our designs on blank sheets of paper. It wasn't always obvious what exactly we had been trying to depict. The paper was soaked and turned to mush, and the table was messy and covered in water. Luckily, in no time, as if by magic, Abla Madiha swiftly cleaned up all the mess and restored the shiny veneer to our desk. As a reward, those of us who managed to produce something that looked like a discernible pattern were given a biscuit, although I cannot recall ever tasting any of them!

The alleyways of Tal al-Kidaiwi were full of kids playing marbles or football – with rudimentary balls made out of shredded rags – or, whenever there was a breeze, flying colourful kites. They played barefoot in the dusty dirt road leading to our house. Father forbade us to mix with them. 'Rough children,' he warned, fearful of our poverty and unwilling to admit to the deplorable condition that our new abode camouflaged.

One of my early hobbies was making toy cars and bicycles with wire that I salvaged from abandoned fences. As I got older that hobby grew into a pocket-money-producing skill, as the toys were replaced by trucks and buses as big as kids' tricycles

– the size would depend on the user's height and budget – with wire wheels and steering columns. They were sturdy enough to be steered around the alleys. They became something for the children who owned one to brag about and to show off. I personalised each of my creations with small touches, like a flag or a steering wheel covered in bronze wire. I used the few piasters earned that way to pay to rent bicycles by the hour, starting with three-wheelers then moving on to a child-sized two-wheeled bicycle. Cycling became my passion, and I became a regular customer at Abu Zaki's bicycle rental shop and a familiar feature in Jericho's flat, tree-lined streets. On becoming a teenager that skill helped get me my first job as a delivery boy at a dry-cleaner's and laundry in Ramallah.

We had neighbours from At-Tur, Deir Yassin, Deir Aban, Ein Karem, Qalunya, Katamon and Lifta. Not all of our neighbours were refugees. The Erekat family lived a few hundred metres away from us. Saeb, one of their sons, later became a well-known politician and chief Palestinian negotiator. Every time my parents mentioned our Deir Yassin neighbours they looked awkward and would preface anything they said with 'May God help them, they are still grief-stricken, no end to their feelings of woe and desolation,' without elaborating. Eventually, the truth about Deir Yassin came out little by little, but it was felt that talking about it openly was disrespectful to the victims and hurtful to the survivors.

Most of the refugees in and around the three camps near Jericho were villagers who had lived off the land in Palestine. Agriculture and cattle breeding were the only skills they knew. They put those skills to use, turning Jericho from an oasis where, with the town's small population, agriculture did not go beyond the town's municipal limits, to farmland that stretched to the banks of the River Jordan.

Refugees from all walks of life also shifted their attention to education, quickly reaching a consensus about its pivotal importance to their children. There was a public school in Jericho, and several UNRWA schools were built in all the adjacent refugee camps. Children of all ages flooded these establishments, forcing

Class photo, Jericho, 1959. I am seated on the floor at the front

some of them to operate two shifts a day in order to cope with the numbers. After spending two terms at Hadanat al-Jeel al-Jadid I was transferred to the state primary school, where I stayed in the first-grade beginners' class for two or three weeks before the teacher discovered how valuable Abla Madiha's teaching had been to me and promoted me to the second grade. Since I was the smallest and the youngest in the class, I was assigned a spot in the front row and continued to be so seated for the rest of my school years in Jericho. This had its advantages. It made it virtually impossible to be distracted, and being in full view of the teachers' surveillance made it easier for me to concentrate on their lessons. That seating arrangement also had unintended effects on my character. It must have contributed to making me an attentive listener. Combined with our harsh living conditions as refugees, it certainly propelled me to the fast track from infancy to adolescence, as I gradually learnt to shoulder the outsized responsibilities normally expected of adults.

☀

Paying the school fees soon became part of the constant strain of trying to keep up appearances, to conform with the standards of the school and the other children, some of whom were from relatively well-to-do local or merchant families. Every morning we would be lined up with regimental precision while the schoolmaster inspected us for neat nails, polished shoes and a clean handkerchief. Peering intently at my nails he would suddenly whack the back of my hand with a ruler, complaining, 'Will you never learn? How many times must I tell you to stop biting your nails?' and disregarding my excuses about my mother having cut them close. Then would come the scrutiny of the shoes. And let us worry about our nails when we have lost our homeland, let our prime concern be the glint of our shoeshine when our home has vanished. Shoes! How many of my friends in the camp even possessed shoes? I had to wear my one large pair for years, unable to go to school if they needed mending, which was increasingly frequently.

Father considered it his right to have the final say over those fit to be my friends but luckily approved of my greatest friend, Mufid, even saying, 'If only you were as good as that boy …' Three years my senior, Mufid was charming, with a deceptively innocent, earnest face. His family were refugees from Katamon, a suburb of Jerusalem. They had a wholesale business, selling fruit, vegetables and fertiliser to local shops and farmers. They were relatively well off and lived in a large house with a small garden not far from us. Sometimes Mufid and I hitched a ride on the lorries his family operated for transporting the farm's produce to Jericho's wholesale market. As we waited for them to be loaded, we ate ourselves sick on cucumber and tomatoes.

Geography was our favourite subject at school. We had an old atlas and studied the maps endlessly. We fantasised about the places we would visit, deciding to be explorers and making up our adventures. My eyes roved compulsively over the map of Palestine, and I marked the location of our village and drew the route my family took, first to Bethlehem and then to Jericho. We spent whole afternoons drawing maps of the countries we were studying at school, sticking coloured papers on them and writing neatly the names of the main towns in a thick ink called Chinese ink. Perhaps in a subconscious expression of admiration to our oppressors, our geography teacher asked us to draw a map of the British Isles. He was so pleased with it he decided to hang it on the wall and use it for his lectures. That encouraging gesture motivated me to learn about other countries and aroused an interest in the outside world.

Another critical drive to my world view came from the Khoury brothers, my two charmingly eccentric English-language and English-literature teachers. They were Palestinian Christians. The elder was called Daoud. He told us, proudly, that during the British Mandate in Palestine he had worked, in one capacity or another, for *The Times*. He had a rounded, slightly lined face and rosy cheeks. His eyes were light brown. He had well-groomed silvery hair. Always elegant, he attached overt importance to his well-polished, classic, English-style shoes. An extrovert and natural orator with a sonorous voice, he acted out his well-articulated words and expressions with open arms. Good-hearted when one of us made a mistake, he would stare straight into our eyes then slide his glasses slowly to the tip of his nose and say, 'That's better. Without my glasses I cannot see you.' At other times he would hurl insults at us in such a comical way that it sent us all into fits of roaring laughter. He would then react by laughing uncontrollably at us laughing at him. Even the smallest mistake would provoke one of his comments, and we were all on the receiving end at one time or another. His favourite insult was, 'Today you speak English like a young colt; tomorrow you will speak it like an old donkey.'

Looking back, I think that the scripts he made us read were

not in the official curriculum. We acted simplified versions of *Julius Caesar* and *The Merchant of Venice*. In one of his early lessons he regularly recited and acted out a rather trivial ditty with such theatrics that, generations later, it is still imprinted on my memory:

Where are my glasses –
O, where, o, where?
Near the window,
Or near the chair?
I am looking here,
I am looking there.
O, where are my glasses –
O, where, O, where?

His younger brother Emil was his complete antithesis. Introverted, with dreamy-looking brown eyes and salt-and-pepper hair parted in the middle, he delivered his lessons quietly, sitting behind his desk. He was so tall that even seated his head towered above ours. When chatter broke out in the back rows he just swivelled his seat around and, with his back turned, continued to silently read his notes, not turning back again until complete silence was restored. To those of us making mistakes or not handing homework in on time, he would write on the blackboard or announce, 'I cannot teach you what you don't want to learn.' That became our favourite way of imitating him and for teasing each other.

We revered these two teachers. The Khoury brothers taught us and motivated us to learn English with a passion, giving us the confidence to practise it, and Mufid and I made full use of that in our contacts with the hordes of tourists who visited Jericho.

Jericho is considered to be one of the world's oldest continually inhabited cities, where human settlement dates to around 9000 BCE. It is endowed with unique ancient sites such as the Mount of Temptation, Hisham Palace, St George's Monastery, and Tal al-Sultan, and coaches filled with tourists were a familiar sight throughout the year.

Proceeds from selling the wire toys helped me pay for the materials needed for drawing maps as well as to learn and indulge in other pastimes that would otherwise have been inaccessible to me, like billiards and snooker. I started off as part of a of doubles team before acquiring enough know-how and confidence to play one-on-one duels. As a prize, the winner would get his tea or drink paid for by the loser. Sometimes the bet would be extended to include paying for the drinks of one or two of the winner's friends. Perhaps as an expression of appreciation, but also because I would often win even against older players, several of those beneficiaries started to call me the snooker champion, which boosted my young ego. The café we played in was called Makha Abu Owaiss. It was there that I also learnt to play various card games, the most challenging and amusing being *tarneeb*, a card game similar to Spades.

Another less glorious pastime I occasionally indulged in with my chum Mufid was to help ourselves to the fruit that grew abundantly in Jericho, especially the oranges. It started as a child's game, but on two or three occasions we actually sold what we'd picked to tourists. We devised a variety of stratagems for our scheme. The simplest was to hook the oranges over the fence with a wire, but all too often the oranges we snagged would fall to the ground on the inner side of the fence. I remember one evening in particular. Riddled with nerves, we anticipated the footsteps of the guardian. When we knew he was far enough away, we climbed the high fence. On reaching the top the fence swayed dangerously under our weight and we jumped, thudding into the forbidden territory, where we stood motionless amid the trees. Quietly, we stretched up to feel the cool oranges that glistened in the twilight before picking them. Then, suddenly, a shuffling and the sound of the watchman's stick tapping could be heard inside the fence. 'Stop!' he shouted. We heard him moving towards us but didn't turn to look. 'Thieves … rascals, catch them!' he shouted. I froze as I heard him call my family name. 'I'll tell your father, you damned boy,' he continued as we sprinted along the road, breathless and terrified.

The next day, as I arrived home from school, I saw Abu el-Abed, the watchman, sitting with my father on our small veranda. My father's eyes bore into me before he demanded, 'Where were you yesterday evening?'

'I was at Mufid's house,' I replied, feigning innocence.

Father's frown relaxed, and he quickly turned to the watchman. 'You see,' he said, 'my son never lies.'

The watchman glared at me. 'I could have sworn it was him,' he said quietly before standing up to leave. He mumbled an apology for questioning our honour, and, as he was about to leave he added in a gruff voice, 'Back in Abbasiya I would never have scolded anyone helping himself to a few oranges from our trees. But now I have to watch over someone else's property. I'm only trying to do my job.'

The blood rushing to his face, he left awkwardly. The tone of his voice and the sincerity of his lamentation left a deep impression on me. I had a sleepless night. The following day Mufid and I decided to put a definitive end to that recklessness and resolved never to repeat it, not even for fun. Immediately after school we decided to confess and apologise to Abu el-Abed. He received us warmly, regretting his overreaction and insisting that from then on we would be welcome to use the orange grove for revision and homework under the cool shade of the trees.

During the winter and summer school holidays Mufid and I used to abscond from Jericho on buses quite regularly, hoping that we would not be spotted by either family. We perfected our technique, standing at the front of the crowded bus, and Mufid, with his innocent-looking blue eyes and dark-blond hair, would tell the conductor that our mother was right at the back of the bus with our tickets.

The tourists who visited Jericho were kept separate from the locals, insulated within their coaches and hotels. Rather than cluster around them peddling packets of tissues or chewing gum, as some other children did, we conceived a plan to penetrate their ranks. One summer's day in 1960 a distraught Mufid, pleading, besieged a coach disgorging its load of Swiss tourists. 'A doctor. We need a nurse or a doctor.'

The stars were on our side. There was a medic on that coach. Coming forward, an earnest expression on his face, Mufid, fourteen or fifteen years old at the time, explained that I had fallen out of a tree, and he thought I might be injured. From a Swiss tree, he added, as some conifers did grow in Jericho. His charm worked, and the man approached me as I lay groaning on the pavement. Aided by Mufid, he carried me to the hotel foyer, a place inaccessible to locals.

It was the first air-conditioned building I had ever been in. The entrance was filled with pots with huge, exotic plants. It was called the Winter Palace, in reference to King Hussein of Jordan's vacations there during the cold winter months. Jericho's warm climate made it a favoured winter resort for affluent Arab families. They put me on a sofa. The porter looked at us suspiciously, but we were safe, protected by the goodwill of these tourists. The medic examined every part of me. I found it difficult to keep a straight face seeing Mufid's expression of concern. Finally, the medic announced that he found nothing wrong. By then the whole group had become involved in this little drama and agreed that we could accompany them to Bethlehem for the day. That providential episode was to play a decisive role in my future. Among this group was a couple, Frau and Herr Haller. Meeting them changed the course of my life.

3

About a year after that encounter, aged thirteen, I switched schools. The UNRWA school at one of the neighbouring camps had garnered an excellent reputation. In addition to having an array of good teachers, the management struck a partnership with two of the best private schools in Jerusalem and Amman, whereby some of the two schools' top instructors started to travel regularly to teach part-time at the UNRWA school.

I found the climate of my new school and classmates more congenial, with a greater political awareness than I had encountered before. All of my new peers lived in refugee camps and were very poor. The camp was a melting pot for pupils from all over Palestine – all with their distinct accents, styles of dress, even cooking. They were united by those differences and enriched by that diversity. That was a silver lining for our families, all of whom were victims of the 1948–9 dispossessions and the dispersals that followed. Our growing awareness of one another's accents and rituals became a vehicle for affinity and an endless source of teasing. Those from lost villages would eagerly share funny stories about older generations and how they received the first arrival of modern technologies such as vehicles or radios into their village in the same way that they would have welcomed a travelling visitor. Some of my friends laughed that their grandparents had poured cups of mint tea down a rattling wireless or sheltered a car in a barn, offering these inanimate new arrivals the best of their village hospitality. We laughed at our provincial roots, but our laughter was full of love and nostalgia.

The most rewarding aspect of the new class was the students' ages. Some of my classmates were twice my age. They were teenagers when they became refugees, and, since they had never been to school before, their parents followed the new trend of embracing education and enrolled them in primary schools. That mix added immeasurable value to our academic discourse and social consciousness.

Our mature classmates would talk about problems they were having at home. Above all, they sharpened our knowledge of the political changes in the region, the rise of Gamal Abdel Nasser – the hugely popular Egyptian military officer who became president of Egypt in 1954 and remained in that position until his death in 1970 – and the schemes to permanently resettle Palestinian refugees in faraway places like Canada. The Jordanian government ruled the West Bank with an iron fist. Freedom of expression was limited, particularly calls for militant action against Israel and for the liberation of Palestine. With the exception of Egypt, Algeria and Syria the same was true of the rest of the Arab countries. There was also a new brand of humour in our interactions with teachers. One day we locked the history teacher out of the classroom as we all sat on top of our desks and huddled together listening to a speech by Nasser transmitted on a smuggled transistor radio, completely ignoring the teacher's pleas to open the door. There was thunderous applause every time Nasser mentioned Arab unity or the liberation of Palestine.

The poor teacher, having lost control of his class, called for the help and the intervention of higher authorities. The headmaster's voice could be heard over the persistent thumping on the door reciting the litany of punishments awaiting us. Once the door was opened and the headmaster strode in, the owner of the transistor radio was immediately identified as Hashem, the eldest in the class. Well-built and taller than most of our teachers, the frown of his thick eyebrows and the glare of his large green eyes was usually enough to cow them into retreat.

'Hashem!' the headmaster yelled. 'Out – and don't come back without your father or your guardian!' Hashem slowly gathered his belongings and walked out without saying anything. The whole class held its breath. What would happen to Hashem next?

Our history teacher went to sit behind his desk, having

regained his composure. He then gave us an impromptu two-question test. The first was to write a summary of Caliph Omar's entry into Jerusalem in 637 and of Napoleon's siege of Acre in 1799; the second was to compare and analyse the two expeditions. Only those passing the test would be allowed to leave the classroom before 4 p.m. that day.

It was the same history teacher who spoke to us about Deir Yassin. I am not sure that it was part of the curriculum, but I recall asking him why every time my parents mentioned Deir Yassin, they just say, '*Haram, Allah yerhamhom* – how terrible, may God bless their souls.' 'Because it was a *madbaha* – butchery,' he replied while making a cutting motion with his hands. 'It was a butchery,' he continued. 'The Zionists slaughtered men, women and children like goats with carving knives.'

One of our classmates was introverted and unusually quiet, but sometimes he asked direct questions. As the teacher spoke the boy's face became red and his arms and head shook. Without raising his hand to ask permission to speak, he shouted suddenly, 'Why? Do Jews eat humans?'

'No,' the teacher answered calmly, 'like us, Jews don't even eat pork. This has nothing to do with Judaism. Those were *irhabyeen*, terrorists. They sought to strike fear into the population to make us leave this land. That's why your families left and you are now refugees.' He explained that they were successful in achieving their aim and that Deir Yassin was followed by other massacres.

About seventy years later classified Israeli information was unearthed detailing the Deir Yassin massacre. Yehoshua Zettler, the Jerusalem commander of Lehi – the radical militants also known as the Stern Gang – did not mince his words when describing the way Deir Yassin's inhabitants were killed. 'I won't tell you that we were there with kid gloves on. House after house … we're putting in explosives and they are running away. An explosion and move on, an explosion and move on and within a few hours, half the village isn't there anymore,' he said. Professor Mordechai Gichon, an intelligence officer with the Haganah, the more mainstream Zionist militant force, was sent to Deir Yassin when the assault ended. He described what he saw as evoking 'a feeling of considerable slaughter … My impression was more of a massacre than anything else … To me it looked a bit like a pogrom,' he said. 'If you're occupying an army position – it's not a pogrom, even if a hundred people are killed. But if you are coming into a civilian locale and dead people are scattered around in it – then it looks like a pogrom.' Yair Tsaban, who later became an Israeli politician, was sent as a teenager with fellow members of the Youth Brigades to bury the corpses of the dead. 'I don't remember encountering the corpse of a fighting man. Not at all … An old man and a woman, sitting in the corner of a room with their faces to the wall, and they are shot in the back … That cannot have been in the heat of battle. No way.' Shraga Peled, at the time of the massacre, was in the Haganah information service. 'When I got to Deir Yassin, the first thing I saw was a big tree to which a young Arab fellow was tied. And this tree was burnt in a fire. They had tied him to it and burnt him. I photographed that.'[1]

That was the first time I heard the term *irhabyeen*. I felt like I was being strangled, and tears welled up. It was a turning point in my life. My innocence evaporated. 'Whatever is the matter with you?' my mother asked when I got home. I put on a cheerful face for her, the beginning of a habit I would be forced to learn, but inside I was in turmoil. My carefree adolescence began to erode. The world was suddenly full of dark uncertainties. That night, images of murdering and murdered humans haunted me. With my eyes open wide in the dark, warm tears flowed down my face.

The following day, during our first break, we stayed in the classroom, all on tenterhooks to listen to Hashem relating the events of the previous day. Our school did not have a canteen or any eating facilities, so during breaks and lunchtime, street vendors with makeshift two-wheeled carts gathered outside the school gate to sell, for a few coins, falafel and pastries. Hashem said that he addressed one elderly man among them and convinced him to pose as his father in return for paying him a shilling, the equivalent of a half day's earnings.

Looking frail and dejected, the man had gone along with this and shuffled into the school, dragging his feet behind youthful, sturdy-looking and defiant Hashem. As they entered the headmaster's office he erupted into an emotional speech about the importance of education for us Palestinians and how he saw all the students as his children and only wanted the best for them. The street vendor was captivated by the headmaster's words. Slowly he stood up. Blinking continuously, he took one step towards his 'son', fixed Hashem with his small black eyes and landed him with a hard slap to his face. At first, Hashem was stunned, then as he absorbed what happened he stood up, looked at the frail man from his towering height, grabbed his shoulders, lifted him until their faces met, shouting, 'Was this our agreement? I want my shilling back, and I want it now!'

When I was about fourteen or fifteen my perspective on life began to change. My boyish distractions and adventures became increasingly unfulfilling, and I grew dissatisfied. I gradually became increasingly solitary and more conscious of the plight of the Palestinian people. Resentment about the circumstances of our displacement preoccupied me. I was more and more anxious to find out about what had happened, to understand the history that lay behind stories of our flight. How could all this have been allowed to happen? How were we ever going to return? How would we reclaim our homes?

Like me, my contemporaries were passing through upheavals, our minds beginning to awaken to the true significance of the appalling situation surrounding us. The pain, the bewilderment, the closed horizons – is it possible, even for those who intellectually recognise the injustice, to understand our feelings? My frustration and anger grew at what the world had allowed to happen to us – neither preventing nor seeking to remedy it.

Our school, the one concrete building in the camp, was a centre of political activity, meetings and discussions, and, despite restrictions and the suppression of freedom of expression by the Jordanian authorities, students took the risk of organising demonstrations to support the Algerian and Egyptian revolutions and to call for the liberation of Palestine. The Jordanian army

At the wheel of a tractor with friends in Jericho, c. 1961

intervened and quelled them violently. Mustafa Radaaha, one of my former classmates, was seriously injured and later had his leg amputated. At that time suppressing manifestations of Palestinian patriotism was part and parcel of the undeclared policy of some Arab regimes to maintain a de facto peace with Israel.

Around Jericho in the late 1950s and early 1960s, the local indigenous farmers, supported by farming-savvy refugees from the camps, turned the barren land into fertile fields as ways were discovered for pumping water up from the depths of the earth. Each year the green carpet was spreading further and further until it covered almost the whole area between the River Jordan and Jericho. Yet, that thriving sector could only employ a small fraction of the burgeoning labour force that was left with no land to cultivate nor any industry that could offer them work.

In the early 1960s West Germany was going through an economic boom. A number of our neighbours went there to work in the car industry. When they returned for holidays I listened carefully to their stories about life there, especially when they told us that some of their co-workers were students who worked part-time while pursuing their studies. Given the high unemployment rates, it was impossible to contemplate combining study with work in any of the Arab cities that had suitable universities. During the final months of school we talked ceaselessly about what we would do afterwards. With the land being saturated with unemployed workers there were no prospects of employment. We felt robbed of everything, including our futures.

The Gulf states were the only ones offering employment in the Arab world. In 1962 my elder brother Yousef moved to Kuwait to work for a construction company and I was not encouraged by the results. He wrote to us about life being sterile with the intense heat and the colonies of single men, there for the sole purpose of trying to earn some money. Despite working hard for long hours, he could only send a small sum of money to Father every two or three months. Besides, by then I had subscribed to the dominant view that, as with Jordan, a correlation existed between the creation of Israel and the economic development of the Gulf states. After the Palestinians' exile in 1948–9 those entities emerged and became a tempting destination for Palestinian refugees to settle and forget about Palestine. But with no alternatives in the horizon, I thought that if I worked there for a limited time I would be able to support my parents and save enough to enable me to pursue my education. This dream was short-lived. During my last year at school, as a sixteen-year-old I applied for several jobs in Kuwait and Saudi Arabia, but as I was not well-enough qualified for the positions on offer, and still did not have a secondary-school diploma, I received a chain of rejections to my half-hearted attempts to find employment there.

Those rejections motivated me to turn to the inspiring idea of combining work with study, as was practised in Germany. Instead of lamenting my misfortune, I saw hope. So I made a solemn decision to prepare myself for a journey, although the destination was still unknown and uncertain. Right after graduating from secondary school I applied for a Jordanian passport, in line with my entitlement as a Palestinian refugee resident in the West Bank. To facilitate the integration of Palestinian refugees and other Palestinians living in the West Bank and encourage them to turn the page on what had befallen Palestine in 1948, Jordan offered citizenship to all West Bank residents. At the same time, Egypt offered identity cards to all Palestinians resident in the Gaza Strip.

With passport in hand, the next step was to identify temporary work opportunities. By the early 1960s Jericho had become an important hub for exporting fresh fruit and vegetables to the Arab countries of the Gulf, especially Kuwait and Saudi Arabia. I was too proud to look for manual work in that sector, where people knew me. The bourgeois town of Ramallah, about twenty kilometres from Jericho, with its 14,000 inhabitants was flourishing as a summer resort and a favoured destination for Arab tourists and Palestinian expatriates from the Gulf countries. Its surrounding villages were also known for their prolific fresh-fruit production, especially figs, plums and apricots. To whole families from the Jericho refugee camps that was the season to escape the town's scorching heat and earn some money picking fruit and camping in the orchards as nightwatchmen. As soon the final exams were over I accompanied a friend's family on one such expedition.

The morning following our arrival in Ramallah I went to the city centre and started my search for work in the cafés and *muntazahat* (open-air cafés and restaurants) until a waiter told me that they were looking for a delivery worker at Rivoli, a dry-cleaning and laundry establishment near the bus station. The owner asked me if I could handle a delivery bicycle with a big back wheel and a huge basket over the much smaller front wheel. 'Like a champion,' I answered. He engaged me on the spot.

It was as difficult keeping the heavily loaded single-speed bike under control while cycling down Ramallah's steep hills as it was pushing it uphill. I was allowed to sleep on the premises. The first morning my body felt so stiff I could hardly stand up. Luckily there were no deliveries that morning. I spent the time observing the boss and his assistant washing, dry-cleaning and ironing. Noticing me stare and my concentration, he asked me if I wanted to learn the trade. I nodded enthusiastically, so he pulled out an ironing board and a bundle of old clothes and asked me to copy what he was doing. I readily obliged, and a few days later was assigned the role of doing the preliminary smoothing of the shirts before passing them over to his skilful hands for the final pressing. Another skill he taught me was the art of invisible clothes mending.

I enjoyed the combination of learning new skills with cycling up and down Ramallah's beautiful streets – albeit less keen on struggling uphill. The town balanced the rural and the urban. There were no high-rise buildings, and people lived in stone houses that blended into the landscape, which boasted well-kept, lush private gardens filled with colourful shrubs, bougainvillea, roses, irises, acacias, pines and fruit trees, including olive and fig trees.

After a memorable month working and living in Ramallah, my savings were still far short of my needs for the ambitions I was nursing. I swallowed my pride and, with Mufid's help and other friends whose families were in that business in the Jericho region, I found better-paid work in local farms or loading and unloading trucks.

On Friday afternoons I met with my Jericho chums – Mufid, Jamal, Juma'a, Fouad and Walid – at a café and proudly paid for their mint tea and soft drinks with *araq jabini* (literally, money earned through my sweat). Our get-togethers always ended with an evening stroll along the conifer-lined Nazzal Street, with orange orchards stretching as far as the eye could see on both

In Jericho (left) with best friend Mufid, 1962

sides of the road, and *muntazahat* offering outdoor drinks and food services, savoured against the melancholy sounds of old Arabic songs.

It was while on such a walk one day in the summer of 1964 that a young tourist, wearing shorts and carrying a rucksack, approached me, introducing himself as Bob and asking where to find somewhere cheap to spend the night. Jericho had only three hotels: two expensive ones and a third that was very small and filled up quickly. Bob told me that he was a first-year medical student from Missouri and was touring Europe and the Middle East on a tight budget. He was thrilled when I invited him to stay the night at our home. We had okra stew for dinner and, notwithstanding my limited command of English, we stayed up chatting until the early hours of the morning. He told me that he travelled light – only one change of clothes and a sleeping bag – and had hitchhiked from London, sleeping in youth hostels or in public parks. I had never heard the words hitchhiking or sleeping bag before. Before Bob explained what they meant I assumed they were trucks or buses in which seats were replaced by bags spread out on the floor and in which the passengers sat or slept.

As I listened attentively to my Godsent guest, I started putting names to the destinations I dreamt about and wanted to reach, tracing the routes in my head. My objective was to hitchhike to Europe, where I hoped to be able to combine work and study. As a first step I had to earn enough money to cover the cost of the journey. The following day we gave Bob a warm farewell, and I rushed to the wholesale market looking for work loading lorries. It took me six months to save about fifty US dollars. With those savings assured, my plan to travel to Europe began to crystallise. A good first destination could be Switzerland, I thought. I combed my tatty notebook and found there in my childish scrawl the address of the Hallers, the Swiss couple whom I had met all those years ago when I had 'fallen out of a tree' in Mufid's company.

I scribbled them a letter in English, asking for help. To my amazement and delight, a postcard arrived from them about a month later. They had enquired about work, but without knowing French, German or Italian, it would be impossible for me to get a job. They added that if I ever were in Europe, I must get in touch with them. They would show me Switzerland.

Switzerland! Mountains, snow and fir trees, lakes and cool weather. I stared out at my surroundings: the endless despondency and struggle. I longed to escape, to shout to the world about us, to try to cure this festering wound that was defining Palestinians.

The idea of access to another world seized me, refused to let go. Someone in Europe knew I existed! There was a link. I showed Father the postcard. 'What does it say?' he asked suspiciously, unable to read English. 'It says that there are good opportunities in Switzerland,' I lied, testing his reaction.

That card became the most precious thing in my life, and from that point on my mind started to spin fantasies about travelling to and studying in Europe. Dreading ridicule or being forbidden from doing so, I did not share those dreams with anyone. I lay on my back looking up at the stars, attempting to digest in my sixteen-year-old brain that hundreds of thousands – no, millions – of other sixteen-year-olds in Europe and America had access to these very same stars and might also be staring at them that very night.

We had relatives who lived in Jordan's capital, Amman, seventy kilometres from Jericho. I had visited them a couple of times during school holidays. My perception of Jordan was tainted by its historical complicity in Palestine's plight. Britain saw Jordan as a buffer and a tool to thwart Palestinian nationalism, and there was much collusion between King Abdullah and the British to that effect.[2] When we visited relatives in Amman I would enjoy playing and wrestling with my cousins, but as soon as those games were over I would nag my parents incessantly to take us on the next bus back to Jericho – Palestine! Despite the fact that around 60 per cent of Jordan's inhabitants were Palestinian refugees, and although native Jordanians were kind and hospitable, I felt a sense of alienation there.

But now, very rapidly, Amman became central to my planned escape to Europe. It was not difficult to convince my family that I needed to spend a few days in Amman to look for work. I would stay with relatives. Shortly after mid-March 1965, with no fanfare, I bade them farewell, and, with a small duffel bag over my shoulder that contained my passport, one change of clothes and my toothbrush, I walked briskly to the bus station.

I felt my ties with family and friends pulling me back as I went, but I carried on, now out on my own completely. With a heavy heart, I forced myself onto the bus, not looking behind me and scarcely believing what was happening, but determined to carry myself as far away as quickly as possible lest I suddenly change my mind.

In Amman I took another bus to the outskirts of the city. I then walked until I reached the main highway connecting Amman to Damascus. It would have been futile to start hitchhiking on that road. Private cars travelling to Damascus were rare to non-existent. There were no marked bus stops. Passengers just waited on the side of the road and waved when the appropriate bus approached.

I chose a strategic spot with enough space for a vehicle to stop off the main road and waited. Buses to nearby destinations pulled over, but I declined to take any of them. After a three-hour wait, a bus with the sign Amman–Damascus came to a halt. 'Where are you going?' the driver shouted. Without answering I swiftly scaled the two steps, leant forward, and told him timidly that I was a boy scout. We were having a competition. The first to reach Damascus free of charge would win the first prize. I could read his mind. He did not believe my story. He looked up into his rear mirror. The bus was almost empty. 'Go and sit down,' that Godsend said kindly.

4

In Damascus I spent the night in a youth hostel. I resisted the temptation to visit the old city with its legendary Souk al-Hamidiyyah, the Umayyad Mosque and the Saladin Mausoleum. I wanted to avoid all accidents or other unforeseen events that might end my dream journey. The following morning I took a bus that dropped me at the junction of the Damascus–Aleppo highway, the point where my hitchhiking started.

It was mainly lorries and a few private cars that passed. These were luxurious vehicles, perhaps owned by government officials or high-ranking military personnel. I accepted any ride, even short hops, as long as they brought me nearer to Aleppo. I was open in mentioning the purpose of my trip and future plans. The drivers were kind and generous, treating me to meals and drinks at every stop. It took half a day to travel the 200 kilometres to Hama. For the last leg of the journey I had a ride in a truck that took me non-stop to Aleppo, with the driver singing along to the radio and insisting that I join in. After reaching his destination he left the truck to be unloaded and invited me to a nearby food joint serving *lahmeh bi-ajin* – Aleppo's delicious speciality, a kind of meat-and-pastry dish topped with pine nuts.

I spent my second night away from home in a youth hostel. All in all, my travels from Amman across Syria to the Turkish border, cost me the equivalent of one US dollar. Bob, the American student from Missouri, had told me that there was normally a *bureau de change* at every country's frontier, and I was amazed how a single dollar was exchanged for a handful of Syrian or, later, Turkish or Italian lira or Yugoslav dinars. In the morning, again resisting the temptation to visit another old city rich in cultural heritage, I followed my practice of the previous day: a bus ride to the city's outskirts, then hitchhiking, with Istanbul as my ultimate next destination.

I acquainted myself properly with the route of my intended journey using that grimy school atlas, smudged with glue and ink, from the days when Mufid and I used to copy maps. The countries fitted together so neatly with their pretty colours, but the map could not convey the effort involved in moving even a millimetre up the page. I had memorised the names of the key places to overcome the language barrier while travelling.

In the first two days, while crossing Syria, a momentum seemed to carry me forward without much difficulty. On my third day I was travelling through underdeveloped Turkish rural areas in a great variety of vehicles, ranging from heavy trucks, churning reluctantly up some hill, to vintage tractors. Perhaps my most memorable ride was with a farmer carrying, painfully slowly, a load of hay on a cart through the fairy-tale countryside of İskenderun – or Alexandretta, to give the place its historical name. As we crawled through the gentle hills, forests, terracotta earth and occasional villages of red-roofed houses, the old man sang and joyfully recited endless lines of Turkish poetry and ditties, none of which I understood.

I walked long distances through that countryside, as vehicles were rarely seen, and one evening arrived in a little village where the curious villagers came into the street to gawp at me. They sat me down and asked the headman to give his permission for me to sleep in the mosque. Around me, the floor was smooth and cool, and I slept the deepest sleep of my journey, my dreams coloured by images of travelling. In the morning I woke to find that they had filled my duffel bag with bread, cucumber and white cheese for the journey. As I left a group of children turned out to wave. I envied these villagers their peace and the same contented pace of life that my family had once known.

It was tough to hitch a ride from İskenderun to Ankara, as private cars were rare on that stretch through Turkey. A few times I had to use public transport. After eventually reaching Ankara, hitchhiking to Istanbul became relatively easier. Altogether the crossing from Aleppo to Istanbul took about a week.

At last, I was in Europe, I told myself, since much of Istanbul is on the European side of the Bosporus. The first thing I did was to buy a sleeping bag. I resisted the temptation to spend a few days discovering that city's medley of mosques and minarets and headed westwards, hitching and surviving on bread, milk, cucumber and tomatoes.

Some of the drivers must have thought me odd, for every time someone stopped to pick me up, using my passable English and sign language, I would promptly ask the driver where they were going and make a quick decision, my sole criterion being whether the lift would take me nearer to Western Europe. After leaving Istanbul my efforts to hitch a lift to Bulgaria ended in vain. It took me two days of trying out different routes – this was, after all, 1965, the height of the Cold War, with Bulgaria firmly behind the Iron Curtain – before being picked up by a Greek lorry driver going to Thessaloniki. I remember that journey in a well-equipped lorry – of which the driver was proud – particularly clearly. He was at first friendly and humorous, trying bits of every language he knew on me, but I was too tired even to respond in sign language, and after a while he grew irritable, having expected me to provide him with some diversion and company on the long journey. He scowled, looking straight ahead, while I kept falling left and right, once even falling against him. He had a sleeping compartment behind the seats, but when I pointed to it he scolded me in a language I could not understand and pulled the curtain between us and the compartment firmly shut. At every eating place we stopped after that he got out alone, slamming the door of the lorry.

Sometimes I felt like giving up, especially when I was travelling through Yugoslavia, and my initial excitement at wayfaring on my own died down. Traffic through those countries was limited to the occasional small car, and those that did pass were usually full or only going a short distance. It seemed an interminable stretch, and I felt so far from home yet still far from Western Europe. The hardship of the trip was compensated every time I managed, through gesticulation and English, to hold a rudimentary conversation with the drivers. They were welcoming and made me realise that we were in Tito's Yugoslavia, one of the champions of the Non-Aligned Movement and a vocal supporter of the Palestinian people.

Since it never rained during springtime in Jericho, I was surprised when, one April evening on the outskirts of Sarajevo, there was a sudden thunderstorm, and my soaked-through clothes clung to me like plaster. I walked to the nearest town, my head lowered against the curtains of rain, and spent the night soaked and shivering on the doorstep of a shop, trying to shelter while water poured all around forming little waterfalls down the steps. The next day it continued to rain, and no one was tempted to pick up a bedraggled young stranger. I spent that night in a tall haystack digging myself a shallow burrow. The haystack creaked and swayed all night, and I thought it might well come crashing down on me, but I was too exhausted to care. From there it took me four days to reach Zagreb and another day before I got a lift with an Austrian driver and decided to go with him to Austria. As we approached the border and the land became higher and alpine with wooden chalets, I grew quite excited – Switzerland would be like this, too – I would soon be seeing the Hallers, and my solitude would end.

At the border an Austrian officer came forward to check cars and papers. He took my passport and quickly returned it to the driver. 'No visa,' he said to me in English. Until that point I'd had no difficulty worth mentioning in being allowed into the countries I travelled through. Perhaps Jordan was on good terms with those countries or I looked inoffensive enough to their border officials. It also helped that travellers by road in those days were few and far between. The driver explained to the officer that I was transiting through Austria on my way to study in Switzerland. The officer took the passport again, leafed through it and threw it back at me, saying, 'No Swiss visa. Get out of the car,' then asked the driver, who had attempted to help me, to move on. I waited for him to examine another car that was behind us. After he had finished I started to walk towards him, when he yelled at me in a language I did not know. '*Vek! Vek!*' he repeated loudly, pointing his finger in the direction of Yugoslavia. (Later

I learnt that he was saying '*Weg! Weg!*' German for 'Get away from here! Off with you!')

It was frustrating to see Austria so close, just past the guards in their uniforms. But it was no good loitering. Dejected, I turned back. The officer's command was carved in my memory. In silence, I kept repeating it as I waited on the opposite side of the road hitching a lift back to Yugoslavia. I became aware of how lucky I was to not have been confronted with any visa problems at the numerous frontiers I had legally crossed before reaching this point.

☀

I consoled myself with the thought that the idea of Italy somehow appealed to me, that leg of land sticking randomly down far into the Mediterranean, so out of place. I hitchhiked to Ljubljana, where I spent the night, and continued the following morning to Trieste, the Italian city on the border with Yugoslavia, encountering no difficulty whatsoever in gaining entry to Italy. Barely a year previously, the pope had visited the holy places of Jerusalem, which was then under the sovereignty of Jordan, and was met with much-publicised euphoria and acclamation. The local press was filled with stories not only about the deep-rooted affinity between the Catholic Church and Jerusalem but also the legacies left after seven centuries of Roman rule over Palestine. Maybe the goodwill created by that visit was the reason for the warm way I was treated by the Italian frontier guards. After a casual glace at my Jordanian passport they just waved me in.

Deciding I would take the next lift wherever it went in Italy, I got picked up by a truck going to Florence, which the two drivers showed me on the map. I jumped up into the cab, and while I sat perched high up in front with a sweeping view all around, they insisted on giving me apples and pears while they sang Italian songs, and being altogether very cheerful, oblivious of my terror as the truck hurtled through northern Italy at breathtaking speed.

It was springtime, and everything seemed in full bloom. We passed green fields painted with wildflowers, vines and numerous crumbling, balconied villas with faded façades and closed shutters. It was a long way to Florence, and it was night-time when we arrived, one of the drivers already snoring thunderously. They tooted loudly as they left me near a bridge studded with lights. The River Arno shimmered, and the bright streets were thronging. A man was selling watermelon, and I could not resist buying a piece and munching it as I walked through the crowds.

I enjoyed that feeling of complete anonymity and did not feel lonely. But, as a solitary traveller for about five weeks, I was beginning to feel homesick. I thought a lot about home – Palestine was the framework within which my life was organised, what pushed my determination somehow to make a success of this adventure and equip myself to be able to help back home. This drive had now become the essence of my identity.

That first night in Florence I rolled out my sleeping bag and slept in a park on the grass under rustling trees. Insects and the screeching of tyres constantly interrupted my sleep. Shortly after dawn I gave up and staggered off to walk the streets and watch the city come to life: people opening shutters, bicycles and cars filling the streets. I feasted on a bread roll and an apple, sitting on a wall by the river and contemplating my next move.

By this time, my fifty dollars had dwindled to about ten, but if I continued to sleep in the open and live simply I reckoned that my money should last a few more days. I started looking for work. I set off full of optimism, sure that there must be an abundance of jobs in the endless cafés with their clusters of umbrella-topped pavement tables. My language formed a barrier, and I could not fathom why the first café proprietor I asked rolled his eyes and drew his finger across his throat in a sawing motion, nor why the next flatly shook his head, nor why the one after waved me away. And so it went on, until finally an Algerian waiter explained to me that without a work permit I was unemployable.

I kept faith that somewhere there must be a compassionate proprietor, but if so, he eluded me that first day, and in the evening

I found myself sitting in a square, surrounded by pigeons fluttering and small children running around while parents dozed on the benches. Somehow the light atmosphere was infectious, and the gravity of my situation did not worry me. But that night, as I lay down on the grass of the night before, I wondered what I would do if everybody turned me down and no job appeared. The best I could muster was 'something must turn up', and I persuaded myself to drop off to sleep.

And it did. Some intuition took me to the youth hostel. A very large Italian lady was sitting at the reception. I told her in English that I was a Palestinian student and was looking for work. She asked me in broken English if I spoke Arabic, and, when I said yes, 'Aldo!' she called. Her husband, with the physique of a wrestler, emerged from behind the reception area. 'See what this Arab wants,' she commanded. He was friendly and started talking to me in perfect Arabic with an Egyptian accent. I told him my story, and he told me his. He and his family were part of the Italian community that had lived and worked in Alexandria during the Egyptian monarchy and only returned to Italy after the 1952 Egyptian revolution. He and his wife were Godsends. They had big hearts, and immediately offered me a job at the hostel.

It was obvious that I would make no fortune there, but all I wanted was to save enough money to continue my journey to Switzerland. My workmates – also roommates – were Greek and Somali, and the *signora* took full advantage of our energy. Early each morning came a loud hammering on the door and cries of 'You're late, *arabo*!' in a powerful voice. I would take a shower, cold of course, which she begrudged me, shouting impatiently down the corridor in Italian. Her voice jarred at first, but after a few weeks I became used to it, just as I adapted to the scrubbing of floors, preparing food in sordid conditions, sweeping the dormitories and cleaning out the bathroom area. As soon as one job was finished she would materialise like a huge spider from whose web we were never free, pushing us to the next.

Since my English was sufficient for registering newcomers, I gave them a hand when needed at the reception, and this was the one pleasant aspect of my work: meeting people from all over the world. People frequently asked me where I came from, and to say I was a Palestinian often evoked little response. Their reaction was a solid proof that with the creation of Israel in 1948 not only had Palestine, as an identifiable country, disappeared from the world map but its people had vanished from other peoples' consciousness. Travellers of my age group very rarely knew who the Palestinians were, and to them Palestine seemed to have only a biblical meaning. They were satisfied merely to know me as an Arab. 'Harem … eh?' they would say, nudging me and roaring with laughter, or they would imitate a belly dancer. Is this all the West knew of Arab culture? And they thought we all lived in the desert, permanently astride camels! I tried to explain that the terms Arab and Palestinian are like the words Italian and Sicilian. All Arabs speak the same language and share the same culture, but they are divided into regional identities – Lebanese, Jordanians, Iraqis and so on – like Italy was once divided into smaller states.

During our precious free time I would sometimes go walking around Florence with my workmates or might take the bus out of the city, winding up the hills and eating at a café there under pines with that beautiful pure light all around us, feasting on pasta and salads. I was struck by the beauty of Florence. As I got to know the city better and started to go behind the doors, more riches were revealed. I knew little about Western art – even the most famous names meant nothing to me – but that may have enhanced my pleasure. Looking at the works opened up a strange and unfamiliar world to me, and I would wonder – sometimes aghast – at some of the pictures in the galleries or churches – semi-naked women and little angels, not to mention all those men in their finery or fighting gear. I had never seen such images, especially since, in traditional Islam, depiction of the human form was strongly discouraged. I would stand mesmerised in these places before running back to my employer, who would become hysterical if I were even a few minutes late. Florence still represents to me the peak of Western creativity and civilisation.

Another favourite occupation of mine was seeking out discarded English or American newspapers, spreading them on any spare surface and painfully trying to improve my English and to keep abreast of events in the world. In particular, I tried to follow the various raids by Palestinian infiltrators into Israel and the Israeli reprisals and incursions into Gaza and the West Bank. I had no books, only the tattered concise Arabic–English dictionary I had brought with me from Jericho. I developed a sharp eye for picking out newspapers in English, and the titles became familiar to me – the *International Herald Tribune*, *The Times* and the *Sunday Express*. Years later, every time I had a letter or an article published in *The Times*, the *Herald Tribune* or elsewhere, vivid memories of those days came flooding back. I would invariably reflect on the temporal, geographical and cultural distance I had travelled since leaving Jericho and on the radical reconfiguration of my world view.

Having saved some money over several weeks, the urge to move on began to stir. I wanted to continue my journey to Switzerland. I would have been very unhappy were I to consider my life in Florence as my endpoint, that I would spend the rest of my days as cheap labour in a country far from home. Looking back, I don't know by what right I had such dreams for my future. I was almost seventeen, with limited education, no qualifications and, apart from passable English, no technical or linguistic skills. For thousands of Palestinians, who had more to offer than me, becoming a foreign labourer was the best they could hope for. What conceit was driving me in a different direction, or was it something more spiritual? Were all those Godsends who had cropped up at crucial times throughout my life pure coincidence?

As if fate wanted to make a point, a couple of days after these thoughts crossed my mind a young man, a Swiss named Matthias Bontems, came to stay at the hostel. He remained for several weeks while taking an art course. There was a rule against stays of longer than three days, but the *signora* made sure it was waived for those whom, in her unpredictable way, she liked.

Matthias was unassuming and earnest looking. He always greeted me while I was darting in and out of the kitchen to the eating area. The first time we sat together he asked if I was Italian, and when I said no he continued to tell me about his interest in Italian art and how regularly he visited Florence. He spoke some Italian, English and French, but German was his mother tongue.

'What does *vek* mean?' I asked.

'It depends on the context,' he answered, and when I told him my story with the Austrian border guard, he said, 'Away! Get out! Go away! Scram! It's written *Weg*. In German, the W letter has a V sound in English.' I thanked Matthias for his Swiss precision. We had a good laugh. I then told him about my hope to travel to Switzerland and why. 'Come with me,' he said simply. He knew his parents would be sympathetic and was sure they would either arrange a work permit or find me a job that did not require it.

And so, after eight weeks in Florence, I was back on the road, this time with Matthias, giving that familiar wave of the thumb. We first took a bus to the city's outskirts and joined the queue of hitchhikers waiting for rides. Only a few cars stopped, and three hours later we concluded that it would be evening before our turn came, if it came at all. Matthias then told me that it was wiser to go back to Florence and catch a train. 'Don't worry, Matthias. I will manage. Just leave me your telephone number, and I will call you when I reach Switzerland tomorrow or after tomorrow. I have time.'

He broke into hearty laughter before saying, 'Of course, we will take the train together.' He had spent little money in Florence and had enough left for both our tickets. Then, he added that he wanted to be with me when we crossed the frontier to shield me from another '*Weg!*'

Frustratingly, we travelled through Switzerland at night. I had wanted to see the mountains gleaming and speckled with white. I do not recall being checked by any border police. Maybe they passed through the train while we were napping or did not pass at all! We reached Lucerne early the next morning, and the air cleared out my lungs.

Hitchhiking in Europe, c. 1965

'Welcome to Switzerland,' Matthias said as we reached out to take our bags and joined the line of sleepy-looking passengers leaving the train. The station was not far from the lake front. We took a short walk along the lake watching the mist, the flocks of birds on the water and the faint impression of mountains over the water, before heading back to the railway station to catch a train to Dornach, a couple of hours away near the city of Basel and the border with France, where Matthias's family lived.

5

Matthias's parents gave us a tumultuous welcome when we arrived at their home. After showing me my room we all sat and had a hearty meal and pleasant talk about our journey and about Palestine. Matthias's father worked as a theatre actor and had a good knowledge of English. His mother was a music teacher and was also fluent in English. Both worked at the Goetheanum, where they had already arranged for me to work, as a *Hilfsarbeiter* (handyman) with a temporary permit. I could start in three days. They saw from my face that I was overjoyed and could not find the right words to thank them. The father then turned to Matthias and asked him to take me on a tour of the Goetheanum the following day.

That evening I asked Matthias to help me telephone the Hallers. He kept looking at me and raising his eyebrows and smiling with excitement while the line crackled. I kept hearing the word Jericho. Then he handed me the receiver.

'Hello,' I said timidly, and the telephone felt as if it would explode with Mr Haller's booming voice. I wished I could understand something of the torrent of words. I remembered that he only spoke some rudimentary English. It was only thanks to the help of that medic acting as an interpreter that we had been able to communicate when we met in Jericho four years before. I listened, only intermittently interjecting '*jawohl*, *jawohl* – yes, yes.' After a short pause I handed the receiver back to Matthias, who explained that we were in Dornach, that I was preparing to start work in three days and how much I wanted to see them. Mr Haller said that he worked at the local railway station in Emmenbrücke on the outskirts of Lucerne, and I would be most welcome to visit them any time. Mrs Haller did not work and

In Dornach with Matthias Bontems and family, 1966

was always at home. Otherwise, they planned nothing special for their forthcoming spring holidays, and I could visit them then.

As soon as we finished talking to Herr Haller, I bade Matthias goodnight and went to my bedroom. I was too exhausted to think about the excitement of sleeping in a room on my own. More thrills awaited me the following morning.

A quick breakfast with Matthias and we were out of the house on our way to visit the Goetheanum. Not long after we'd left the family's house we could see on the horizon a massive edifice perched on top of a hill towering over Dornach. The Goetheanum was designed by Rudolf Steiner, an Austrian disciple of Goethe, also an architect and philosopher. The rounded building looked as if it had been carved out of a mountain in one piece. As we approached I felt dwarfed. It was as if it had been built for giants.

The Goetheanum is a structure of 7,735 square metres, forty metres high, built in 1925 of reinforced concrete. As we entered I was awe-struck by the colossal interior. A strange scent lingered in the building, and everything was immaculately tidy and polished. The people, too, were neatly dressed, and some looked as if they had not seen the light of day for years, with yellow skin and exhausted eyes. They walked along the corridors as if in a trance, so absorbed in themselves that the merest greeting suggested a serious interruption of some deep thinking.

There was a large reception area with a vast cafeteria, exhibition rooms, a library, a bookshop, administrative offices, a museum, two auditoriums (one with 1,000 seats and the other 450), narrow corridors, dimly lit rooms with high ceilings and a pipe organ in the Great Hall. I am detailing all this because, on the way there, Matthias explained to me that my job would entail cleaning that whole expanse together with Joe, another *Hilfsarbeiter* from Venezuela. On seeing the expression on my face after entering the building, he added that during conferences and festivals, four or five more workers would also join in. There was much to see and learn at the Goetheanum, but we were both tired and decided to go home to rest.

The first thing that struck me about the family's house was its almost uncomfortable orderliness. I became conscious of my worn jeans, which had become like a second skin to me, and my pullover, frayed around the cuffs. At first I felt some apprehension about touching anything or sitting on their fragile-looking chairs. Herr and Frau Bontems were warm and welcoming, but I was concerned about the possibility of them finding it hard to adapt to their son's scheme to have me stay, disrupting their routine.

I had a room to myself, overlooking the garden, and the first day I stretched my leg down when I woke as I used to do when I slept in the top bunk in that cramped little room in Florence. I had never known such luxury as now. There was gushing hot water, a huge television set, an immaculate garden with lawns and exotic shrubs. But luxury and material comfort never ranked high on my list of personal priorities. After an evening snack, as I sat up in my bed, it hit me. I suddenly felt immensely homesick. Despite all the comforts and serenity here, I missed my family, my friends, my Palestine. Restless, I started fiddling with the little transistor radio Matthias had lent me, trying to pick up Arabic stations. When I succeeded, and those waves of melancholic music and songs came and went, or the voice of someone reading poetry, or a news bulletin, my homesickness became unbearable. Surrounded by a caring and hospitable family, I was not alone, but I felt weak and lonely, a forsaken exile.

In the morning, when I expressed my concerns to Matthias about being in the way, he laughed, as he had done in Florence about the train ticket. 'Relax,' he reassured me. 'First, you are not in the way. Second, you are moving to new lodgings tomorrow.'

Later that day we went to the Goetheanum to meet Herr Kumm, the maintenance director. He gave us a cheery welcome and continuously talked to me in German, notwithstanding the fact that, as I discovered later, he was proficient in English. He showed us the cellar where all the cleaning products and machines were kept then took us to the *Heizhaus* (boiler house). It consisted of two floors. The ground floor housed the furnace and the boilers that provided the nearby Goetheanum with central heating and hot water, while the first floor housed the workers' residential quarters, which had a hall with eight cot beds, an adjoining kitchen and showers. That uniquely designed house became my home for the following ten months. From the outside the building had the form of a spring onion with a high chimney built in the shape of a flame, giving a sensation of heat and smoke.

Herr Kumm then accompanied me to an adjacent wooden building decorated with carvings that housed the Goetheanum's administration offices. There I met Herr Emil Estermann, the general manager, and I signed the work contract.

I started the following day. Two days later Herr Estermann drove me himself to the local immigration office. After a short meeting the officer in charge nodded his head, telling us that

Heizhaus at Goetheanum, Dornach

my temporary permit would be sent by post. Without saying a word to me during the whole journey there and back, Herr Estermann dropped me back at the Goetheanum to resume my work. As I pushed open the giant, wooden, carved doors I felt I was entering a new world where humanity functioned so calmly and with such precision that you could hardly hear its murmur.

My work at the Goetheanum consisted of a variety of jobs: cleaning and polishing floors and toilets, stacking books and moving furniture. I did that for four months. Once a week I attended an evening class at the Migros School to learn German. Migros is a supermarket chain that initially opened a school to teach German to its foreign workers before later expanding to incorporate a variety of subjects. When possible I also made efforts to learn about the Goetheanum, anthroposophy and Rudolf Steiner's esoteric philosophy, but without much success. The Goetheanum was a 'spiritual school', open to all but frequented mainly by adherents to anthroposophy. For anthroposophists spirituality is the necessary corollary to the way people talk, choose colours, paint, think about the now and the hereafter, sculpt and study the cosmos. Anthroposophists were also forerunners in bioagriculture and homoeopathy. Many years after leaving the Goetheanum, I learnt that Rudolf Steiner was critical of Theodor Herzl's goal of creating a Zionist state in Palestine and against the principle of any ethnically determined state anywhere.

One day I was waxing the floor of one of the halls from wall to wall, running to align my speed to that of the machine, when there was a sudden power cut. I started shuffling around in the dark when I heard someone's footsteps. When the lights came on again I saw Herr Kumm standing near the door. 'Don't switch on the machine – you're finished!' he said.

'I still have half the hall to polish,' I answered.

'No, no. Leave it. Someone else will finish it. From now on you will work as a stagehand assistant. After an intensive training course you will start in two weeks with a better salary.' He handed me a leaflet written in English about the impending two-month theatre festival. That night I stayed up late reading it, excited by the sudden turn of events in my life. It was cosy resting at the *Heizhaus*; the humming of the boilers lulled me into a deep sleep.

*

Two days later came the long weekend I had been waiting for: a visit to the Hallers. My years of frustration in Jericho and dreams about the world outside had built up an image of Herr and Frau Haller. When I met them, arriving at their house in July 1965, they seemed shrunken from the portraits I had carried with me. Frau Haller was a preoccupied-looking woman with permed grey hair who would talk in rapid bursts, seemingly laden with anxiety. Her husband, whom I remembered as a jolly man, was in reality now rather gloomy and silent.

We sat around a dining-room table neatly laid out with cakes, biscuits and teacups on a pretty lace spread. My non-existent German and Herr Haller's barely elementary English made communication difficult, whereas all those years ago in Jericho the attempts at sign language and groping for words had been exuberant and fun. But not now. When Frau Haller eventually showed me the bedroom where I was to stay, she stood watching me in the doorway like someone mentally wringing her hands. The room was laid out as if someone lived there and had just gone out. In the corner stood a pair of skis; a pair of climbing boots was nailed to the wall. Like a shadow, Frau Haller crossed the room to the bookcase on top of which stood a framed photograph. She picked it up and brought it to me. It showed a young man with fair, brushed-back hair standing in the snow. '*Mein Sohn*, Bernhard,' she said quietly – the words were close enough to English for me to understand she was pointing to her son. '*Tot. Unfall. Zwei Jahren.*' I looked blank. 'Dead. Accident. Two years.' She raised her thumb and forefinger and gestured the past. The boy had been killed two years ago. My heart sank, not knowing how to express my sadness, with neither of us sharing a common language. She sat on the bed staring down at the floor, then suddenly stood up, tears streaming down her cheeks. She walked to the door, closing it gently and saying something like goodnight.

The next day the Hallers lent me a pair of well-worn walking boots – Bernhard's? I wondered – and took me on an expedition to Mount Pilatus where we had a picnic. It was a spectacular vista, but Bernhard was present throughout, and I knew what was going through the minds of his parents.

That evening Frau Haller sat me down on the sofa and took out pictures of her son, her eyes moist and her thin lips trembling. She laid them out and talked endlessly in Swiss German, sighing, seeming to forget in her agitation that I did not understand what she was saying. Her husband would try to talk to her, but she would ignore what I took to be his pleas to put the photographs away. I felt he was resentful of my presence. This stirring-up of memories was doing neither of them any good. I decided that I would cut my visit short, and the following morning I said goodbye to the Hallers and took a train back to Dornach, feeling powerless. I couldn't put out of my mind the extent to which the Hallers, without them knowing it, had been instrumental in shaping my dream of a new and different life. And circumstances now – language barriers and, above all, Bernhard – had prevented me from expressing my deep gratitude to them.

☀

The theatre festival was different. It was only held during July and August and featured plays by major playwrights, including Shakespeare. Every four years (and that year happened to be one of those) they staged an unabridged version of Goethe's *Faust*, a performance that lasted twenty-three hours and played to full houses. It was a once-in-a-lifetime opportunity. With the help of Matthias and conversations about the play with his parents, watching *Faust* from backstage broadened my horizons and stimulated my intellectual curiosity as nothing before. *Faust* is a rich opening to complex questions about morality and life's meaning. Everything is nuanced and absolute truth illusory. It is claimed that Goethe himself did not understand the complex character of Dr Faust. Faust learnt everything about the world and human nature without gaining any understanding. What a place to start for learning and unlearning about the world,

I thought! Another Godsend! Such exposure motivated me to learn more about the Goetheanum and the philosophy behind it.

☀

Among the foreign students who came to work during the theatre festivals there was Peter, an English student. He lived at the *Heizhaus*, and we talked a lot about our prospects. He told me that to be accepted to study at a university in England after secondary school, students had to have passed A level exams, normally with high grades, although the requirements varied slightly between universities. He encouraged me to try doing the same.

It had never crossed my mind that I might study in Britain. Only princes and lords studied there, I thought. I had been thinking of continuing my work at the Goetheanum and at the same time trying to enrol at the University of Basel, ten kilometres away. But, when I made enquiries, they told me that I would first need to bring my basic colloquial German to an academic level and estimated that that alone would take a year. Then, given that my secondary-school certificate from Jericho was not recognised in Switzerland, I would need a year or two of foundation courses before standing a chance of having it recognised as equivalent to the Swiss school diploma. Studying in Britain or Switzerland, both options would be difficult for me to achieve, although my by now fair knowledge of English played in favour of prioritising going to Britain. I kept spinning those choices in my head, daydreaming about them. I made a mental tour of the UK, moving slowly over the map of the British Isles I had drawn in Jericho, and felt excitement about that trip and dreamt about studying there.

One day there was an art exhibition at the Goetheanum, and during my afternoon break I went to look at some of the paintings. I noticed Professor Hiebel, the head of the arts and humanities department at the Goetheanum, standing inside with some of his students. I had met him soon after my arrival during my first exploration of the building. I had found myself walking into a large room and wandering over to look at a huge wooden sculpture, when a gentle-looking and elegantly dressed man approached me and said in English, 'Are you interested? This is the sculpture of Rudolf Steiner. It shows a man being pulled between earthly and spiritual forces, a symbol of the balance between art and science.'

'Yes, I am very interesting,' I replied.

'*Ach so!* You are very interesting!' he exclaimed and peered at me, smiling quizzically. 'Then tell me more ...'

Excitedly, he led me to his office, pushing open a door with the words *Professor Hiebel* written on it in strange letters. He was a distinguished man with rather penetrating eyes and silvery hair. We both sat down.

'So,' he said and asked me to tell him about myself. After a brief exchange I realised I was sitting in that room due to a linguistic mistake, but he still listened to my narrative and expressed satisfaction when I told him that I was working at the Goetheanum as a stagehand. Following that first chance encounter, Professor Hiebel took an interest in me, introduced me to his sculptor wife Beulah and sometimes invited me to his home in Dornach. When he saw me at the exhibition he gestured, asking me to wait. I had talked to him earlier about my desire to study and the options I was exploring.

'Come and have lunch with us this Sunday. I want to introduce you to an English lady.'

The lady in question was the wife of one of the guests. She told me that she had a friend who worked at the British Council in Bern. He was willing to help me get a place at a college in Essex.

'*Marhaba*,' he said, when I arrived at his Bern office two days later. 'I learnt my Arabic in Jerusalem,' he continued. He had worked there until the end of the British Mandate in 1947 and had many Palestinian friends. I told him that many refugees from Jerusalem had been our neighbours in Jericho, and I mentioned some names. He knew one of the families I mentioned quite well. He assumed that money was not a problem, muttering to himself, without expecting an answer, that 'If you can afford to study in Switzerland, you certainly can afford to do that in England. The cost of living there is much lower than here.' He also knew Miss Manning, the secretary of the Jordanian ambassador in London. She had good contacts with the college he had in mind for me.

Yet another Godsend. It took less than two months to get me a visa and an offer from Braintree College of Further Education, eighty kilometres outside London. We were in late April 1966, but the college suggested that I join classes for a break-in period as a listener towards the end of May. I was thrilled but had no clue as to how I was to pay for that promising adventure. '*Inshallah*,' I said to myself, 'studying and working is a formula that also works in England.' A few days later, after booking my ticket and a place at a youth hostel in London, I bade farewell to the dear friends I had made at the Goetheanum and left Switzerland for London on the night train.

II

Studying, Working and Identity in Exile

With friends in Braintree, Essex, 1966

6

On arriving at London's Victoria Station, the first thing that struck me was the ethnic diversity of the people. The whole of what was, until the Second World War, called the British Empire was there: Asians, Africans, Caribbeans but remarkably few Arabs. That first impression was amplified on my Tube ride to Covent Garden, where the youth hostel was located. There was a huge map of London, stuck with little red pins, hanging on the wall facing the reception. Would this vast maze of streets and the occasional expanse of green ever make sense to me?

My course in Braintree was starting ten days later. I decided to spend that time exploring London. On the first evening I studied London's underground map. Figuring out directions, especially in Central London, could be handy for working there during school holidays. I improvised a simple formula for memorising the map and started implementing it the following morning. It consisted of taking the Tube from point A and getting off at point B, the next stop, then walking back to A to discover the above-ground area, then again taking the Tube from A, but this time getting off at C and walking back to B, and from there taking the train to D and so on. Within one week, I could visualise Central London in my head. Sometimes, in the evening, I walked slowly without any purpose along streets that glistened from the inevitable recent rainfall, ignoring the buses flashing past, spraying water from puddles the likes of which I had never seen before. Despite my financial difficulties, one evening I went to see my first movie in London, *My Fair Lady*.

From my ten months' work at the Goetheanum, after sending a monthly stipend to my family in Jericho, I had managed to save about a hundred and twenty pounds. I had to cut my expenses to the minimum possible. It was late spring, and when there was no rain some days were sunny and warm in London. I left the hostel and moved into Regent's Park. When it was properly dark I spread my sleeping bag on a plot of long grass I had spotted during the day and lay down watching the bright stars flickering and glittering – those same stars I had previously gazed at in my Palestine. Feeling light-headed, I dozed off. Gradually I arrive in the year 1187. I am a knight at the Battle of Hattin. We are galloping behind the sultan, Saladin, fighting against the crusaders, when I am knocked off my horse. I lie on the cool grass, holding my aching shoulder and watching the belly of my stallion. 'Watch out!' a woman shouted, waking me from my dream. 'You almost crushed someone lying on the ground,' she called to her riding companion. I opened my eyes, and the soft trotting died away into the distance.

'You must be an incarnation of a cat,' I said to myself. I was still tired and wanted to go back to sleep, but fear drove out exhaustion. Determined to enjoy myself, I decided to spend that day walking, exploring London: Trafalgar Square with its majestic fountains and huge flocks of pigeons; Piccadilly Circus with its famed advertising lights; Oxford Street; Leicester Square, studded with plush cinemas and nightclubs, completely inaccessible to me with my meagre resources. London was a city of contrasts, a glittering velvety world of artificial glamour that came into its own after dark, a city of drabness with monotonous strings of grey houses, a city of green parks, a city of sinister back streets and drunkards. I looked on London with a mixture of fascination and a growing sense of alienation. Exasperated, yet dependent on the place, I was overwhelmed by the scale of it all.

Braintree was such a contrast to London. A small town surrounded by flat fields, it was my home for the following year and a half. Its main highlight was the college where I studied for my A levels in four subjects: British politics, classical Arabic, economics and mathematics. I lived in a house with four other students, each having his own bedsit. We all shared a big television room, located on the ground floor. My tuition fees were fifty pounds per annum, and my rent was two pounds per week.

One Saturday Mustapha Kalaji, one of my housemates, invited me to accompany him to London on one of his monthly visits there to have his hair cut by an Italian hairdresser in Soho. I watched the gregarious Sicilian attentively while he cut my friend's hair. After his haircut we proceeded to Jermyn Street, where he bought some shirts. While wandering around that area, I spotted in one of the shop windows a display of blade clippers and photos showing how practical they were for trimming hair. They were sold combined with a pair of professional hairdresser's scissors. I knew that some of my rich Arab fellow students in Braintree went to the hairdresser every four to five weeks. Little did I realise how significant that little escapade to London and that purchase would become to my life story.

With my one hundred and twenty pounds in savings, I could only get by for a term. I needed to find work. I found an evening job washing dishes and saucepans for two hours at a restaurant located in a bed-and-breakfast boarding house. The work was stressful, but I enjoyed the company of my workmates. They dreamt of becoming rich and having holidays in sunny places but channelled their hopes for achieving that by betting on horse races and playing the football pools. I must have clashed with their preconceived idea of Arabs as portrayed by Hollywood. How could an oil-rich Arab be working in a restaurant? We laughed each time a waiter placed orders for steaks in an exaggeratedly posh accent: 'One steak for a lady, and one steak for a gentleman.' They claimed that, in line with British tradition, a lady was expected to eat half the quantity consumed by a man. Maybe they were pulling my leg.

After the end of term most of my fellow Arab students went home to spend their summer holidays with their families. I went to work as a forklift driver in a factory in Maldon, about twenty-five kilometres away, where they manufactured agricultural machines, and whenever possible, I doubled up as a strawberry picker at weekends. My workmates – wherever it was – were curious. I was the first student they'd seen working there. They thought all foreign students must be rich to come and study in England. That was certainly true in the case of students from

Saudi Arabia and the Gulf, where oil production (and wealth) was rising rapidly. For young men from these places (and they were all men) studying was often the excuse rather than the reason for their stay in England. It was not so for most of my fifteen fellow Arab students in Braintree, comprised of Jordanians, Iraqis and Palestinians, mainly children of hard-working professionals or with a government scholarship.

One day, during a break for what my work comrades called 'a cuppa tea and a fag', Mr Jarvis, the foreman, asked me where I came from, and when I answered that I was Palestinian, he gave me a tender look with an ironic smile.

'Oh yeah, mate, we British should know something about Palestine.' After a short pause, he added, 'You can come back and work here any time.'

He was as good as his word. At the end of my eight weeks there he asked me if I needed a job during the spring holidays. I hesitated, before adding that the factory was not on a direct bus route from Braintree. It took an hour to travel the twenty-five kilometres, even longer in the evening. 'Then come and live at the workers' hostel. It is a token rent. There is also a live-in nurse who controls the hygiene level there.'

To my fellow Arab students this sounded like a fairy tale. When I said it wasn't, some of them wanted to try it. They were mostly well off, but two of them couldn't resist having an original experience to brag about and did join me the following spring for a stint at the factory. I was later told that Mr Jarvis kept the tradition of engaging Arab students for many years after my departure.

Then, in mid-September 1966, the new term started, with me following the same pattern I had established the previous term: full-time student during the day and working part-time in the evening.

*

Back in Braintree my Arab friends had returned from visiting their families the week before. We sat down, heard stories about their holidays and shared some pastries they had brought back, especially *kunafah*, a popular Palestinian sweet made of stringy, spun pastry layered with goat's or sheep's cheese, rose water and sugar syrup.

At the end of the academic year, I would be sitting my A level exams. As the exams came closer I wondered how I would overcome the obstacles ahead. Only those obtaining high grades stood a chance of being admitted to university. Even if I did pass my A levels, would I even be able to go to university? If I were lucky enough to get a place I did not know where the money would come from. With my savings I reckoned that I could get by without the evening job during the last term, when intensive revision would be needed. But these calculations fell apart when Prime Minister Harold Wilson's government announced an increase in annual tuition fees for overseas students from fifty to two hundred and fifty pounds. I had to find an urgent solution. I started to promote my hairdressing skills and brand-new equipment to my fellow Arab students. The response was amazing. Within a couple of weeks I had most of them and a few others, including our physical education teacher and his wife, as regular clients. The balance of my account began to look healthier. Then Mustapha Kalaji gave me the compliment of abandoning his monthly trip to his Soho Sicilian hairdresser. Performed with a certain cadence and all the necessary rituals, the hairdressing sessions started with a spurt of scissors clipping the air before turning to the client's hair, performed to the tune of anecdotes about this and that, just like at any other hairdresser, hyphenated by moments of silent hair trimming and more air clippings to signal the end of the suspense and the resumption of the storyline.

☀

One evening in May 1967 I was returning home feeling utterly drained after a day of revision. On entering the house the door of the television room was wide open, and I could hear the news about King Faisal of Saudi Arabia's visit to London the following day. I went inside to hear a detailed report about the arrangements that were being made and about the type of special food the government was providing for its royal guest. I ran up the stairs to my top-floor bedsit. It was tiny, with a bed, a desk and a small sink. I felt tension building up inside me, as if waiting for the starter pistol before a sprint. I scrutinised everything there was for inspiration. There was a wooden ruler lying on my desk and a few felt-tip pens scattered around it. 'I have it,' I shouted between my teeth and got to work. To implement my idea, I needed a second wooden ruler. At that hour all the shops in Braintree were closed. I rushed to see my friend Gaby Khoury on the floor below and was thrilled to find that he, too, had a wooden ruler. During my school years in Jericho, other than drawing maps, I sometimes earned some pocket money by offering my services to shopkeepers and cafés as an amateur calligrapher in Arabic. I tore open my pillowcase, took my collection of felt-tip pens and wrote in Arabic calligraphy, in the largest letters that the space allowed, *Welcome Your Majesty*. Then I nailed the banner to the rulers, folded it, snatched a few hours of sleep and took the first train to London.

As the commuters filled the carriage, I watched them absent-mindedly as I pondered my next step. All that walking around London was now bearing fruit. I started with the Ritz on Green Park, asking about the Saudi delegation. Seeing the confusion on the face of the receptionist, I mumbled an apology and left swiftly, heading towards Park Lane. Arriving from the direction of Hyde Park Corner, I saw the Dorchester Hotel with its majestic entrance. I rushed through the imposing doors. 'Sorry,' I said to the receptionist, 'I overslept and cannot see anyone from the Saudi delegation. Do you know where they went?'

'They went to the Islamic Centre in Regent's Park. Can I get you a taxi?'

'No, no,' I said. 'I am not yet ready to go.' I thanked him, mingled with the crowd, and, when he was talking to someone else, I dashed out.

There were half a dozen journalists and cameramen standing in front of the Islamic Centre's gate when I arrived. A small

Holding a banner at King Faisal's press conference, London, 1967

group of men dressed in dark suits watched me from a distance. I was holding my folded banner and a small envelope in my hand. One of the men in black approached, asking in a whisper if we could talk. He wanted to know what I was carrying. He was from Scotland Yard. I told him, rolled out the banner, and showed him the letter, written in Arabic, asking the king to pay for my studies. He looked carefully at the writing. After a few more questions about who I was, what was I doing in London and what the writing meant, he left. I became the journalists' focus of attention. They had been waiting for a long time and were bored. Perhaps the king had another morning engagement before the Islamic Centre. I told them that I was there to welcome him. I was a student, a Palestinian refugee and was unable to pay the recently quintupled college fees. They were sympathetic. One of them, Paul Martin of the *Daily Mail*, promised to raise my case during the upcoming press conference with the king. I was the only member of the public welcoming his arrival.

Surrounded by photographers and flashing cameras, when the king's motorcade was in sight, I raised my banner.[1] He asked the driver to slow down, lowered the limousine's window, read it and smiled. The motorcade proceeded inside, with everyone chasing the cars except me. A security guard raised his hand, signalling me to halt. Alone, I waited outside the gate for thirty or forty minutes before seeing a security guard walking toward me. 'Come on in,' he called. 'The king wants to see you.' Astonished, I was ushered in and asked to sit in an armchair next to where he was seated. I handed the envelope to the king, summing up what was written in the letter. He passed it on to one of his advisers, telling me that someone from their London embassy would contact me. When I returned to Braintree, dazed by my apparent success in at least making contact with the king, life seemed very humdrum. My friends saw what happened on the news and were thirsty for more details. The following morning the story and my picture were on the front page of the *Essex Chronicle*, the local paper. The *Daily Mail* filled half a page with the king's visit, highlighting the question, 'What will you do for the Palestinian student?' and the king's answer, 'I will pay for him from my own pocket.'

☀

My excitement was short-lived. That week, in the early summer of 1967, the simmering crisis in the Middle East was threatening to boil over. Headlines from the newspaper stands shouted the latest – Israel would be wiped off the map by Nasser – accompanied by patently one-sided coverage. The writing was on the wall. Israel was preparing to make a new attack while posing as vulnerable and about to be flattened by a sea of Arabs. People were demonstrating in sympathy with Israel all over the United States and Europe, some holding posters with racist slogans demeaning the Arabs. In Amsterdam thousands of cars sported *I'm backing Israel* stickers. No doubt these people felt they were righting a wrong in doing so. Feeling free from 'prejudice' enhanced their self-image. In the same breath they described the Palestinians – victims of Europe's sins against the Jews – as terrorists.

By the end of May 1967 it was against such a background that the talk of war was becoming increasingly frequent. To appease their public the Arab countries, especially Egypt, substituted their actual inferior military power with supposedly superior rhetoric that played right into Israel's hands. But what none of the Arabs understood was that the overpowering memory of the Jewish experience, culminating in the shameful events of the Jewish Holocaust, gave what was now called the Jewish State of Israel an unbeatable – although completely flawed – propaganda advantage that they and their backers exploited to the hilt: namely that the Arab insistence on preserving a Palestinian homeland was nothing less than another attempt to eliminate the Jewish people from their midst. In early June 1967 Western public opinion was overpoweringly pro-Israel. Western media told them that Israel combined the best features of (Western) capitalism and (Western) socialism and that its citizens were making the desert bloom. A few Americans and Europeans volunteered to defend tiny Israel from annihilation. But Israel knew the truth about the Arabs' military weakness and that the Arab countries were caught in a trap. In reality, their military prowess came nowhere close to matching their rhetoric. Theirs were largely conscript armies of barely literate, poorly trained, unmotivated villagers mixed with an urban underclass recently migrated from rural areas. Their most effective armour was the slogans fed to them by their leaders, which proved useless in the face of trained, highly motivated and much better equipped fighting forces.

Early in the morning of 5 June 1967 200 Israeli fighter jets staged a surprise attack that swiftly destroyed 90 per cent of Egypt's air force. The ill-judged fiery rhetoric of Egypt's President Nasser was deemed by Israel's leaders to pose such an existential threat as to justify a pre-emptive strike to fulfil their latent ambition of creating a greater Israel. Major-General Mattityahu Peled, one of the twelve members of the army general staff during the 1967 war, later explained that 'The thesis, according to which the danger of genocide hung over us in June 1967 and according to which Israel was fighting for her very physical survival, was nothing but a bluff which was born and bred after the war' and that 'by falsifying the causes of the war and confusing its true motivations, the Israeli government was seeking to render acceptable to the people the principle of partial or total annexation.' Haim Bar Lev, another of the leading twelve generals, said, 'We were not threatened with genocide on the eve of the Six Day War and we had never thought of such a possibility.'[2]

With Egypt incapacitated, Syria and Jordan fell like autumn leaves. By 10 June Israel was in control of the Egyptian Sinai, the Gaza Strip, the Jordan-administered West Bank and the Syrian Golan Heights. That victory brought radical changes to the cartography and demography of Israel and the surrounding Arab countries, but it did not change the perception of Western public opinion, which continued to view Israel as the vulnerable island of democracy encircled by a sea of hostile Arabs.

We – my Arab housemates and I – did not go to college; we stayed home that week. We kept the curtains of the house drawn and went virtually without sleep, one of us occasionally venturing out to get milk and newspapers. We were living through every minute of that war ourselves. Every so often we would hush while the television news was on, and in the evenings we tried to get the Arabic radio stations on a small transistor radio. It was impossible to concentrate on anything.

We were numbed. We felt humiliated and violated. Worst of all, we felt helpless. As we stared at pictures in the newspapers or reports on the television, we could see that all around Israel's borders people's lives were destroyed, houses and cars smashed and bodies mutilated, while Israeli troops in tanks and armoured vehicles raced through Sinai triumphantly waving their flags, with the decomposing corpses of Egyptian soldiers lying along the sides of the dirt roads.

Through my total exhaustion the same questions kept hammering at my mind: where was my family? Were they even still alive? There had been reports of refugees fleeing across the River Jordan; the Jericho area had been bombarded, and people fled. I saw television footage of Palestinian refugees stumbling in panic across the wrecked Allenby Bridge over to Jordan.

I tried contacting my family by letter and telegram. Nothing worked. In one of my letters, after expressing my hopes that they were well and safe, I wrote: 'Whatever happens, don't leave. Stay in your home in Jericho. The mistake of fleeing Beit Nattif in 1948 must not be repeated.' As it turned out that war offered Israel another opportunity to continue in Palestine a policy and a practice that later, and in another context, came to acquire its own label: ethnic cleansing. Faced with aerial bombardment of Jericho my family joined the lines of those fleeing for safety across the Allenby Bridge. They left their house in a state of panic, leaving everything behind, including my address in England. It took more than three months before I could finally locate them in Amman.

Israel's attacks against three Arab countries on 5 June was premeditated. Referring to Israel's destruction of Egypt's air force, Israeli general Mordechai Hod, then commander of the Israeli Air Force, told *The Sunday Times* on 16 July 1967 that: 'Sixteen years' planning had gone into those initial 80 minutes. We lived with the plan, we slept on the plan, we ate the plan. Constantly we perfected it.'[3]

According to the archives of the *Los Angeles Times* that June fiasco ended with an estimated 777 Israelis killed against 18,594 Egyptians, Jordanians and Syrians killed. Tens of thousands were unaccounted for, and wounded soldiers were left to die from heat, thirst and hunger under the blazing sun of the Sinai Peninsula. The war also caused the flight of 350,000 new Palestinian refugees.

*

In the midst of all my grieving at the news a letter arrived one morning at the end of June 1967. It was from the Saudi Embassy asking me to go and see them. It failed to lift my spirits, but I nevertheless roused myself and took a train to London the following morning, sleeping deeply all the way. At the embassy I was curtly received by an attaché, who was evidently unsympathetic. He held my letter to the king in his hands. It was a factual letter, no colourful language, written by a proud Palestinian.

'How much money do you need?'

'The college fees and a budget to cover my living expenses,' I answered.

'You were living in England before the rise in fees. They rose by two hundred pounds,' he stated smugly.

From Braintree railway station I walked back to my tiny room. I was battered, not the same person who had met the king a month earlier. I dismissed meeting the king as a mirage in an Arabian desert. Any personal hardships or losses were trivial in comparison with our national tragedy, I reminded myself. Two weeks later I received a letter from the Royal Diwan in Riyadh with a cheque enclosed, saying that on the embassy's recommendation they were happy to make a one-time gift of two hundred pounds from His Majesty. I kept that letter as a souvenir.

7

Following the war and its devastation, my renewed financial worries forced me back to the drawing board. The havoc of the war and its aftermath did not spare me. My hopes of dedicating the months of May and June to revising for my A levels were shattered. I had to revise my plans and put some order into my life, urgently. I decided to go ahead and sit the exams but to view the present round as a practice, a preparation for the real ones a year later. That meant postponing university by a year, during which time I would work while monitoring the news for more Arab royals' visits to London.

I heard about a cigarette factory that was paying good wages to summer workers. I signed up as soon as I could leave Braintree and moved to Bristol, where I rented a room at a Greek Cypriot landlady's house and soon started work at the Embassy cigarette factory. It was not a place for daydreamers. A slight turn of the head away from the conveyor belt to sneeze could result in a pile-up of cigarettes and a fine equivalent to a week's pay. I enjoyed the challenge but often felt like a character from Charlie Chaplin's *Modern Times*. The most stressful was the short break during which we all stood in line waiting for our turn to urinate, with the foreman standing at the entrance to the toilets, intermittently shouting, 'Hurry up, lads. If you shake it more than three times, you are playing with it.' Returning one minute late from a tea break would raise a jeering ''Ere, mate! Get on with it, will you!' I soon adapted, and my work comrades were generally friendly. I joined in with their gossip, laughed at their jokes and they fantasised about mine, colourfully depicting students' lives and the exotic world of the Middle East.

Outside of work I kept up with news from the real Middle

East through my transistor radio and the national daily newspapers. The *Guardian* published several articles written from Jerusalem by Michael Adams. They spoke about Israel's demolition of Palestinian homes in the Old City, the destruction of nearby Palestinian villages Beit Nuba, Imwas and Yalu, and the expulsion of their inhabitants. It was the first time I had read anything critical of Israel since my arrival in the UK. I wrote to Michael Adams, expressing my appreciation. He answered me with a friendly note saying that he was often in London and invited me to meet him on one of his future visits. We did meet about two months later, and a friendship was born; he went on to play a significant role in my life. He was a gentle, unpretentious man, with a wide-ranging knowledge of the Middle East. I told him about my story with King Faisal, and, without any fuss, he arranged for me to meet Shaikh Salem al-Sabah – the son of the emir of Kuwait and his country's ambassador in London – a few days later. The ambassador told me that the bilingual press attaché's deputy was on maternity leave and her replacement only knew English. I could work with her, monitoring the Arabic press. Surprisingly, her work was limited to cutting articles and filing them. She told me that plenty of publications were also delivered directly to the ambassador's and press attaché's offices. It was not difficult to work out that none of them would have the time to thoroughly read the volume of material received by the embassy. Not long after being hired I started writing a daily summary of articles relevant to the Middle East and sending it to the ambassador and press attaché, which they both found useful.

One section of the embassy was in Park Lane, housing the offices covering education and health. The Kuwait Health Office looked after Kuwaiti citizens coming to London for specialised treatment, mainly at the London Clinic and Harley Street's private surgeries. After the return of the press attaché's deputy I was sent as a reinforcement to the team of three interpreters that accompanied the Kuwaiti patients. We were all Palestinian.

Some of the patients were seriously ill and needed urgent care; others were rewarded with a holiday in London for services rendered back home. With the latter our role as interpreters was reduced to that of tourist guides or shopping assistants. They came from a cross section of the population, and I learnt a lot from them about their distinctive traditions. On the matter of education I could see that their school system was based on a rote-learning system, which rarely challenged them to think for themselves. I am sure that constructive reforms have been introduced since, but I still remember some amusing encounters from that time. For example, when one of those patient-tourists arrived with his whole family, he told me that in two years his fifteen-year-old son would be finishing high school and was planning to go to university. He asked me to spend some time with him as he needed advice.

'I want to study ambassador,' the son told me.

'Good, but what subjects will you apply to study at university?'

'I don't like other subjects, only ambassador.'

Still lost, I said relevant subjects could be history, geography, literature, international relations, economics, that there was no subject called ambassador as such.

'No, no,' he disagreed knowingly, he had a relative who was studying ambassador.

Early in 1968, Michael Adams wrote to me saying that I had a new chance to meet an Arab royal. He was interviewing Shaikh Zayed al-Nahyan, ruler of Abu Dhabi, in London and thought I could accompany him as his interpreter. We saw the shaikh at his suite in the Dorchester. He was sitting surrounded by half a dozen people, with a television on with the volume down. The shaikh nodded to his companions to leave. In the ensuing hustle and bustle, one of the companions approached and whispered in my ear, asking me to hang around the hotel's foyer after the interview. The shaikh spoke about his ideas for modernising Abu Dhabi and spreading the benefits of the newly found wealth to his citizens. Michael Adams and I exchanged looks when the shaikh said that he planned to stay in London for a few weeks to see some consultants and recruit some experts.

I accompanied Michael Adams to the foyer. He was pleased that there would be other opportunities to see the shaikh and told me about the Council for Arab–British Understanding that he had founded with Christopher Mayhew MP, when I felt Mr Anonymous was watching us from the corner.

As Michael was leaving, he was already walking towards me wearing a big smile. 'Sure, you don't remember me. I am a few years older than you.' I let him continue, giving my memory time to refresh. 'Jericho, Hisham bin Abel-Malek school. Don't you remember? I am Nabil Hijazi.'

'My goodness, yes. Now I remember. Your family lived on al-Kharouf Street.'

He told me that he was working at the Abu Dhabi Government Office in London. On hearing my story he said that the shaikh rarely had appointments in the evening and welcomed new guests at his dinner table. Once or twice a week I became one of a dozen people who dined with the shaikh, exchanging shop talk and funny stories. On one of these occasions Nabil arranged for me to sit next to the shaikh. I told him that I was hoping to go to university in the autumn, but without financial aid that would not be possible. Not wanting to repeat the Saudi fiasco, I gave him a precise figure of the total cost. He signalled to Nabil to join us and asked him to arrange for my name to be added to their list of government-sponsored students.

The speed with which a solution was found to fund my university education was in itself remarkable, but, in retrospect, what was even more astonishing was the calmness of my response. My self-confidence, bordering on conceit, in finding a solution was such that when it did come I perceived it as nothing more than what was to be expected. Perhaps it was the arrogance of youth – this was 1968, and I was now twenty years old – that has no bounds.

That evening I invited my friends to an Indian restaurant in Chelsea, and the following day I went to work as usual at the Kuwait Health Office. Since my first job in Dornach I had been sending monthly payments to my family that varied according to what I was making at the time. With my studies secured, I doubled the amount I had been sending them since moving to London and moved from Finsbury Park to a small bedsit in

South Kensington, where I spent the evenings revising for my A levels. I also filled in the usual UCCA application, which allowed a student to choose, in order of preference, six universities. I put Durham as my first choice. It had a collegiate system and a reputation that appealed to me. Two months later Durham rejected me. Except for Oxford and Cambridge, where candidates' interviews are compulsory, other universities made their decision based on A level results already achieved or on the student's potential to obtain them.

Without waiting for a reply from the other five universities I wrote to the principal of St Cuthbert's Society, the Durham college that had sent the rejection. Professor Leslie Brooks called me for an interview. When we met a couple of weeks later I could see that he was forcing a severe expression onto his gentle-looking face.

'Quite frankly,' he said, 'when I started reading your letter I thought you must be a pest to dare question our decision. But your story was so compelling I read it to the end.'

I muttered something about having to struggle for things other students took for granted.

My Godsend was upstanding and dignified and did not want me to go through the process of offering degrading explanations. He shifted the conversation, saying apologetically that I might have to share a room with another student, as all single rooms had been provisionally allocated.

Back in London, I celebrated that happy outcome by inviting my friends to dinner, this time at an Italian restaurant in Soho.

*

That summer of 1968 I went to visit my family for the first time since my departure from Jericho three years earlier. The flight landed at Amman airport in the afternoon. I had told no one about my visit. Outside the arrivals terminal, a little boy followed me. 'Hey, *touristo*!' he cried, a skinny arm extending towards me. His eyes looked at me hungrily. He was dressed in rags. I looked at my suitcase with its London labels and bent down to speak to him quietly in Arabic. Before I could give him a little coin, he scurried away confused. I had never liked Amman. Now, it was worse. The streets were filled with people, mostly refugees in a pitiful condition. No news bulletin, no television camera, could have conveyed the oppressive atmosphere of Amman in that summer following the ignominious defeat of June 1967.

I had been unprepared for the change I saw in my parents; they looked tired and frail. In their letters they had been underplaying the harshness of their condition. The war turned them old before their time, making them disconsolate and nostalgic. My father's hair had gone completely white, and my mother's face had become drawn and haggard since I last saw them. It was a very emotional reunion in that dingy room where they now lived on the outskirts of Amman, where other refugees from Beit Nattif had lived since the first exodus. The war had reunited them, as if something had turned full circle, the catastrophe completed.

We talked as if I had left the day before, as though we had never been parted. With a fixed, sad look on her face, it was an effort for Mother to blink or to open her mouth. Sensing that my disapproval of them leaving Jericho was still burning inside me, Father described their panicky departure. Then, his face twisting with anger, he told me how they had been bombarded even as they ran. Some people had been hideously burnt; children screamed with terror as they tried to claw the deadly, highly inflammable, sticky napalm from their bodies.

The following day I asked a relative working as a taxi driver to drive me to the Baqa'a refugee camp on the outskirts of Amman. From a distance the camp looked like some rampant fungus, spreading patchily over the lower reaches of hills, as bare and wrinkled as elephant hide. The driver gestured to the camp ahead as the car bumped along the track. He gripped the steering wheel hard. The land around us was barren, a stony waste. I felt the chaos pressing in on me from all sides, families huddling together, quarrelling voices shouting angrily at each other and music piping mournfully from a doorway. Against the wall sad-eyed men and women crouched hopelessly, like a huge refuse pit for unwanted humanity. They were second-time refugees. After 1948 in the Aqbat Jabr and Ain el-Sultan camps outside Jericho, now in this one outside Amman. With the outbreak of the 1967 war fear had spread through the Jericho camps like wildfire. A father told me of his little daughter who had fainted while they crossed the Allenby Bridge. She still had not recovered. She would not eat, had shaking fits and would scream in her sleep. I saw her huddled in her mother's arms, speaking with a whimper, her eyes huge and frightened. The mother turned away weeping as my eyes met hers. She was broken.

Our taxi was quickly surrounded by a crowd of desperate people. I spoke to some relief workers. They did their best, but it was like trying to empty water out of a sinking ship with a leaky bucket. The problem was massive, the physical discomforts vast. There was a repugnant stench, sanitation being virtually non-existent. Water was in very short supply. It would arrive daily by truck, there being no water distribution network in the camp. The degradation was sickening. The camp was the worst of slums: its residents lived in ramshackle housing or tents, and children played in rubbish-strewn alleyways polluted with raw sewage. If someone had attempted to devise an environment that would induce a slow cancer of the spirit in a pit of physical degeneration, they could not have laid a better plan. This was surely psychological torture. How could anyone living in these conditions ever hope to recover?

Meanwhile, back in Palestine were our cities, villages, houses, churches and mosques. I knew we were no more suited to live in these threadbare tents and wretched shacks than any other people on earth. I was done with waffly arguments made by politicians seeing us as pawns in a chess game or as atonement for hideous crimes committed far away from our world by European fascists. The impassioned, reasoned appeals of friendly states or conscientious human-rights advocates so often heard at the UN were in concrete terms as impotent in achieving change as so many goldfish mouthing mechanically behind glass. And here was the living proof of that impotence.

That visit to the refugee camp in Jordan helped to crystallise not so much my perception of the injustice meted out to Palestinians, but rather the sheer irrationality and cruelty of the position in which they now found themselves and the double standards it reflected. This has stayed with me ever since. It is something I cannot shake off.

A glaring illustration of these contradictions and inconsistencies can be discerned in terms of the implementation of UN resolutions on Palestine. It was the UN General Assembly (GA), where all member states cast a vote, that made a non-binding recommendation in 1947 to partition Palestine based on a simple majority vote. This recommendation, which did not even consider the legality of partition itself and was adopted without the consent of the inhabitants of Palestine, gave the basis for the creation of the State of Israel.[1] But an independent Palestinian state never emerged. Instead, militarily superior Zionist forces swiftly took control not only of the territories that the GA had 'granted' to Israel under the Partition Plan but also of a significant part of the territories intended for the Palestinian state. The fate of the Palestinians was then left to the Security Council, whose five permanent members represent the superpowers and have the right to veto any resolution. There the United States, for its own geopolitical reasons, has routinely vetoed any resolution even remotely calling for Israel to uphold international law vis-à-vis the Palestinian people. To overcome this blockage, and given the GA's historic responsibility for the creation of the Palestine problem, a vote was called at the GA in November 2012, at which 138 out of the 193 member states (71.5 per cent) of the GA voted in favour of the recognition of Palestine as a state. Nine members voted against: the Marshall Islands, Micronesia, Nauru, Panama, Palau, Canada, the Czech Republic and, of course, Israel and the United States. That vote for recognition was not implemented on the ground, however, as it did not lead to a withdrawal by Israel from the occupied Palestinian territories. By contrast, when thirty-three out of fifty-six member states (58.93 per cent) voted in favour of partitioning Palestine in 1947, their recommendation was promptly implemented to create the State of Israel, thanks to US influence and pressure.

*

To move my family to a better house, I cut my trip short and rushed back to London to work at the Kuwait Health Office and earn the needed funds before starting my studies at Durham.

On my flight back to London I was seated next to a friendly and talkative middle-aged Canadian. He was in the mood to chat, and I wasn't. I excused myself. I had slept little the night before and just wanted to rest. My body language and mumbled responses made no impression on him. He was up for a conversation. Apparently before the 1967 war he had been an unquestioning supporter of Israel's position but, after the war and the tour he had just made in the area, what he thought he knew clashed with the reality he saw. He felt that a biased media and the absence of Arab voices had created a culture of ignorance in North America. He thought that the war in June 1967 had sparked interest in the region and that Arab immigrants in Canada were becoming more vocal. It was talks with Arab neighbours in Ontario that helped my chatty new travel companion to understand better and encouraged him to visit the area. He assumed that people were better informed in England. That would be natural, he answered his own question. 'I saw *Lawrence of Arabia*. Great film,' he continued. 'Relations between Britain and the Arabs go way back. They must know a great deal.'

'Some do,' I answered casually, 'but those who know are not heard, and those who do not know, are shielded from knowing.'

8

Durham's collegiate system suited me. I could pursue my tutorials in social sciences with students from different colleges studying my subjects while living with peers from other academic disciplines, whose subjects ranged from physics to theology. For the first year we all lived and ate in college and shared various activities.

Our tutorial classes were very small, between three and five. All those in my class worked on the same assignments, with one tasked with writing the essay, which would then be circulated to the rest of the group so that they could prepare for a discussion during the tutorial. The first class was with Dr Charles Reynolds. He gave a piece of advice that was repeated by all tutors teaching other subjects: 'Our mission is not to stuff you with data. You can do that alone. Our mission is to help you think for yourself.'

For our first tutorial in international politics I was asked to write an essay on nuclear deterrence. Perhaps as a nod toward me as a Palestinian, the second essay was about the UN, with special emphasis on the Security Council. It was an opportunity for me to unburden myself of all the frustrations that were building up inside me reflecting what I considered an unbending Western perspective on what had happened in the Middle East. About how every Palestinian child knew that the UN had had no legal right to partition Palestine. That it only did so as a reflection of the then prevailing balance of power that was hugely favourable to the United States and the Soviet Union, who were first to vote for that partition. How the United States harboured ambitions to replace Britain on the international arena and viewed appeasing the Zionist agenda as useful for achieving that objective.

And how the Soviet Union, too, saw an opening for spreading its influence in the strategically important Middle East and felt an ideological affinity with some socialist aspects of the Zionist movement. That some of the thirty-three countries that voted in favour of the 1947 non-binding recommendation to partition Palestine (in the form of UN GA resolution 181) did not know or care where Palestine was on the map. That they had voted in favour in order to receive material benefits and to appease the United States.

The Palestinians also knew that on 20 July 1949 the Security Council admitted Israel as a member state of the UN on the condition that Israel would implement resolution 181, which had provided its birth certificate, as well as resolution 194, which called for the repatriation of and compensation for the Palestinian refugees. They also knew that this same Security Council remained passive and paralysed in the face of Israel's refusal to abide by these resolutions. Instead, Israel annexed half the territory assigned to the Palestinians under the partition plan and rejected the right of return for Palestinian refugees. Yet it remained a UN member state.

I welcomed the opportunity to share my frustrations about the UN with such a bright audience. I wasn't convinced I would make any headway, however.

Durham was throbbing with student activities, including those related to nuclear disarmament, Vietnam, Latin America and the Middle East. There were numerous student societies that organised cultural, musical and political activities. Arab students numbered about fifteen plus two lecturers, both Palestinian, Dr Abdallah Dabbagh and Dr Jamil Hilal. We called our association the New Arab Society to distance ourselves from the old Arab regimes that we saw as failures, and I was elected president. We held regular debates, Palestine being the main focus. To publicise them we designed eye-catching banners and hung them on the walls of strategic spots, but they would be swiftly taken down by those sympathetic to Israel. In vain I started adding a line on the posters stating 'Opponents are welcome', but the efforts to silence our voices were persistent. So, in the land of

John Stuart Mill, we began to display our banners late at night to make it harder for our adversaries to remove them.

I became aware of how widespread the inbuilt prejudgements and distorted perceptions of the Palestinian problem were. After the Second World War, as the horrific details of the Holocaust became known in the West, naturally, and for understandable reasons, sympathy with Jewish victims of Nazism was at its apogee. That sympathy was accompanied by a wave of guilt in the West, because many recognised that the Holocaust was a kind of natural outcome of the centuries of anti-Semitism that Jews had faced in the Christian West. Not surprisingly, advocates of Israel were able to successfully portray Zionism, settling in the already inhabited land of Palestine, as a national Jewish liberation movement. Many decent, fair-minded people then uncritically accepted that flawed premise and began to view being anti-Israeli as being anti-Semitic. That common syllogism has blurred outsiders' vision of what Palestinians and many others see as injustices committed against the Palestinian people and had lethal ramifications for their cause. Systematic campaigns were launched and gained traction, portraying Palestinians as villains and the occupiers of their land as victims and champions of freedom and democracy.

It was then that I started my conversation with the British public. In 1970, my second year at university, I financed – from my Abu Dhabi grant – and published *Palestine or Israel?*, a twenty-two-page pictorial booklet that summarised the history of the conflict and formulated hopeful ideas for resolving it. I wrote the text and the captions summing up the messages with drawings by an artist friend of mine. I placed short ads about it in *The Times* and in local papers in Durham and Newcastle. I explained the booklet's objectives in an interview with the *Northern Echo* with wide-eyed enthusiasm:

> The aim was to give people the chance of reading facts affecting both sides before they made any judgement. I wanted to give something people can read in a few minutes and get a fair idea about what, why and how the conflict between Israel

and the Palestinian people came about. Though emotionally involved, I have tried to be as impartial as possible.

Palestine or Israel? was well received. The 6,000 copies printed were quickly sold. Encouraging letters arrived, the majority from English readers but also from Arab students and diplomats. In June, Bassel Aql, a director of the Arab League office in London, expressed the majority view by writing in Arabic, '*Khayr al-kalam ma kalla waddal* – Good brevity makes good sense'. On 28 August, Elizabeth Collard, director of Middle East Economic Consultants and publisher of *Middle East Economic Digest* wrote: 'What an excellent publication ... I shall certainly try to see that it gets a wide distribution.'

The most touching letter was received fifty years later. It was written on 14 May 2019, the seventy-first anniversary of Israel's creation, by Richard Miles, a fellow former student at Durham University:

> You probably do not remember me. I was a student at St Cuthbert's Society in Durham from 1968 to 1971, and it was there that I ... bought a copy of *Palestine or Israel?*, which I still have. I have been brought up as a Christian with an eschatological world view that required the Jewish people to 'return to' a Jewish homeland in Palestine, and was therefore pleased that progress had been made with that ... It was you that helped me to begin to understand the plight of the Palestinian people and gross unfairness of the division of land in Palestine. I felt great sympathy for Jewish people who had suffered huge trauma through the Holocaust and who had been displaced and scattered ... but I was ignorant of even such basic understanding that you referred to in *Palestine or Israel?* ... I came to realise ... that whatever the desire or even justification for Jewish people living in Palestine, the behaviour of the Zionists towards Palestinians was thoroughly inconsistent with my growing understanding of Christian values. I could begin to distinguish between my sympathy for Jewish people and my distaste for the behaviour of their Zionist political

> leaders; and to appreciate the injustices and deprivation experienced by the Palestinian people. Fortunately, I have held on to my Christian faith, but it no longer requires the 'certainties' of eschatological interpretations about events in Palestine ... and for that I thank you. I admire your attempts to encourage and bring about reconciliation and peace.

The message of *Palestine or Israel?*, as outlined in its foreword, is still relevant today. That's why it is reprinted below, verbatim:

> Most people outside the Middle East cannot understand why the struggle between the Arabs and the Israelis has gone on for so long. Why, they ask, cannot the Arabs recognize that Israel is here to stay and get down to solving their urgent social and economic problems? Why is so much material wealth and capital wasted on bitter and apparently hopeless fighting?
>
> What is so easily overlooked by those outside the struggle is that Israel came into existence as a state by the displacement of a whole people – the Palestinian Arabs. How did this come about? This [is] a story which goes back to 1917, when the British Foreign Secretary, Lord Arthur Balfour, promised support for the creation of a Jewish National Home in Palestine. Palestine was then part of the Ottoman Empire. Encouraged by Britain, Jews from all over the world flooded into Palestine. Zionism appeared as a new nationalist movement and was supported by wealthy Jews in the major Western countries. The Fascist persecution of the European Jews evoked sympathy from Western liberals and strengthened the desire for a National Home where the Jews could build a new state and live without fear. The tragedy was that they could only achieve this using the same weapons which so often in the past had been used against them – terror and force.
>
> The indigenous Palestinian Arabs had lived side by side with Jews for centuries in peace and mutual tolerance. But with the influx of the European Jews of a radically different way of life, imbued with aggressive nationalism, and with their terrorist organisations, the Arabs reacted by forming a

resistance. Consequently, during the British mandate, strikes and demonstrations were common in Palestine, until the colonial administration broke down altogether and the problem was handed over to the United Nations. The United Nations was faced with a vastly changed situation from that of 1917, for since that time large numbers of Jews had migrated from Europe. On 29th November 1947, a settlement was recommended which created a Jewish State and gave 56% of Palestine to the Jews, 43% to the Arabs and declared an international zone including Jerusalem and its environs on the remaining 1%. The fighting which broke out in 1948 resulted in the Jews occupying 78% of Palestine.

Effectively Palestine had disappeared from the political map. But its people could not disappear and they remained either in huge refugee camps or became political exiles in other Arab countries. The freedom of political expression, the right of self-government, and the civil and personal liberties achieved by the Jews were taken away from the Palestinians. They left their homes, land and possessions behind them in what became Israel.

It is a sad irony that liberty for one means a loss of liberty for another. Since the deprivation of the Palestinians, the struggle against the state of Israel and Zionism has continued. It will continue, not because of the support given to it by other Arab nations and the Soviet Union or because Israel has taken more and more territory through her conquests, or because of an unfavourable international situation, but because a whole people have been unjustly deprived of their basic freedoms. It is the belief of the writer that justice is indivisible and that what is justice for the Jews must also be justice for the Palestinians.[1]

It was during my time at Durham that my thoughts about identity, and specifically about my identity as a Palestinian, began to develop and form into some sort of adult coherence. These thoughts always began with a puzzle. I never ask people their nationality, for fear of being asked about mine. But why should I be so reticent about revealing my real identity? In retrospect, my reasons are clear.

My Palestine was emblematic of a failure, weakness, hopelessness and alien 'otherness' that was far removed from Western norms and their paragons of virtue. This was in contrast with the newly established State of Israel – a country perceived in the West as a shining embodiment of courage, rebirth, hard work, success and a haven of Western values and democracy. Yet here in reality was the West redeeming itself after more than a thousand years of shameful behaviour towards the 'Christ-killing Jews', which saw industrial slaughter within the heartland of Europe's Christian civilisation. These heinous acts of violence against the Jews had not been committed in the Middle East, let alone in Palestine. There was no question that Jews had every reason to feel anxious about their relations with the Christian West and that the sovereign Jewish territory that could function as a haven of security to mitigate such anxieties had its own logic. But there seemed no logic in selecting Palestine as the locus for European redemption, thus depriving the local population of their lands, property, livelihood and presence in their ancestral land.

Palestine was struck off the world map in 1948, yet Palestinian national identity continued to run in every Palestinian's veins. To outsiders, however, it became an abstraction. In May 1948 the Zionist movement, emboldened by the UN vote to partition Palestine, embarked on an immediate drive for expansion, and, after eighteen months of fighting, ended up, as I mention in *Palestine or Israel?*, with 78 per cent of our country. The remaining 22 per cent fell under the control of two neighbouring Arab countries: the Gaza Strip under the control of Egypt and headed by an Egyptian military governor; and the West Bank incorporated into Jordan, with all its Palestinian population becoming de facto Jordanian citizens.

The geographical fragmentation of Palestine eclipsed its name. For millennia the place has had a distinct political geography. Throughout ancient history and classical antiquity, as well as during the Byzantine Christian period and up to modern times, the most commonly employed name to refer to the geographical region between the Mediterranean Sea and the River Jordan and various adjoining lands has been 'Palestine'. The ancient Egyptians and Assyrians, classical Greek writers, Romans, Byzantines and medieval Arabs all used this name. For example, in the fifth century BCE, the Greek historian Herodotus referred to the land as Palaistine in *The Histories*. The British, who occupied it in 1917, continued to call it Palestine throughout the thirty years of their Mandate, referring to its population as Palestinians and issuing them with British passports bearing the word Palestine on the cover page.[2]

That was the cherished name within which we tucked our ancient heritage, culture, a wide variety of dialects and our ethnic and religious diversity. Our religious identity mirrored our deep-rooted and dynamic history. We cherished its legacy with pride. Invaders came and went. We, the indigenous people, did not budge.

Archaeologists believe that the land was first inhabited 20,000 to 50,000 years ago.[3] As the coveted crossroad of the ancient world, it saw all the great powers of the time knocking at or knocking down its gates. A new reign would settle down until a more powerful rival emerged and set out to dislodge them. Historical records only go back to 1710 BCE when Palestine, inhabited by the Canaanites – the forebears of the Palestinian people – was invaded by the Hyksos, in turn dislodged by the Egyptians in 1480 BCE, followed by a chain of invasions/liberations by the Hittites (1350–1290 BCE), Egyptians (1290–1154 BCE), Jews (1000–586 BCE), Babylonians (586–538 BCE), Persians (538–330 BCE), Greeks (330–323 BCE), Egyptians (323–200 BCE), Seleucids (200–142 BCE), Jews and Seleucids (142–70 BCE), Armenians (70–63 BCE), Romans (63 BCE–614 CE), Persians (614–628 CE), Romans (628–638 CE), Arabs (638–1085 CE), Turks (1085–1099 CE), crusaders plus Seljuks and Arabs (1099–1291 CE), Egyptian Mamelukes (1291–1517 CE), Ottoman Turks (1517–1918 CE), Great Britain (1923–1948 CE), and Israelis (1948–).[4]

Ranking these powers in terms of their length of domination over Palestine, the Muslims would come first with 1,088 years of total control, followed by the Romans with 687 years of hegemony. That compares with seventy-three years of total rule by the Ancient Hebrews (the extended kingdom of David and Solomon on which the Zionists base their territorial claims) and 413 years of partial control.[5]

Should the proven ancestors of any of these people now decide to use this legacy as a justification for reclaiming total supremacy over Palestine, their decision would amount to a declaration of permanent war and would be a flagrant injustice to those who had 20,000 to 50,000 years' continuous presence in the land – the native Palestinians, moulded through the ages by an admixture of the multitudes of peoples that at one point or another ruled over Palestine. Obviously, the history of Palestine is multilayered and no one layer can be singled out as the sole proprietor to this area's collective and complex history with its many centuries-old traditions. Jewish-American psychoanalyst and social philosopher Erich Fromm wrote in 1959 that 'the claim of the Jews to the land of Israel cannot be a realistic political claim. If all nations would suddenly claim territories in which their forefather had lived two thousand years ago, this world would be a madhouse.'[6]

Our society was composed of Jews, Christians and Muslims. Although Jews constituted 3 per cent of our population in 1882, the Zionist Movement that emerged fifteen years later called for the creation of an exclusively Jewish state in Palestine. Palestine's complex and multi-ethnic history was overlooked by both the Zionist movement and the British Empire in 1917 and has been neglected ever since. Britain's thirty-year occupation of Palestine left the country and its indigenous people in tatters.

As soon as Israel was created in 1948 its leaders proceeded energetically to erase any vestige of our centuries-old Palestinian existence by demolishing villages, changing street names, and confiscating land deeds, tax receipts and any evidence proving that we ever existed, even to the point of appropriating our food culture and national dishes.

As my thoughts evolved and my understanding of the general importance of identity took shape, I was also conscious of another aspect of my reality. Here I was, having made new friends and embarking on a promising new life that should lead to some degree of prosperity, comfort and security in a world that was a universe away from the miseries I was leaving behind in my Palestine, and yet ... and yet that pull of Palestine. Could the alienation I felt in this European apparent paradise ever be reconciled with the alienation I was beginning to feel from my Palestinian roots? But that very awareness of a drift away from my Palestinian identity seemed, strangely, to reinforce that identity. It was as if dwelling on my dichotomy actually drove me closer to the idea of Palestine, my Palestine. So, every time I thought about my identity I sank deep into despondency, consumed by mixed emotions. My European friends would constantly ask why we, the Palestinians, didn't do as other migrants and refugees had done and adopt the countries we now lived in? I tried to point out how the Palestinian problem was different from the experiences of other migrants and refugees. In other cases, where war, upheaval or economic crisis had displaced people, there was usually an option for the displaced to return home – or, at the very least, a practicable right to return, whether they chose to exercise that right or not. Masses of Sicilians might have emigrated to America, impelled by economic needs; Ethiopians might have crossed into Sudan in search of relief from famine; Vietnamese might have taken to rafts to escape torture and war; and Russians might have fled from Bolshevik repression and firing squads. But Sicily remains Sicily, Ethiopia is still Ethiopia, Vietnam is still Vietnam and Russia and its culture are still very much in place.

In our case, with Palestine, it was different. A conscious, systematic strategy had not just deprived us of our lands, it was trying to erase our individual identities and our nation's identity. Israeli school textbooks deny the existence of the occupation, labelling maps of the whole of historic Palestine, including the occupied territories, as Israel, or, at best, they attempt to normalise it.[7] Palestinian traditions have been rebaptised. Falafel, a popular Palestinian dish, was now presented to visitors as an Israeli delicacy. Palestinian embroidered dresses were worn by the Israeli national airlines' flight attendants as symbols of Israeli craft. It is just so much Dead Sea salt in festering sores.

In 1948, Palestine was turned into a theatre for power games. Its partition was a power play, as was its fragmentation and demarcation of the new frontiers – a power play involving genuinely aggrieved and concerned European Jews, a United States determined to reinforce its authority with regard to an increasingly muscular and ambitious Soviet Union, a Western Europe scurrying to retain the favour and protection of the US while seeking to hold influence on the world stage and an Arab world devoid of power. Those rare opponents to writing that ghastly chapter of Palestine's history, such as Count Folke Bernadotte, ended up paying with their lives. Bernadotte, the UN-appointed mediator in Palestine, was assassinated in Jerusalem on 17 September 1948 by the Zionist terrorist group Lehi for daring to raise questions about the distribution of equity and fairness in Palestine.

With Bernadotte's assassination the Palestinian cause received an enormous setback. Bernadotte was a Swedish aristocrat who, during the Second World War, had been instrumental in securing the release of tens of thousands of Jewish and non-Jewish prisoners from the Nazi camps. He had been appointed in May 1948 as the official United Nations mediator in Palestine as a desperate attempt by the international community to resolve the conflict between one community seeking security from the violent, centuries-old experiences of their past in Europe and another community being denied their ancestral rights and removed from their lands and homes to accommodate the perceived needs of the first.

Bernadotte had established a reputation as a fair-minded, principled individual with a tough spine, able to secure just outcomes for what he perceived as unjust situations. In the summer of 1948 he had prepared a set of principles that sought a peaceful solution to the Palestine crisis between the Arab and Zionist Jewish communities. Within his proposals he expressed his perceptions of the dilemma that underlay the crisis:

> It would be an offence against the principles of elemental justice if these innocent victims of the conflict were denied the right to return to their homes while Jewish immigrants flow into Palestine, and, indeed, at least offer the threat of permanent replacement of the Arab refugees who have been rooted in the land for centuries.[8]

Bernadotte's assassination brought to a shuddering halt any hint of optimism that still lingered within the Palestinian community. United Nations mediator Ralph Bunche succeeded in negotiating the Armistice Agreements in 1949, but Bernadotte's final words ended up counting for nothing.

☀

Since Israel's creation in 1948, annual calls by the UN for the repatriation of the Palestinian refugees have gone unheeded. According to Article 13 of the Universal Declaration of Human Rights, 'everyone has the right to leave any country, including his own, and to return to his country'. That right has never been revoked or amended.

I couldn't imagine my parents spending the rest of their lives in a miserable exile. They were so attached to their land. It was the basis of their identity, as were the agricultural seasons which defined their traditions and customs. Their deep attachment to the land and its produce was reflected in the touching gesture of blessing and naming old fig, almond and olive trees as if they were branches of their own family. Away from Beit Nattif they were lost and felt like fish out of water. Even while remaining in what had been Palestine, having their cherished fields and orchards seized from them was like uprooting a flourishing olive tree and transplanting it into an indoor pot forlornly sitting in a darkened room. It would soon simply shrivel.

Before 1948 shifts in power in Palestine had limited bearing on the Palestinians. When in 1917 the Ottoman Empire crumbled and Palestine slipped under British rule after the First World War, my family switched to paying their land taxes to the British authorities. Ottoman land deeds and British tax receipts later decorated the walls of their living-room as solemn reminders of the land they once rightfully owned.

☀

To obtain an Arab perspective on world events, our New Arab Society subscribed to a few Arab magazines. My favourite was *Al-Hadaf*, published in Beirut and edited by the Palestinian journalist, writer, painter and novelist Ghassan Kanafani. Like me, he was educated at an UNRWA school, but in Damascus, where he lived with his parents as refugees. He wrote his acclaimed first novel, *Men in the Sun*, in 1963 at the age of 26.[9] *Al-Hadaf* was a progressive analytical magazine in which leading Arab intellectuals expressed their views. It had an affiliation with the radical faction of the Palestine Liberation Organisation (PLO), the Popular Front for the Liberation of Palestine (PFLP), and Kanafani became the official spokesman. I did not personally know anyone working there, but I decided to send them my essay on nuclear deterrence with a note allowing them to use it if deemed interesting. To my surprise, a month later they published a translation of the whole essay on the back cover of *Al-Hadaf* and sent me a message welcoming more contributions.

Immediately after the end of term in June 1970, I took the first possible flight to Amman. Since the last visit I had saved enough money to move my family out of the hovel they lived in. I had already lined up a few houses to visit in Jerash, a small town fifty kilometres north of Amman, famous for its Greco-Roman ruins and mild climate. During the week I stayed in Amman while preparations were made to settle my parents in their new home; I found the atmosphere chaotic and oppressive. What shocked me most was seeing Palestinian commandos speeding in open jeeps across residential areas as if they were battlegrounds.

As soon as my parents were settled in Jerash, I travelled to Beirut, where I had planned to meet Ghassan Kanafani. By then *Al-Hadaf* had already translated and published three of my essays and a few other articles on the Israeli economy and current affairs. Both Kanafani and *Al-Hadaf* were well regarded in the Arab world, and I was seriously thinking of passing a year or two working in journalism after graduation. When we met, after the usual pleasantries, I told Kanafani, among other things, about my visit to Amman and how eerie it was seeing people at the airport waylaying travellers and imploring them to visit *fedayeen* camps as if they were tourist destinations. He told me that the resistance groups were growing too quickly, and they lacked the necessary structure and governance to cope with such a sudden growth and protect themselves from malicious penetrations and outside manipulations. He asked me to write a summary of my observations and introduced me to his deputies, Bassam Abu Sharif and Adnan Bader.

'Don't forget the summary; we might even publish it. Come and work with us when you graduate,' were Kanafani's last words to me on leaving them a few hours later. I summed up my critique and posted it to Adnan Bader soon after reaching London in mid-July 1970.

The simmering situation finally boiled over in mid-September and a tragic armed conflict, later to become known as Black September, broke out. This time it was a civil war between various Palestinian liberation groups – particularly the PFLP and the Democratic Front for the Liberation of Palestine – and Jordan, whose leader King Hussein was determined to expel the Palestinian *fedayeen* from his country and to enforce Jordanian control over the West Bank at their expense.

Bader answered me on 7 October, saying that the transgressions I listed were encouraged by some outside quarters to undermine the popularity of the Palestinian revolution. Although in agreement with the factual points detailed in my memo, they did not publish them for fear of them being exploited to discredit the whole Palestinian resistance movement. They were also overtaken by events. The situation deteriorated quickly and, with the usual politesse in correspondence conducted in Arabic, he counted on my friendship to forgive him both for not publishing the piece or replying sooner.

I later did come to understand what Adnan Bader was getting

at: that the fraught situation of Black September was not the best time to critique aspects of the Palestine resistance movement.

Like all inter-Arab conflicts, fighting between Jordanians and Palestinians benefited no one except their enemies. A futile blame game followed, which dragged the bloody confrontations on for almost another year. Instead of focusing on what went wrong and how to resolve it, precious time and energy were wasted by both sides as to who was right and who was wrong. At least in part they were blaming others for their own incompetence, superficial grasp of realpolitik, and disunity.

I was overcome by a deep sense of sorrow and shame. The drive to restore Palestine and the rights of its citizens was in the hands of self-serving incompetents who had no vision or understanding of the damage they were inflicting. I lost the fervour with which I managed my first two years' studies and extra-curricular activities. In that third and final year I handled my courses and preparation for the final exams with a dull sense of duty. The only stimulating essay I remember writing that year was about disarmament, President John Kennedy and the Cuban Missile Crisis. As for my political and social activities, they were substituted by hopes and prayers for an Arab awakening.

9

A soon as my final exams were over in June 1971 my Shaikh Zayed scholarship came to an end, thrusting me back to relying on myself. I moved to London and resumed working at the Kuwait Health Office. I was accepted by the Faculty of Economics at University College London (UCL) and won a five-hundred-pound scholarship to read for a twelve-month taught master's degree. That amount, combined with my part-time work as an interpreter, enabled me to pursue my studies and sustain my family responsibilities.

In those early 1970s the British media's focus shifted to the question of Soviet Jews emigrating to Israel. A determined campaign was waged by the Zionist movement pressuring the Soviet Union to 'let them go'. The Cold War hostility between the West and the Soviet Union, coupled with the heavy-handed Soviet restrictions on travel for all their citizens, provided an ideal opportunity to depict the Soviet Jews as victims. As for Israel, the pool of Soviet Jewry was an obvious resource with which to boost the Jewish population of the country, which many demographers were predicting would face long-term problems given the faster growth rate of Israel's indigenous Palestinian population. So expressions of support for the cause of Soviet Jewish migration became a frequent topic of media attention and international political discourse. The paradox was striking. I had to point this out and wrote a letter published in *The Times* comparing the indifference that met calls for the return of the Palestinian refugees driven from their homes twenty years earlier with the urgent passionate pleas calling for the emigration of Soviet Jews to Israel on the grounds that they were the descendants of Hebrew tribes that had lived in parts of Palestine more than 2,000 years earlier.

In response I received dozens of letters from all over the country expressing sympathy for the Palestinian refugees. Some spoke of their frustration with their government's lack of action to protect the Palestinians, others blamed Arab governments for not using their great leverage to contain Israel and influence their Western allies, but the majority criticised the British media for its bias and expressed surprise that *The Times* had printed my letter. The most poignant was a letter that encapsulated well what had always puzzled Palestinians: how could Europeans justify that it was others – living 4,000 kilometres away with no involvement in the strife that took place in Western Europe – who should end up losing their land and political rights and now live as refugees.

As my studies progressed, and as I was becoming increasingly aware of – and engaged with – world affairs, the ironies, paradoxes and contradictions that had shaped the Palestinians' plight over the previous quarter of a century began to gnaw at me more and more. To lament the injustices was becoming a cliché, but how else to describe Israel's obvious measures to deliberately deny Palestinians their basic rights and freedoms and even their identity and existence? The chutzpah – that wonderfully evocative Yiddish word that says it all – of successive Israeli governments knew no limits. Any Jew from anywhere, including a recently converted Lithuanian or Louisianan, was entitled to show up in Israel and receive full citizenship rights. By contrast, as refugees, my parents and their parents were denied the right of return to their homeland, dead or alive. Their yearning to be buried in the family plot in Beit Nattif could never be satisfied. Not only did the creation of Israel deprive the Palestinian people of their centre of gravity but it also ruptured their ability to honour some of their centuries-old traditions and customs. Commemorating our dead and performing our basic and sacred rites in exile turned into a constant reminder of what we as Palestinians could no longer be. 'But we are exiles from our fathers' land,' to quote an anonymous Scottish poet. And it has always been a particularly painful exile for my Palestine.

☀

During the spring term of 1972 I applied to Oxford University to read for a postgraduate degree. Oxford was associated in my mind with the British aristocracy, tradition and great scholarship. I viewed going to Oxford as a big fantasy and grinned with amusement when I imagined myself wandering around the colleges with a learned expression on my face, a mortar board perched precariously on my head and a gown flowing around me. To my delight, it was not long before I was called for interviews.

At first sight Oxford was not quite the dreamland I had expected. A sign reading *Welcome to Oxford, the Home of Pressed Steel*, greeted me at the railway station, and the road from the station was as drab as any. But as I approached the centre, the old Oxford started to appear: the spires, the ancient profiles of buildings, the colleges with their quads and distinctive characteristics, each like a small fortress snuggling behind its walls. I slowly made my way to St Catherine's College where I was to be interviewed, drinking it all in, unable to believe that such a place existed in the modern world.

The porter greeted me as 'sir', something that made me feel awkward. He told me how to get to the middle common room. 'Once there, a scout will show you where to wait.' The 'scout' turned out not to be a boy, but an elderly fellow in a starched, stiff white jacket with a deferential military manner. He pointed to a table where three other candidates were seated. They were younger than my twenty-four years and looked shy and nervous – one of them seemed so young that it was almost as if this was his first day in long trousers. We were surrounded by the college's graduate students looking overconfident, talking incessantly about people they knew with names like Clarissa, Rupert and Justin.

In between interviews at St Catherine's College, St Antony's College and the Oriental Institute, Dan, a very gentle Sri Lankan graduate student, offered to show me Oxford. It seemed a dreamlike fantasy, the ancient buildings with their unique architectural character preserved over eight centuries; the students milling around or cycling down narrow lanes looking purposeful, many with their academic gowns flapping in the breeze. There were the walks through college cloisters, along by the river down past the Magdalen College deer park where the deer roamed without a care under ancient trees. Dan told me about the Bodleian Library, much of it concealed in a vast underground network about which legends were told of people vanishing forever in the labyrinth of books.

It had been difficult to prepare for the series of interviews. Some were fairly straightforward chats while others were more a battle of wits. Nevertheless, a strange confidence gripped me. If I had come this far, why shouldn't I go all the way?

I took the last train back to London and was thrilled when a letter arrived three weeks later with an offer of a place beginning October 1972. I celebrated the news with my UCL classmates in a Chinese restaurant near Warren Street. We were a small group that studied and socialised intensely. Academically, the MSc course at UCL, taught through seminars, was invigorating. We huddled together for long hours debating the paramount role methodology played in determining the quality of research outcomes or the comparative merits of applying quantitative or qualitative analysis for understanding and predicting human behaviour. Our tutors – particularly John Burton, John Groom and Dennis Sandole – shared their vast knowledge with us, imparted with a rigour and passion that gave textbooks like Kaplan's *The Conduct of Inquiry*, Kuhn's *The Structure of Scientific Revolutions* and Popper's *The Poverty of Historicism* an aura of sanctity.

Immersed in enthusiasm for my studies, I began to detect – or thought I could detect – a connection between strategic planning and the way Zionist political and military leaders executed Plan Dalet, a blueprint, formally adopted on 10 March 1948, for the expulsion of Palestinians from vast swathes of Palestine. You calculate the probability of the reactions to your action and draw up plans to deal with the chain of those reactions as they occur. So it was possible to see that by launching their Deir Yassin attack and spreading news of a subsequent massacre there, the

Irgun accurately calculated the risk-and-reward ratios of their action and the waves of panic it would trigger, which, in turn, would trigger a mass exodus from small towns and villages. In the event, and as a result of other attacks and expulsion orders, more than 250,000 Palestinians had been expelled or found it necessary to abandon their homes and properties, even before the start of all-out war in May 1948.

Israeli historian Benny Morris described Plan Dalet as 'a strategic–ideological anchor and basis for expulsions by front, district, brigade and battalion commanders'.[1] He also noted that from the beginning of April 1948, 'Clear traces of an expulsion policy on both national and local levels with respect to certain key districts and localities and a general "atmosphere of transfer" [were] detectable in statements made by Zionist officials and officers.'[2]

Whether the mass flight that followed Deir Yassin was the result of strategic planning, or simply of common-sense reasoning – whereby Palestinians hearing of the massacre expected, not irrationally, that they would themselves fall victim to a similar fate and thus decided to seek safe refuge – it is undeniable that the events of Deir Yassin had a devastating impact on the collective psyche of hundreds of thousands of small-town Palestinians who got up and left, clutching what possessions they could.

☀

One of my classmates was Shukry Bishara, a Palestinian Christian.[3] Before coming to Europe I never referred to my compatriots' religion, whereas my personal experience in Europe showed that identifying one's religion is common. Even with a first name like mine, I was occasionally asked, once by a senior American journalist, if I were a Christian. A few of my neighbours and classmates in Jericho were Christians. We celebrated each other's feasts and came together in times of grief. Our elders told us that before the advent of Zionism the same harmony prevailed between all religious communities in Palestine.

Shukry and I quickly became close friends. We often worked on our papers and assignments together. Naturally, we talked about home and the plight of our people. We had both read Leon Uris's book *Exodus*, the novel widely acclaimed in the US as a historical document, and which even David Ben-Gurion, Israel's first prime minister, deemed 'the best ... propaganda ... ever written about Israel'.[4] It was so skilfully written that it was normal for any ordinary reader to be left with the sentiment that the Zionists were entitled to Palestine and should be left in peace to develop that 'fruitless, listless, dying land' and not be surrounded by a sea of Arabs with 'little song or laughter or joy in [their] life'.[5]

In fact, Palestine was an exporter of agricultural products to Europe well before the advent of Zionism in the late nineteenth century. Reclamation of new agricultural land came naturally with expanding populations. Even in the inhospitable climate of the Arabian Desert bordering the Persian Gulf, with wealth and new technology, countries such as the United Arab Emirates, Bahrain and Saudi Arabia have turned previously arid areas into successful cultivable land. And besides, even if the immigrant Jews did show themselves to be highly effective cultivators of crops, on ethical and legal grounds, how can someone's supposed efficiency justify robbing another's property?

The novel – which sold twenty million copies between 1958 and 1980[6] – and the 1962 film version both portrayed Palestinians as lazy degenerates: 'listless men sat around or lay on the ground as their wives tilled the fields. Some played backgammon. The air was foul with the mixed aroma of thick coffee, tobacco, hashish smoke ...'[7] The film was a box-office hit and provoked sympathy and support for the state of Israel from millions of viewers.[8]

Inspired by that success, Shukry and I conceived launching a plan for a reverse exodus. Its objective was to mobilise thousands of Palestinian refugee families, joined by foreign sympathisers and journalists, who would board a ship from a Mediterranean port and sail to Israel asking for the Palestinians' right to return to their homes and land. We conceived several probable Israeli reactions and drafted appropriate scenarios detailing the steps to be taken for countering each of these hypothetical reactions.

For more detached feedback, I sought and later received the opinion of Henry Tudor, one of my ex-tutors at Durham and a specialist in history of political thought. His reaction convinced us to modify that plan. He wrote:

> To illustrate my reservations, I want to start by reminding you of this: Marx referred to Hegel's remarks somewhere that all facts and personages of great importance in world history occur, as it were, twice. Hegel forgot to add: the first time as tragedy, the second as farce. One should never attempt to re-enact past events. Repetition, unless done for the purposes of art, always has something of the ridiculous about it. Marx, in the passage above, was referring to Louis Napoleon's attempt to revive the empire of Napoleon I. The first Napoleon made Europe tremble, the second succeeded only in making Europe laugh. A second edition of Exodus, even in Arab dress, will have the same effect. All meaningful and effective action that is not ritual in character must be original in the sense that it must come as an appropriate response to present conditions.

On Henry Tudor's advice, instead of replicating *Exodus*, the plan changed to propose a mass march by Palestinian refugee families to the Allenby Bridge carrying banners reading *I Want to Go Home* and crossing the River Jordan into the West Bank. No other slogans, just those banners.

The march would follow in the wake of the Black September conflict of September 1970 to July 1971, when, facing defeat, the PLO were forced to remove their leaderships, fighters and administrative structures from Jordan. Our plan afforded an opportunity to restore some measure of attention towards the plight of the Palestinian refugees away from the distraction of a fight with Jordan.

In early July 1972, a year after the end of Black September, I sent that plan to Ghassan Kanafani, to whom I had recently submitted my essay on nuclear deterrence and which he went on to publish in *Al-Hadaf*. I asked for his feedback and the role *Al-Hadaf* could play in rallying support and sharpening people's awareness. I reproduce here the reasoning that I developed in my letter to Kanafani because it reflects so accurately my thinking and my frustrations twenty-four years after my Palestine was disrupted:

> Since the tragic events of Black September, tension deepened between Jordanians and Palestinians, and I expected Jordan would be willing to support an initiative that throws back that 'hot potato' to where it came from: Israel's doorstep. The whole world could become our constituency. We must drop our insistence on getting Arab consensus for any action. It will not be forthcoming. How can it be otherwise when Arab countries have different agendas, diverse alliances and interests? We have been hearing rhetoric about the liberation of Palestine and rebuffing of Israeli aggression and expansion all our lives. They promised that it would come at the right place and right time, but after twenty-four years they have not yet found the needed compass. The best we saw was popular demonstrations in main squares of Arab capitals calling for the liberation of Jerusalem, some shooting in the air, followed by people walking back home or to business-as-usual routines, while Israel tightened its grip over Palestinians' lives and confiscated their land under all sorts of pretexts, from security imperatives to divine commandments.
>
> I am aware that this plan might be seen as going against the noble objective of having a unified Arab front. Alas, Arab disunity is a fact of life. If the Arabs have serious plans for waging a campaign of liberation against Israel, the Palestinian people need to hear it. Since its birth in 1948, Israel has turned violations of international law and bilateral agreements into a national sport. In the meantime, it is unreasonable for the Arabs to ask the silent majority of the Palestinian people to sit still and just wait for Godot. The PLO has resorted to armed struggle, not out of love for violence but because it was marginalised by Israel, and the world was not willing to hear anything about the dispossession and injustices committed against the Palestinian people. After the 1967 fiasco,

> Israel sought peace with the Arab states, completely ignoring our very existence. They reduced our tragedy into an inter-state dispute about frontiers and sovereignty. This peaceful plan could stir a storm that blows away their sinister schemes aiming at relegating us and our national rights to oblivion.

I never found out whether Kanafani ever saw that plan and my accompanying letter. On 8 July 1972, at the age of thirty-six, he was blown to pieces outside his home in Beirut by an under-cover Israeli operation in retaliation for a massacre committed at Israel's Lod Airport, the gateway to the country, five weeks earlier by members of the Japanese Red Army Brigade, recruited by the PFLP, in which twenty-six people were killed and eighty wounded.

*

Exams for the UCL MSc course were due in mid-September of that same year, 1972. There was a vast amount of information to revise and digest; it was said that the course crammed two academic years' learning into a single calendar year. Some weeks before the exams I gave up my job as an interpreter, and Shukry and I worked out a revision strategy that required iron discipline to achieve. We were motivated to achieve our respective goals – and we did. Shukry was immediately recruited by the London branch of an international bank, and I was on my way to Oxford. I went back to working at the Kuwait Health Office until the end of September and planned to rejoin them again early December for work after the end of my first term. I was going to be self-funded at Oxford until further inspiration.

10

I carried my financial worries with me to Oxford. It was a heavy bag. I hid it in a closet in a remote corner of my mind and, with that irritating problem shut away, I channelled my energy into exploring and enjoying the thrill of being at Oxford. The first (Michaelmas) term in 1972 was spent meeting people and discovering the wide range of extra-curricular activities offered.

Academically, I wanted to do research for a DPhil on a Middle Eastern topic. I did not have the constraints of daily classes and homework. My meetings with tutors were on a one-to-one basis and were conducted in a relaxed and friendly manner. The tutorials were followed by reading or research in the library and writing papers that took the form of outlines rather than comprehensive essays. During that period, apart from my college tutor Wilfrid Knapp, I primarily saw my supervisor, Albert Hourani, and also Roger Owen and Derek Hopwood from the Middle East Centre at St Antony's College and Professor P. J. Vatikiotis from the School of Oriental and African Studies, University of London, who often visited the centre.

The night before the end of the first term in December, to avoid major problems, I recovered my worry bag from that hidden corner of my mind. It was intact. Opening it cluttered my mind with worries; it was difficult to sleep. Early the next morning, almost as a distraction, I wrote a letter to Ambassador Shaikh Salem al-Sabah of Kuwait. I had lost contact with him since he had been transferred from London to Washington, DC a year earlier. I then shuffled what was not needed in London into storage , packed up my personal belongings and took the first train to London to resume my work as an interpreter.

I worked throughout that vacation. It was dark and rainy when

I arrived back at college six weeks later, just before the beginning of term. I was dragging my luggage through the college gate when the porter noticed me from the lodge just inside the entrance.

'Evening, sir,' he greeted me. 'Bet you wish you were back home on a perishing night like this.' He rubbed his hands together vigorously. 'You have plenty of mail. Your pigeonhole is full.'

I took out the letters, flipping through them quickly. I noticed one stamped with the Kuwait Embassy seal. I often stopped and chatted with the porter. That evening I just wished him goodnight and went straight to my room. Inside the envelope there was no letter, only a handwritten postcard, expressing Shaikh Salem's congratulations and telling me of his decision to pay, as a gift, the full cost of my first year at Oxford. After unpacking and dispensing with the rest of my mail, too excited to sleep, I lay on my back on my bed, thanking the heavens for that Godsend.

I was happy to be back among my family of friends at college. One term sharing the same facilities with other students, eating, sleeping, playing sports, studying in the same place, was enough to form a sense of belonging. St Catherine's College – Catz to the students – was known for its relaxed atmosphere and good food. Students only left college to share lectures at various academic departments or use common university laboratories or libraries. We would gather again in the evening for dinner in a big hall with fellow students and all the college's academic staff. It was like the coming together of a tribe. We all had to wear black gowns, which varied according to academic status, before sitting down for a three-course dinner served by scouts wearing black bow ties. These practices were common to all other colleges of the university.

Anthropologists study the rites of remote tribes, but perhaps they should also turn their attention to this strange ritual that unfolds night after night in one the most lauded seats of learning in the world. Long tables stretched along the body of the dining hall, lined on each side by figures clad in black like rows of crows. The crows cawed and chattered until a sudden silence

At St Catherine's College, Oxford, 1973

descended and the figures froze in whatever position they happened to be. Then, a slow procession of older and wiser-looking bats appeared walking across the platform on which lay the High Table, solemnly taking their places. One of them incanted '*Benedictus benedicat!*' This was performed by a different person every night, each one giving those two words – loosely translated as 'May the Blessed One bless us and our food' – their own characteristic rendering. Then, as the so-called High Table sat down, there would be a din and scraping as the student mass in the dining hall took their seats, and a great commotion of voices would burst out, instantly followed by a procession of white-jacketed scouts emerging bearing trays and distributing the dishes among the tables.

Before coming up to Oxford (and it was always coming or going 'up to' Oxford, whereas London only rated a 'down to') I had expected everyone to be fired with answers to the world's problems and engaged in passionate argument about their views. There were certainly plenty of those around, but there were also those content to be steeped in their academic subject, eating and drinking in silence and solitude.

At the end of the meal people would start drifting away to work in their bedrooms, or the college library, or to chat and argue in one of the common rooms over more drinks. The college had three categories of common rooms: the senior common room, used exclusively by the college dons and their guests; the middle common room, for the college postgraduate students and their guests; and the junior common room for undergraduate students and their guests. St Catherine's was one of the various colleges that, together with the various shared academic departments and institutes, the Bodleian Library, the Oxford Union, parks and sports facilities, made up Oxford University. Students joked about some tourists insisting on visiting the university campus, when in fact Oxford University is a concept with no physical centre.

The academic year had three terms of eight weeks each. Michaelmas term ran from October to December, Hilary from January to March and Trinity from April to June. The Hilary and Trinity terms of my first year were spent on tutorial seminars, symposia and lectures. By the end of Trinity term I had not identified a topic for my research. That had to wait until the following year.

At the end of the third term I decided to stay in Oxford and drop my plan to return to my interpreter role in London for two reasons, which, combined, gave me a fulfilling summer. The first came after seeing an advertisement by a construction company that was building an extension, eleven kilometres from Oxford, of the M40 motorway connecting London to Oxford and beyond. They were offering attractive wages. I applied and was called for an interview. I am medium height and do not have a wrestler's body.

'You don't look like a bulldozer driver,' the foreman said when he saw me.

'The machine does all the lifting,' I answered, smiling.

He called out to Jim, the big man in charge of the drivers' team. 'Try the f—r out,' he bellowed.

It was an enormous dumper truck, and the driver's cab could only be reached by climbing a ladder. Sitting behind the steering wheel I must have looked like a bird to Big Jim's eyes.

'What the f—k are you waiting for? Show me your f—n' skills.'

I paused, stared at him and said, 'Listen, Jim, I've never driven a truck in my life, but I am willing to learn fast. I am a student and need the money.'

He looked at me with the tenderness of a father. 'Not to worry, son,' he said, with no F-words. 'I've got just the right machine for you. It needs concentration and patience. It's called a grader. I'll teach you how to drive it myself.'

I thanked this Mr Godsend and spent an hour with him as he revealed to me the secrets of his trade. The work rhythm was like that of the Bristol cigarette factory. A pause or stop could trigger a chain of unwanted consequences. They were working three shifts. For eight hours a day I was stuck in a jungle of girders and trucks, stirring up storms of dust that choked us, while scooping up earth in great mouthfuls, dumping it and going back for the next helping. None of this depressed me. I had a huge toy, and I was having fun with it. We only had short breaks, enough to feed ourselves with huge helpings of sausages, fried eggs and baked beans, washed down with giant mugs of tea. I used to get back from the shift with aching muscles, longing to lie down. Instead, after a shower, I would sit behind my desk and let my body rest while my mind drifted into a different universe.

Then there was the second source of fulfilment during that summer of 1973. After the assassination of Ghassan Kanafani, the 5th of June Society, a Beirut-based cultural association, decided to launch a literary competition, offering prizes to short novels or plays with a Palestinian theme written in English or French. The submission deadline was the end of October 1973. As a sign of respect and admiration for Kanafani's contribution to Palestinian literature, and as a contrast to the manual labour on the motorway, I decided to participate in that competition.

I was preparing myself for the beginning of Michaelmas term 1973 when war broke out in the Middle East. Since 1967 tensions

Constructing the M40, 1973

between Israel and its neighbours never abated. Sporadic fighting continued, particularly on the Israel–Egypt front, causing heavy economic and human losses. There were several futile initiatives to work out peace agreements, but none succeeded. On 6 October Egypt and Syria mounted a massive surprise attack on Israeli forces stationed in the occupied Suez Canal zone, Sinai and the Syrian Golan Heights. At first their armies had the upper hand, then the US stepped in and tipped the balance in Israel's favour through massive airlifts of arms, equipment and supplies, to match and exceed the sophisticated arsenal that the Soviet Union had provided to Egypt and Syria. Once again, for the third time in seventeen years, the Middle East was a theatre of rivalry and conflict between the two superpowers. It took three weeks for a ceasefire to be negotiated.

*

In December 1973 I was invited to talk about the situation of Palestinian refugees at a meeting of the Oxford branch of the

United Nations Association. I gave a short description of what happened and a detailed account of my case as an example. I explained how I was a student in England when the June 1967 war happened and how I was not allowed back on the grounds that my family was no longer living in Jericho. I recounted how I explained to the Israeli embassy in London that my family fled Jericho out of fear for their lives and wanted to go back after the hostilities stopped, but that they were refused entry, and how I also told the embassy that I, too, wanted to return home in my own right as someone who was only studying abroad when the war broke out. After the talk an earnest-looking man approached me and asked me to give him more details about my family's plight and mine.

He was Professor Walter Zander. He told me that he was Jewish and was moved by my story and wanted to help. He had a friend called Shmuel Toledano, who was the Arab-affairs adviser to the Israeli prime minister. He asked me to prepare detailed information and meet him the following day at St Antony's College where he was a senior associate fellow. A few months after he wrote to his friend, Mr Toledano arranged a meeting for me with the military governor of Jericho. As soon as a date was set and a permit issued for the visit, I took a flight to Amman and, after a brief visit to my family, shared a taxi to the Allenby Bridge crossing. When my turn came and I presented my passport to the Israeli immigration officer he flicked through it quickly and returned it to me with a yellow slip of paper protruding from it. As I proceeded with the rest of the passengers towards customs a young girl in civilian clothes singled me out and directed me to a waiting area filled with Palestinian-looking Arabs. Everyone was taken aside for interrogation. When my turn came I was asked about the purpose of my trip, where I would stay, the places I intended to visit, who paid for my ticket and so on. Then I was led into the chief's office. More questions, often the same ones repeated, playing classic good cop, bad cop with me. More waiting followed by the same questioning, often punctuated by officials abruptly going in and out of the small room where I was being probed. It then dawned on me that my answers were futile. My interrogator was deep into an exercise of intimidation and was not listening. Evidently Israelis and Palestinians did not talk to each other but across each other. After two hours of that ordeal I was allowed into the country, a tourist in my own homeland.

The governor received me in his office in Jericho's prison, a derelict vestige of the British Mandate. He was wearing a military uniform and dark glasses and spoke to me while stroking the neck and back of his German shepherd dog with the tips of his fingers. He was gentle but firm. My family could not come back, he said, unless they had a close relative who could initiate procedures for their return under a process called 'family reunification'. I could not be that relative because I had lost my residency in Jericho. I tried exploring with him an exit out of that catch-22 dilemma by arguing that I had never renounced my residency in Jericho and was only absent for the legitimate pursuit of studying abroad. Besides, Article 13 of the Universal Declaration of Human Rights gives everyone the right to leave and return to their country. Perhaps to break out of the circular argument he initiated, he told me that the West Bank needed qualified people, and I should be able to obtain a permit to return to Jericho after completion of my studies.

Professor Zander, later described by Sir Isaiah Berlin as probably the purest-hearted man he ever met,[1] was genuinely upset when I told him about the failure of my mission. I am sure that he continued his efforts to find a solution, but in the absence of the desired outcome – judging by the sad look on his face – I started to feel that our chance encounters caused him pain and embarrassment. I understood better those feelings years later on reading a memorial speech delivered by his son Professor Michael Zander in May 1994 – when he was a professor of law at the London School of Economics (LSE) – that brought to life the depth of his father's humanity. These are excerpts from Michael Zander's speech sprinkled with generous quotes from his father's writings: 'The cardinal problem of the Palestinian issue,' he [the late Professor Walter Zander] wrote, 'can be summed up in the single sentence that we Jews had to build our

National Home in a country in which another people is living.' Resolving this problem, he suggested, was the paramount task. 'But instead of concentrating on this task all our efforts and creative energies, we have treated the Arab question, when it was remembered at all, as if it were of secondary importance.' He quoted the words of Ahad Ha'am, the guiding intellectual presence and chief internal critic of Zionism. Ahad Ha'am was a Zionist with a small z, a thoughtful visionary who recognised the need to navigate through the contradictions of Zionism and the Palestine problem with sensitivity and intelligence rather than blundering forward clumsily:

> How careful we must be in dealing with an alien people in whose midst we want to settle. How essential it is to practise kindness and esteem towards them … For if ever the Arab could consider the action of his rivals to be oppression or the robbing of his rights then, even if he keeps silent and waits for his time to come, the rage will remain alive in his heart. [2]
>
> Since the beginning of the Palestinian colonisation we have always considered the Arab people as non-existent.[3]

Walter Zander continued:

> To justify our claims, we have put forward strong and most impressive reasons. We have pleaded, with all the power which deepest conviction can give, the need of our homelessness. We have pleaded all the miseries of persecution … the millions of our dead … With all this, we have aroused sympathy, but have not convinced the Arab peoples that the country is ours. Even Mr Gandhi, a saintly man, maintained that his 'sympathy does not make him blind to the requirements of justice'. What could we expect under these conditions from the Arabs? They regard themselves as the possessors of the country for more than a thousand years, and if that is true, even the most heartbreaking need of the Jewish people does not deprive them of this fact and all the rights arising from it.[4]

The October war caused shock waves throughout the Western world, particularly when, in solidarity with Egypt and Syria, the Arab oil-producing countries imposed an embargo on oil exports to Britain, Canada, Japan, the US and the Netherlands, extended a month later to Portugal, Rhodesia and South Africa. Interest in the West towards the Middle East conflict started to rise in direct proportion with the price paid at petrol stations. International, especially American, diplomats shuttled frantically between Arab capitals and Israel. Henry Kissinger, notwithstanding his dismal record in Cambodia – 500,000 tonnes of bombs dropped and countless civilian casualties – became the star peacemaker.[5] As President Nixon's *eminence grise*, he had the first and last word. Setting himself up as a mediator and peacemaker with his so-called shuttle diplomacy, Kissinger was never able to persuade Palestinians and other Arabs that he intended, or was even able, to exercise any degree of impartiality. The interests of Israel were paramount, and these certainly did not include any concern for the fate of Palestine or the plight of its people.

☀

I was elected president of St Catherine's College's middle common room, a position that gave me more exposure to college and university life. The university student body, although teeming with alert minds, was not immune to the effects of the Kissinger touch, which meant that Palestine did not loom large as a topic of concern for most of them. Some among them were activists who did care about the contradictions and injustices in the Middle East and persuaded the Oxford Union Society to schedule a debate in the Hilary term of 1974 on the centrality of the Palestinian problem to that region. The motion before the house was 'In the Arab–Israeli conflict in the Middle East, the balance of right lies with the Arabs'. I was invited to speak in favour, alongside Dick Newby and Nick Prescott. Against the motion were Professor Max Beloff, Charlotte Raeburn, Patrick Roche and Mary Honeyball.[6] One of those who spoke from the floor in support of the motion was Benazir Bhutto. We spoke to a full house. The BBC broadcast an Arabic translation of my speech in full.

Read in retrospect, the speech does not make any dramatic, fresh revelations, nor does it contain many eloquent flourishes, but it does summarise the main points of the Palestinians' case as it appeared in the spring of 1974, setting out what we considered to be the incontrovertible logic of our position. As such, I reproduce it here in its original form:

> It is easy for a student of politics to make a convincing speech about any issue, and certainly about as multifaceted a problem as the Arab–Israeli one. I therefore decided to shy away from the all too familiar arguments heard so often in discussing the Middle East and will instead concentrate on what I believe, and I am sure many of you must agree, to be the vital issue – the human problem.
>
> I shall assume that you are all familiar with the historical background to the Middle East conflict. A brief reminder of some of the facts, however, might not be out place. The most significant fact to remember is that at the time of the emergence of the illiberal doctrine of Zionism that called for the creation of an exclusively Jewish state in Palestine, Palestine was a flourishing country with a predominantly Arab population. The second important fact to bear in mind is that the Zionists had no scruples about obtaining support for their aims from anywhere willing to help. They approached Germany's Kaiser, Czarist Russia and, as we all know, were finally supported by Britain with the issuing of the infamous Balfour Declaration in 1917. When Britain's colonial empire started to crumble, the Zionists wasted no time approaching and later receiving unconditional support from the new imperialist power, the United States. Thus, the last fifty years witnessed the rise of Zionism as a colonial force, masquerading under the front of religious aspirations. Zionist support for imperialist causes has been highly consistent – they supported the American invasion of Vietnam, the Portuguese in Angola and are confirmed supporters of the racialist state of South Africa.

The motion tonight does not allow me to elaborate further on Israel's international role – instead, I return to the Middle East region where one of the most outrageous injustices history has ever known has been committed. It seems to be fashionable nowadays to dismiss moral considerations as being irrelevant to the making of political decisions. My thesis is to the contrary – universal principles of justice should be recognised and adopted as the foundation of politics.

It is the immorality of our Machiavellian politics that has led to the imprinting of patches of shame on our modern history. It is this immorality that made possible the exterminations of millions of Jews by a fascist European power. Ironically, it is this same immorality that made the expulsion of the Palestinian Arabs from their homeland appear acceptable to the Zionist Jews, and indeed to much of the world. Living with the problem of the Palestinian refugees must have seemed an acceptable price for the Zionists to pay for the realisation of their 'dream' of an exclusively Jewish state. How else can one explain Israel's attitude to the United Nations that has been calling for the repatriation of the refugees ever since their expulsion in 1948? To us, the Palestinians, to live as refugees appeared as a transitory period of our lives that we had to endure, a period during which we would not abandon our hopes and our struggle to return to our homeland and re-establish the peace and harmony that were, until recently, its main characteristics.

The Palestinians did not sit idle in their squalid conditions to await the arrival of a Messiah to help them out of their plight. Their striving for education and hard work has superseded their numerous environmental and economic difficulties, and their considerable achievements came as a surprise to many but to themselves. Those skilled Palestinians now occupy the highest seats of learning throughout the Arab world. Yet these achievements did not diminish their determination to return to their homeland. It is perhaps ironical that the nucleus of the Fatah resistance movement was originated in Kuwait by a group of Palestinian teachers and engineers, which included Fatah leader, Yasser Arafat.

> Ladies and gentlemen, if you vote for the motion before you this evening, don't imagine that, to use the popular cliché, you will be voting for the extermination of the Israelis or the 'driving of the Jews into the sea'. Nor will you be voting for this or that Arab government or politician. You will be voting for a people who have been deprived of their homes, land and, most important of all, their political and civil freedom. But, if you vote against the motion, you will be voting for the likes of Moshe Dayan, who have made militarism into an established instrument of foreign policy. You will be voting for a state that has made a mockery of the noble values of Jewish ethics. You will be voting for the state which is refusing to allow me and thousands of others like me to return to our homes.

Ultimately, the motion was defeated by sixty-three votes.

*

Academically, during Hilary term, I narrowed my research to the role of the military in politics, taking Iraq as a case study and the 1936 Bakir Sidqi *coup d'état* that unleashed a trend that has persisted in parts of the Arab world until today. I had the privilege of having the distinguished and extraordinary – later my friend and mentor – Albert Hourani at St Antony's College as my supervisor.

The situation in the Middle East continued to deteriorate, but, given its importance for the international economy and world peace, it continued to be in the crosshairs of the world powers. It did not take long for Egypt's President Anwar Sadat, who had inherited an economy that had been badly affected by the 1967–1970 war of attrition between Israel and Egypt, to behave like a marionette controlled by Kissinger. Kissinger dominated and flattered Sadat, isolating him from any independent-minded advisers. That suited Sadat's ego. He started referring to Kissinger by his first name and bragging about Henry being his friend. Gradually developing a heady autocracy, Sadat removed a potential challenger by sacking General Saad el-Shazly, chief-of-staff and architect of the crossing of the Suez Canal by Egyptian forces followed by Egypt's initial successes in October 1973. He was given a golden exile and transferred to the UK as Egypt's ambassador.

Shortly after his arrival in London el-Shazly held a closed meeting at the Egyptian Cultural Centre with Arab journalists and intellectuals, where he briefed the audience about the war. He said that after years of analysis, planning and countless simulations, the initial crossings went according to plan. Then Sadat, with few military credentials, started interfering in the war's management before sweeping aside the minutely detailed war plan, taking over the general command of the army and adopting an impulsive, reactive and politically based strategy, which resulted in the early victories turning into a chaotic defeat.

A few weeks after that meeting, Egypt recalled its ambassador from London. Samir Radwan, an Egyptian economist, signed with me a letter to *The Times* protesting that move and underlining how heartening it was to see such a competent person representing part of a region where for many decades an individual's competence had not always been the determining factor in the selection of foreign delegates.

*

With the quadrupling of oil prices in 1974, oil-producing countries, particularly Saudi Arabia and the Gulf nations, began to see a substantial surplus in their current accounts. It was not always wisely spent. There was shameful waste and a startling disregard for priorities. I was angered on reading news of tiny Gulf states spending billions of dollars on buying arms, a pattern that could be found in all Arab states in the Gulf. It was the era of petrodollar recycling: American dollars buy Gulf Arab oil, which fuels the American economy and American factories, which make products sold to Gulf Arabs for those original American dollars, and the circle is complete. It was a heads-I-win, tails-you-lose situation. With or without their newly acquired military toys, these little statelets were incapable of rebuffing a serious attack on their territory without heavily relying on outside support. Even the Saudis with their larger landmass and significantly bigger population simply lacked the personnel skills to properly utilise what they were buying at exorbitantly high prices. The security of these countries would have been better safeguarded by fostering and consolidating relations with sister Arab countries. They also had wide scope for reinforcing inner cohesion within their societies by increasing political participation and introducing transparent governance, accountability and independent judiciaries. The value of those post-1973 arms transactions alone was enough to set up endowment funds to pay for the education of a whole generation of all young people throughout the Arab world.

Early in spring 1974 the Arab oil-producing countries were persuaded to call off their embargo. But that 'oil shock', as it was named, still left its imprint on the world economy and on consumers everywhere. The hike in oil prices caused by the embargo also rekindled worldwide public awareness and sensitivity, not only to the strategic importance of the Middle East but also to the root causes of the Arab–Israeli conflict. To us, the Palestinians, we felt that those subtle shifts ever so slightly lifted the heavy veil that shrouded our existence and stifled our narrative. It had been impossible for us to draw the attention of world public opinion to our plight without being derailed by fake accusations of anti-Semitism, a fundamentally European phenomenon. The ethnicity or religion of the soldiers demolishing a Palestinian home was totally irrelevant. Our criticism of Zionism as an ideology and calls for its abolition needed to be seen in the same way as calls to end capitalism in Britain or communism in North Korea. Besides, there were books written by Jewish authors calling for the de-Zionisation of Israel. As the Jewish author Alfred Lilienthal wrote: 'had public opinion been adequately and impartially informed, it is doubtful whether Zionism would even have succeeded in the United States or in Britain'.[7]

The Palestinian message was simple, and, when not muzzled, getting it across was not hard. The difficulty came from trying to squeeze into a game that had already been played and largely won in the arena of public relations. Palestinians, on the whole, were clueless about the world of PR and simply did not participate in it. The Zionists, on the other hand, mastered it early on and coined the term *hasbara* – which roughly translates from Hebrew as 'explaining' – to describe their project of state-sponsored public diplomacy campaigns and propaganda. From the outset PR specialists became a vital pillar of Israel's state apparatus. They relied on the common belief that if you repeat something over a long period of time, and persuade the mainstream media to applaud or echo your proposition, sooner or later your contention will be assimilated into the public psyche – a technique ironically first successfully deployed and perfected by Joseph Goebbels in 1930s Nazi Germany.

The result was that we could not be seen and recognised as a people by Western public opinion. That public opinion now seemed to have fallen victim to Israel's dehumanising campaign against the Palestinians and largely accepted the Zionist narrative, which saw a new population building a Plato Republic – essentially a justice-for-all society ruled by wise men – in the barren desert of Palestine, despite all the vicious assaults against them by nefarious Palestinian Arabs, who, by the way, did not exist in any form except as marauders. That narrative was so systematic, so skilfully crafted and delivered that, at one point in my life, I started to doubt the reality of my own existence. Every time I visited Palestine/Israel as a young man or even later, reality clashed with the distorted images that kept surging in my head.

Countering this *hasbara* had its problems. It was not simply that its arguments, albeit replete with distortions and downright falsehoods, were always cleverly presented but also that any counter-arguments were forcefully challenged to the point of deploying defamation, not to mention threats to careers and livelihoods.[8] Nothing, not even initiatives in line with the UN Charter and the Universal Declaration of Human Rights, could escape vilification that would emanate from the Israeli opinion-generating machines.

When in the mid-1970s the Iraqi government launched a campaign, through advertisements placed in the *Guardian*, *Le Monde*, *The New York Times* and *The Times* calling upon all Iraqi Jews who had left the country since 1948 to return to Iraq and enjoy all the rights accorded to Iraqi citizens, that initiative was met with harsh criticism of the newspapers that published those ads and with more cries of anti-Semitism.

I wrote a letter published in the *Guardian*,[9] which quoted a confidential despatch dated December 1934 from the British ambassador in Baghdad at the time, Sir Francis Humphrys, who stated: 'Before the war they [the Jews] probably enjoyed a more favourable position than any other minority in the country. Since 1920, however, Zionism has sown dissension between Jews and Arabs, and a bitterness has grown up between the two peoples which did not previously exist.'[10] I ended by assuring its editors that 'no Palestinian I know would subject your paper to any form of abuse were you to accept an advertisement from the Israeli embassy inviting the Palestinians to return home'.

As active members of United Nations Association, three of my Oxford contemporaries, Michael Attwell, Peter Mandelson (later Lord Mandelson) and Dick Newby (later Lord Newby) visited Israel and its neighbouring Arab countries. They came back convinced that the status quo between Israelis and Palestinians was untenable and much work was needed to dispel mistrust and preconceived ideas. Attwell and Newby reported meeting officials of the Israeli students' union who expressed disbelief that Jordan had a university or Syria an economic development plan. Mandelson wrote a more optimistic view in the magazine *Middle East International* (January 1976) referring to Israelis he met succumbing to international backing for the PLO and agreeing to a settlement that included the creation of an independent Palestinian state. Years later, in his memoirs, he recalled writing home after visiting a Palestinian refugee camp during that trip on the outskirts of Beirut:

> The conditions are as gruesome as reported. Thousands of people living in unbearably cramped conditions … Of course,

> they will not leave the camps until they are given the opportunity to return to Palestine. It is the middle-aged and younger ones who seem most committed to return to Palestine. They are good humoured, patient and with a will of steel. It is a desperate situation.

He continued to say that he recognised that Israel's situation was not easy either and that he 'did not take a return to Palestine to mean the end of Israel ... but that the Palestinians had a national identity, and national cause, of their own seemed to me unarguable'. After his return to the UK he wrote in a *Jewish Chronicle* article that 'until there were two states, one Israeli and the other Palestinian, there would never be peace for either people'.[11]

*

Growing awareness of the Palestinian narrative continued to gather momentum, culminating in November 1975 with the UN General Assembly adopting a resolution asserting that Zionism was a form of racism and racial discrimination. It was met with the same reactions as those to the Iraqi government advertising campaign.

For me as a Palestinian, Zionism had evolved into a dogma that stifled free thought. It was glaringly obvious, in words and deeds, that Zionism viewed the Palestinians, whether Christian or Muslim, as inferior. The distinguished Jewish professors Israel Shahak and Norton Mezvinsky wrote several books and articles – quoted later in this book – amply documenting those attitudes which they deemed as racist. We were ethnically cleansed from Palestine not only because we were the weaker party in a power game but because we were perceived as nonentities whose aspirations for a dignified life were beneath consideration. These attitudes within Zionism were not so much theoretical notions but rather lived realities, demonstrated inter alia by denying us Palestinians the right of return to our birthplaces. Abba Eban, the former Israeli foreign minister, published an article in *The Times* challenging the 1975 UN resolution about Zionism and racism. I responded to Eban in a letter published in the same paper by asking what I had asked him previously during an Oxford Union debate, namely to explain why he, a South African, had more rights than me, a Palestinian, to live and settle in Palestine? Abba Eban, who could talk the hind legs off a donkey, had recoiled and waffled back at my straightforward question. Neither his remarkable eloquence nor his immense intellect proved enough for him to articulate a coherent answer.

Early in spring 1976 I was asked by *Millennium: Journal of International Studies*, based at the LSE, to review a book entitled *Open the Gates* by Ehud Avriel. *Open the Gates* was a detailed account of the intricate operations involved in smuggling Jews out of Europe, particularly those living under Nazi occupation, and relocating them to Palestine at a time when Britain had imposed limits on Jewish immigration to Palestine. As an agent of the Haganah, the author was himself a chief operator in organising these missions. He relates numerous dramatic espionage ventures involving Greek shipping agents, diplomats, journalists, princes and members of other secret agencies, among them the Gestapo.

A reader unfamiliar with the history of Palestine under the British Mandate would be left with the impression that Palestine was a deserted country whose coasts were guarded by British sailors and soldiers unwilling to have anyone share that rough treasure with them. No mention was made of the reasons for Britain restricting Jewish immigration to Palestine, namely to avoid provoking hostility from Palestinian Arabs already concerned about the takeover of their country, or of the fact that the indigenous Arab population was actually apprehensive and unwilling for Palestine to receive a flood of immigrants with the self-acclaimed intention of colonising their country.

The same omission is found in Avriel's account of the Évian-les-Bains Conference that was convened in July 1938 in response to President Roosevelt's appeal to discuss the emigration of political refugees from Austria and Germany. Except for the Netherlands and Denmark, all thirty-three countries attending the conference, including the United States, declined to lift their restrictions on Jewish immigration. Although there were no Palestinian representatives at that conference, the author concludes that 'the one country that felt it did not have enough Jews was Palestine'. Most intriguing was the book's reference to the direct collaboration between Zionist figures and the Nazi authorities. At the peak of Nazi persecution of the Jews, the Haganah still gave full priority to Zionists' political aims, and humanitarian considerations were given an inferior ranking. The following encounter between Avriel and Eichmann is particularly striking:

> 'Progress is too slow,' he [Eichmann] barked at me ... It was time to make the place *judenrein* [Nazi term meaning 'cleansed of Jews'] – and soon!
>
> 'We do all we can,' I said ... Sometimes, however, his office delayed these urgently needed papers ... [and] it was increasingly difficult to obtain ships ...
>
> 'Mere excuses,' Eichmann shouted ... I was protecting a political interest. We moved so slowly because we insisted on young people only ... I insisted that the only reason for our selectivity was the hardship of the trip. The passengers had to be able to jump into the sea near the shore to escape the British.[12]

The Zionists' agenda to colonise Palestine was the overriding priority. If the Zionists' predominant concern was rescuing the beleaguered Jews then the refugees would have been better off in any other part of the world outside Germany. The real reason for Mossad's selectivity was that they wanted people young and fit enough to fight and help achieve their conquest of Palestine. This conclusion was corroborated by the fact that, even among the refugees who were young and fit, the Zionist movement confined its help to those of them willing to emigrate to Palestine, and Palestine only. Palestine's domination was their foremost priority. This was notably expressed by David Ben-Gurion in 1938:

> If I knew that it was possible to save all the [Jewish] children in Germany by transporting them to England, but only half of them by transporting them to Palestine, I would choose the second—because we face not only the reckoning of those children, but the historical reckoning of the Jewish people.[13]

*

My thesis on Iraq and a research project I was working on required me to undertake fieldwork, and I conducted several interviews with Arab intellectuals and veteran politicians. In spring 1975 I spent five months staying in or travelling by road between Beirut, Damascus, Amman, Baghdad and several Gulf countries. In Beirut I stayed with my precious friends Mona and Rashid Khalidi.

Those countries' boundaries made no sense at all. They were the result of two European civil servants, the British Mark Sykes and the French Georges Picot, sitting together negotiating and drafting a blueprint for chopping up the land expropriated from the defunct Ottoman Empire that came under the Allies' control after the First World War and placing it under the domination of their respective imperialist countries and Russia.

At that time the Arab people were in a situation somewhat similar to that faced by the Germans and the Italians in the mid-nineteenth century, when both peoples were living in disunited and sometimes conflicting city states, kingdoms and principalities. Visionary leaders in both Italy and Germany, realising that unity is power, patiently negotiated the arduous and hazardous road to unity. The underlying common good of their missions was understood and supported by their peoples, and two new nations were finally formed, Italy in 1861 and Germany in 1871.

Left to their own devices the Arab people would have likely followed a similar path, in line with Britain's 1915 trade-off agreement with the sharif of Mecca, Hussein bin Ali, when Britain promised him recognition of a unified Arab state in return for his breaking away from the Ottoman Empire and fighting against it on the side of the Allies. Under the Ottomans, administratively the Arabs of the eastern Mediterranean and the Arabian Peninsula lived in different provinces but with no actual frontiers separating them to obstruct free movement of goods or people. Above all, there was no language barrier, and internal political rivalry and religious schism were no worse there than they had been in Germany or Italy before unification. With the abundance and diversity of their natural resources and their strategic geographical position on the Red Sea and the Mediterranean, the Indian and the Atlantic Oceans, and with an elite formed and trained in different capacities during Ottoman rule, the Arab people had all the makings to build and develop a viable and prosperous Arab confederation. Their history has shown that it was only after uniting Syria with Egypt that Saladin succeeded in finally defeating the crusaders and liberating Jerusalem in 1187.

The colonial powers knew about these Arab aspirations for unity and that the fall of the Ottoman Empire created an optimal time and space for achieving it. The Arab world was ready to make a restart, revive its vitality and its once major contributions to world civilisation. Indeed, the promise to support those objectives was the joker played by Britain to seduce the sharif of Mecca to revolt and join its fight against the Ottoman Empire. Alas, realpolitik trumped the ethics of honouring commitment; for the British and the French, material and strategic interests were paramount.

Mark Sykes and François Picot concocted a secret agreement, the infamous 996-word Sykes–Picot Agreement, that dealt a fatal blow to the Arabs' prospects for any sort of unity post-First World War. Sykes severed the artery of what was an organically linked Arab society, while Picot punctured its air pipes. That lifeless mass was then sliced up into bite-sized portions, and, as failed states, became prey to the two principal European powers – Britain and France – determined to take over the reins of a defeated Ottoman imperium for their own economic (oil) and geopolitical purposes. Sykes and Picot's 1916 provisions contained all the ingredients for perpetual conflict. They crafted arbitrary frontier lines and proposed allocation of political and economic power in ways guaranteeing that a cultural and national cohesion would remain a mirage. In the process, Sykes and Picot played a decisive role in paving the ground for the French government to accept and the British government to adopt in 1917 the Balfour Declaration supporting Zionism.

Their agreement resulted in Arab tribes such as the Shammar finding themselves divided between what became modern-day Syria, Jordan, Iraq, Saudi Arabia and Kuwait; or, like the Kurds, being split between Iran, Iraq, Syria and Turkey. These divisions made no economic sense either. Had that region been united, with its fertile land, water and human resources, economies of scale combined with the usual multiplier effect would have turned it into what it once was: one of the most prosperous regions of the world.

Most of the Arab states that came into existence after the First World War were a legacy of this infamous agreement. The states emerging from this scheme were born weak, with enough ethnic, class, religious and tribal tension within and between them to condemn them to lifelong dependency on the imperial powers that conceived them. They were ruled by regimes desperately lacking in legitimacy. Not only did their ruling oligarchies systematically employ all kinds of coercion against their citizens but they also helped themselves to their countries' national wealth as if they were the only shareholders, without so much as a hint of any binding social contract. The longevity of these regimes enabled them to entrench their absolute power and perfect their widely used repressive techniques. That state of affairs left Arab societies in total ossified disarray.

Fearing for their safety and deprived of any legitimate means for opposing their oppressive regimes, ordinary citizens commonly sank into a state of despair and apathy. Some sought meaning through religion, while for others the main goal in life became simple survival or an exaggerated pursuit of personal wealth. On the whole the Arab world, which was once a beacon of civilisation, had by the early twentieth century fallen into a generalised impoverishment and decline in all fields and trailed far behind other regions in the world that were not as well endowed with natural and human resources. To say that in many fields the Arab world was not taking full advantage of its huge potential would be an understatement. All kinds of theories have been advanced to explain that skewed situation. These range from lack of unity and collective purpose, uneven distribution of wealth, corrupt leadership, outside interference, the disruption of regional stability created by the insertion of a non-Arab state – Israel – in the midst of contiguous Arab states, lack of true independence and absence of democracy to the downright silly hypothesis claiming that there are idiosyncrasies unique to the Arab mind. Whatever the reason, with genuine Arab solidarity, focusing on the many things the people have in common, it was certainly plausible for these countries to reincarnate as a collaborative community of peoples and nations, perhaps one day morphing into – who knows? – a political and economic union of the kind the Europeans have managed. It was, after all, in the not so distant past that people, goods and services moved freely within their frontiers while, as provinces of the former Ottoman Empire, they also enjoyed a relatively high degree of autonomy. Meaningful alignments and streamlining would enable them to enhance their productivity and empower their countries to become self-sufficient in most fields. In such a setting, prosperity, justice and dignity would not be offered by the state to a select number of cronies as perks but would be claimed by all citizens as their entitlement.

During my frequent crossings of the Iraqi–Syrian border the suspicions with which the frontier guards treated each country's citizens was palpable. Both countries were ruled by the Ba'ath Party, with the same slogans for Arab fraternity and unity. It did not need much analysis to see that hostility between the two states did not come from differences in political ideology but from rivalry and indoctrination by ruling clans that rendered both sides unstable and vulnerable and ready prey for outside manipulation.

It was depressing to see and feel the omnipresence of the military and its dominance in all spheres of life. In Baghdad in 1974, for example, I met some great minds – academics, politicians and journalists – and wanted to discuss with them my thesis,

The Role of the Military in Politics: A Case Study of Iraq to 1941. Although my questions were confined to my academic research, it took a long time and a lot of effort to build trust with these otherwise convivial and outgoing people.

Once the ice melted and shields dropped, my stay in Baghdad became both enjoyable and rewarding. I became aware of how our fraternity as Arabs is superficially suppressed and that not much is needed to revive it and restore its vitality. My travels and fieldwork in the region convinced me that the aspiration for Arab unity was widespread among the people but not shared by governments. The only prospect for such an aspiration to be transformed into anything meaningful is, therefore, through a bottom-up approach, which, as things stand, governments are blocking. Time and again it has been proven to me that person-to-person the Arab people were as capable as anyone else, if they could only break loose from the chains wrapped around their necks by lingering imperialism and the failed states they were left with. This is a fact of life, not 'Arab paranoia'. De facto imperialism exploits others through the continued exercise of power, albeit in different forms, with the aim of ensuring the survival of quasi-colonial control even after the official departure of the colonists. I remember once prefacing a comment in a conversation with a prominent veteran British politician, whom I prefer not to name for reasons of privacy, that 'you might think that we Arabs always look for the hidden hand behind our miseries, but the invasion of Iraq looks like a complot to me'.

'Not at all,' he countered, 'conspiracies and manipulation are commonly used mechanisms for advancing foreign policies.'

During my time in Baghdad my friends and I would often go out for drinks or meals at the romantic row of riverside restaurants spread along the Tigris, to the background sounds of Iraqi verses and songs delivered by legendary Iraqi singers like Afifa Iskandar, Nazem al-Ghazali and Fadel Awad.

While the city's idyllic atmosphere conjured up conversations about Baghdad's five-centuries-long Golden Age and its rich cultural heritage, interspersed with quotations from Arab poets, proverbs and folkloric tales, talk would inevitably turn to the reality of the current Arab condition. We would lament the prevailing archaic political system, that sterile mode of governance entirely based on personality cult, largely applauded by a subservient media. Throughout the region a typical television news broadcast would open with a national leader or one of his ministers shaking hands with an endless line of dignitaries. These programmes were deliberately rendered lifeless and uninspiring. Even the newsreaders' voices betrayed a weariness at what they were being fed. That same flat, monotone voice would produce a matching tone for bad or good news, for exchanges of congratulations or condolences. There was rarely a radio or television programme that addressed concrete and pertinent sociopolitical issues or offered suitable platforms for debating them. Favourite themes were sea-world or other wildlife documentaries – all safe and uncontroversial. Human rights, equality, freedom of expression, women's rights were hinted at but never frankly discussed.

My travels in Iraq, Syria, Kuwait, Abu Dhabi, Jordan and Lebanon during those five months of fieldwork confirmed my worst suspicions about the widespread economic and political inequalities and corruption in those countries and the glaring discrepancies in the living standards to be found in the region.

After my return to the UK in summer 1976, and filled with pessimism about the Arab predicament, I read in the press about Arab businessmen bidding to buy the site of the Battle of Hastings, where the invasion of England by William of Normandy had begun in 1066. I expressed my dismay at this wanton folly in a letter to *The Times* and my conviction that 'the overwhelming majority of thinking Arabs would view it [this bidding] with the contempt it deserves, just as they would had the purchaser been an American or Japanese businessman bidding to acquire the site of the battle of al-Qadisiyah or al-Yarmuk'.[14] I was incensed, and I was convinced that the lack of creditable social and economic development in the Arab world, complemented with a lack of efficient and long-term planning, would inevitably lead the Arabs, once the oil wealth had evaporated, back into poverty. Then the struggle for economic and cultural survival would need other battle grounds than those of Hastings.

*

I had a good working relationship with *The Times*. I was privileged to meet one of their brilliant editors, Edward Mortimer, and found him to be a man of rare intellect and personal integrity.

Mortimer told me an anecdote that summed up *The Times*' general editorial policy. Apparently, one evening the journalist in charge of writing an editorial had had too much to drink and dropped off at his desk. When they found him the following morning he was still asleep, and only one word was written on his otherwise blank sheet of paper: nevertheless. *The Times* was aware that there were at least two sides to any argument, but often that fundamental principle was overlooked in the Israel–Palestine case.

The Times' sympathies with Zionism could be traced back to 1917 and the intensive lobbying preceding the Balfour Declaration. At that time most of the British-Jewish elite stood firmly against Zionism, and in May of that year the two heads of Anglo-Jewry, Claude Montefiore and David Alexander, along with a number of their colleagues, wrote to *The Times* protesting the government's intention to espouse a pro-Zionist stance regarding Palestine. Henry Wickham Steed, foreign editor of *The Times*, friend of Theodore Herzl and sympathiser with Zionism, coordinated the publication of immediate rebuttals from Zionist supporters.[15] The same was done with the *Manchester Guardian*, whose editor C. P. Scott was also close to pro-Zionist Jews, including Chaim Weizmann, Nahum Sokolow and Leopold Greenberg.

Ever since that time *The Times*' legacy of supporting Zionism outweighed the sum total of its journalists' opinions. For example, on 28 October 1969 the paper's foreign editor, E. C. Hodgkin, wrote an article critical of Israeli repressive measures in the occupied territories. It spoke of torture, destruction of homes, disproportionate use of force and capital punishment. It was met by a torrent of letters from readers supporting the article and others ferociously opposing it, accusing *The Times* of anti-Semitism. One of the supportive letters came from Saida

Nusseibeh, relating her own experience with Israeli repression during a women's demonstration in Jerusalem in April 1969. On their way to deliver a letter to the Israeli military governor, first they were attacked by Israeli forces, kicking them with their boots and hitting them with anything they had to hand, then arresting them, telling them they were no better than prostitutes and taking each of them separately to an underground cell and interrogating them for three hours in a shift system.

To put out the fire, on 1 November 1969 *The Times* published a leader entitled 'To Be Fair to Both', unapologetically proclaiming the paper's support for Israel. While admitting that Hodgkin was right in showing that the Israeli forces reacted with severe repression, penalising both the guilty and the innocent, that editorial back-pedalled by adding that such practices were a common reaction by an occupying army and linking the repressive measures to guerrilla or terrorist attacks, completely ignoring violent suppression of peaceful demonstrations such as that attended by Saida Nusseibeh.

Following its 'nevertheless' doctrine, it also criticised attacks from Jewish politicians claiming that *The Times* was friendly to the Nazi government and referring to its 'sinister and terrible anti-Semitism'. *The Times* leader argued:

> [That was] obviously hysterical. If a calmly argued report of the conditions of the Arab people in the occupied territories is equated with the anti-Semitism of the Nazis, then nobody except an avowed Israeli propagandist can be allowed to discuss the state of Israel at all ... It does Israel harm by pretending that she is a special kind of state which either can do no wrong or, when she does wrong, must not be criticised because of the memory of the wrongs that have been done to the Jews by other nations ... The wrongs of the Jews cry out to heaven, but they do not cry out so loud that the wrongs of the Arabs need not be heard.[16]

My own experience with *The Times* corroborated the existence of constraints, sometimes self-imposed, that led to editing out the Palestinian narrative, the overrepresentation of Zionist views and the downplaying of Israel's violations.

In November 1974 I submitted an op-ed article to *The Times* entitled 'Image and Reality of the Arab–Israel conflict'. It was accepted at first, but then a second letter arrived a month later telling me that the editor felt that they were overdoing the Middle East. A cheque for forty pounds was enclosed as remuneration.

Some years later, after I had had some articles published in the *International Herald Tribune*, I was thrilled to receive a postcard from Edward Mortimer saying, 'Congratulations on your excellent articles in the *IHT*. I'm really ashamed that we haven't been able to publish any of them in *The Times*. But the American audience is more in need of your pedagogy, I think. Carry on the good work!'

Other British media outlets adopted similar attitudes to those of *The Times*. In 1979 I submitted an opinion piece to Christopher Hitchens, then foreign editor of the *New Statesman*, whom I had recently met. He was well informed about the Palestinian cause. He replied with this message:

> Thank you for a very generous and enjoyable lunch. It was very good to meet you and I have a feeling that the meeting was the first of many. I certainly hope so. I'm enclosing the piece I got Edward [Said] to do as a birthday present for Israel last May. Very beautifully written apart from anything else, and I think the most daring statement of the case we have published. I'm sorry to say that it doesn't look as if the editor is going to publish your own piece. Is there anything you would like me to do with it – send it on to Michael Adams for instance? Let's hope to meet soon ... Fraternally, Christopher.

My reading of Hitchens' message – perhaps speculative – was that the editors had already allowed a point of order by a Palestinian but that the monologue must continue. The Zionist stance had to be allowed to be repeated with no significant interruption.

In July 1976 the Bar Association of the Libyan Arab Republic invited 500 'scholars, lawyers, writers and journalists' from eighty countries to a four-day international conference on racism and Zionism. It was held at the Beach Palace Hotel in Tripoli from 24–28 July. I arrived at the hotel in the early evening and was at first told by the receptionist that I had no reservation. After a couple of hours' waiting and showing proof of my booking, I was given a shared room with another person. When that other arrived later I was happy to discover that he was none other than Edward Said. We had never met before, but I had recently read an article of his in *Newsweek*, and he had read a letter of mine on Iraqi Jews in the *Guardian Weekly*. If he was displeased at having to share a room, he never showed it. In fact, we got along well, and we were together most of the time during the conference. Following the conference, on his way back to New York he stopped over in London and came to stay with me in Oxford.

In Tripoli not all four days were spent at the conference. We were taken to visit Leptis Magna. On the bus there and back and while strolling along the cobbled street, through the magnificent amphitheatre, basilica and the marble-and-granite-lined Hadrianic Baths, Edward Said and I had lively talks about whether the PLO should be a national liberation movement or an independence movement. At that time the PLO was calling for the creation of secular non-sectarian democratic state in all of historic Palestine in which Israeli Jews and Palestinian Arabs would enjoy equal rights. In his book *The Question of Palestine,* published three years after that conference, this issue was covered in depth. By then the PLO's discourse had undergone a change from a 'goal of general liberation to particular liberation – that is, from the hope of a secular democratic state in all of Palestine to a Palestinian state on the West Bank and Gaza'.[17]

11

By the end of 1976 I had finished my research of the primary sources at the Public Record Office in Chancery Lane, London, and in Baghdad and was ready to start writing my thesis. I felt the need to step out of my daily routine and tackle that challenge in a new environment with its own stimuli.

I bought a second-hand VW campervan from an Australian couple who had used it to travel overland from Australia to London. It was fully equipped with a folding sofa, wardrobe, bookshelves, even a small tank for running hot and cold water. My destination was Paris. It became my mobile home when I arrived there in early January 1977.

Every evening I would park close to one of the grand hotels, using their facilities to keep clean. At the recommendation of my college tutor Wilfrid Knapp and his alumnus student, Francis Ghilès, who was working at the *Financial Times*, I contacted some people at l'Institut d'Études Politiques de Paris (Sciences Po) who arranged for me to the use the library there and access to other academic institutions in the city.

Paris in January 1977 was freezing cold, and it did not take long for the novelty of van life to freeze up, too. Within two weeks I managed to find in a dream street – Rue de la Montagne St Geneviève – a *chambre de bonne*, a 'maid's room', one of several tiny rooms on top of a large bourgeois building that had been used by the servants in years past. All occupants of such rooms would share a minuscule bathroom. They also had their own entrance to the building, called *entrée de service*. I had to climb eighty-seven steps to get to my room, which was just large enough for a single bed, a small writing desk and a sink. It had a little window that overlooked the back wall of another building.

The only sign of modernity was a telephone. All its grim features were quickly forgotten every time I stepped out of the building and into a neighbourhood that encompassed the Polytechnique, the Panthéon and Rue Mouffetard with its famous market, mentioned by Ernest Hemingway in his novel *A Moveable Feast* as that 'wonderful narrow crowded market street'.

Soon the fact that I was living in Paris's Latin Quarter became a pull for some of my friends from Oxford and London. They would come over for weekends and spend their days visiting the many tourist sites Paris had to offer, then join me for dinner at Chez Hamadi, a warm Tunisian restaurant in Rue Boutebrie, for a couscous royale washed down with *thé à la menthe* served in small, colourful glasses, all for ten francs. After one such copious meal, a visiting friend expressed his satisfaction by pulling out of his pocket a wad of crackling two-hundred and five-hundred-franc notes and waving them in the air, saying, 'That's what I thought I would spend this weekend. Now I have to exchange them back into pounds sterling.' The rent for my room was 400 francs per month!

For me, and for Henry Scott Stokes, a friend living in Paris and freelancing for *The Economist* and the *Financial Times*, dining at Chez Hamadi was a treat. Henry preferred to spend his erratic earnings on living in a spacious apartment in the Rue des Beaux Arts, one of the trendiest streets in Paris's sixth arrondissement. Many a time we met for a meal and feasted in my two-by-two-metre room with him bringing the baguette, me the Camembert, or vice versa.

Early in spring 1977 the *Financial Times* asked him to write an article on the phenomenon of the consortium banks that was developing in Paris. He obtained an appointment with Roger Azar, a director at Banque Arabe et Internationale d'Investissement (BAII), which was located in the imposing Place Vendôme near the Ritz.

Henry asked me to accompany him, and I accepted. I thought I might find a part-time job there as an Arabic–English interpreter. As we pushed open the heavy carved doors of the entrance, the hidden courtyard revealed itself, more fitted for bejewelled and bewigged courtiers and princesses than the golden boys we saw swaggering along its uneven cobblestones. We were warmly received. Azar viewed the three consortium banks in Paris with Arab institutional shareholdings as pioneers and wanted the *FT* readers to know about them. I had no interest in banks or banking whatsoever. I let them talk while I almost dozed off on a sofa at the far end of the spacious office.

After the interview ended they both came and sat with me for a coffee and a chat. Azar was an exuberant and easy-going character. He was clearly the bank's young star. Out of courtesy he wanted to know what I was doing, and I told him that I was working on a thesis. 'Bah,' he said, 'spending valuable years writing a thesis! Imagine what three or four years working for a bank like this would bring you.' Henry interjected that I was visiting from Oxford University, where I was working on said thesis. This struck a chord with our host. He started talking with visible nostalgia about having attended a one-year course there that had affected him deeply. Then he, too, struck a chord with me when he added that he spent that year at St Catherine's College. After some reminiscing about his year there, he looked me straight in the eye and asked, 'Do you really want to do academic research?' Noting my pause, he offered me a job there and then. I was stunned. Another Godsend, I thought. But me, in such a capitalist institution? I could not match myself with banking. It was a contradiction.

Our discussion drifted to the purpose of life, from pursuits with a sense of mission to self-aggrandisement, from altruistic dedication to self-indulgence. That meeting did stir doubts in me. There were obviously questions about my future which I had constantly deferred. So what were my objectives? On that occasion, my Godsend swung merrily between 'problem' and 'solution'.

'I need time to think,' I said. He agreed but insisted that I meet separately with the heads of the main departments of the bank: Corporate Finance, Foreign Exchange, Portfolio Management, Real Estate and Trade Finance. He encouraged me to ask them questions and hear from them how the work of an investment bank was different from the negative images I had of banking and how crucial their role was for economic development.

All of them set up long morning meetings in their offices, followed by longish lunches. The speed at which all of this occurred was dizzying, especially the change from having to negotiate my way between files and books scattered on the floor of my tiny room to working in palatial offices surrounded by beautifully carved and polished mahogany furniture. Still more striking was that each of these directors took me out to lunch at a different restaurant from the others. These ranged from L'Esplanade at the Ritz Hotel, to Café de la Paix at Place de l'Opéra, to Fauchon at Place de la Madeleine – a far cry from Chez Hamadi.

I was in the middle of two clashing dynamics, construction and demolition, while reason was tuned to play the arbiter. There was the problem of synchronisation, and I needed the best arbiter of all, time. As agreed, after the five days spent with his colleagues I went back to see Azar. He was looking for a straight 'yes' or 'no', not the dithering 'well, maybe' I gave him. But things were not clear in my head, and I was rather confused. I had pushed the idea of a long-term career to the back of my mind. All I wanted then was a temporary job that covered my expenses until I finished writing my thesis. The bank was four years old and was expanding rapidly. I thanked Azar for the rewarding time and generosity of his colleagues and said that I needed at least two more weeks to think the matter over. To my surprise he agreed.

I used that time to consult with Albert Hourani and Wilfrid Knapp. Both were very encouraging. On the appointed date at 9 a.m. the phone rang: a call to make a choice. It was Roger Azar with an elaborated offer. From June to December 1977 intensive training and exposure to all the bank's departments with a never-dreamt-of salary, followed by six months' fully paid sabbatical to finish my thesis, then rejoining the bank with a new open-ended contract with a title and an intensive finance and management course at the Institut Européen d'Administration des Affaires in Fontainebleau. Only a fool would decline such an offer. I didn't and, as proposed, started my training in June. I was not psychologically prepared for such a radical change in my life but finally decided that a banking position would improve my capacity to help my family and other needy Palestinians financially, and, by learning French and being exposed to French culture, Paris could be a good place for me to live and in my free time take my freelance writing on Palestine to a higher level.

*

That intensive learning period, followed by the demanding writing of my thesis, did not leave me any time to stay tuned to the bubbling diplomatic activities that were taking place that year, and which finally ended with the signing of 'Peace' Accords between Egypt and Israel at Camp David on 17 September 1978.[1]

That treaty was a depressing testimony to the reality that war remained an ever-effective instrument of diplomacy. In the final analysis the Accords extracted a validation from a tamed Egypt to Israel's territorial gains from the June 1967 war and fulfilled its drive to acquire legitimacy from the leading Arab country. President Sadat caved in to American and Israeli pressure without resolving the core issues. He negotiated from a position of weakness without making a serious effort to take advantage of the 'oil shock' and use it as leverage for consolidating the political position of Egypt and the Arab world. His concessions set a dangerous precedent that jeopardised any prospect of genuine peace agreements between Israel and the Palestinian people – for whom peace still remains elusive today.

The Accords dealt a blow to Egypt's status among the Non-Aligned Movement countries, and replaced its solid international relations with a fragile bilateral alliance with the United States. The grounds for the Accords had been prepared earlier in the 1970s by Henry Kissinger, whose endgame had consistently been perpetual Israeli dominance in the Middle East alongside a continually divided Arab world.

It was telling that the month after the Camp David Accords were signed, Israel's premier, Menachem Begin, announced a plan to expand settlements in the occupied territories. To appease Israel and its allies in the West, Sadat added icing to the cake by declaring on 26 December 1977 that Israel's June 1967 war against Arab countries was a defensive one. Menachem Begin must have laughed on hearing that declaration, as he and Yitzhak Rabin had already admitted that the decision to go on the offensive was Israel's and that one month before the war started the CIA had told Israeli officials that their army could easily defeat any combination of Arab armies.[2]

The concessions did not stop there. According to President Carter, during negotiations at Camp David a full agreement was reached to include the following paragraph concerning Jerusalem:

> Jerusalem, the city of peace, is holy to Judaism, Christianity, and Islam, and all peoples must have free access to it and enjoy the free exercise of worship and the right to visit and transit to the holy places without distinction or discrimination. The holy places of each faith will be under the administration and control of their representatives. A municipal council representative of the inhabitants of the city shall supervise essential functions in the city such as public utilities, public transportation, and tourism and shall ensure that each community can maintain its own cultural and educational institutions.[3]

Carter continued to say that 'in the last minute, however, after several days of unanimous acceptance both Sadat and Begin agreed that there were already enough controversial elements in the accords and requested that this paragraph, although still supported by both sides, be deleted from the final text'.[4]

That left Jerusalem exposed to the whims of Israel and paved the way for it to be unilaterally annexed by Israel in 1980 and declared its 'complete and united' capital.[5] Through such 'generous' concessions Sadat may have hoped to win the hearts and minds of the Israeli public and their Western allies. If so, then Sadat's calculation of rivalling, or even replacing, Israel as America's favourite ally in the Middle East was pitifully naive. Rightly or wrongly, for strategic as well as cultural reasons Israel was perceived as a strategic asset by US administrations on both sides of the aisle, and that could not be changed by Sadat's goodwill gestures and concessions to the Israelis. Turning his back on the Arab world was an exercise in self-delusion, where both Egypt and the wider Arab world were, ultimately, the losers. Egypt's considerable sacrifices for Arab causes and her defence of Arab independence were numerous, but it was precisely the role as champion of Arab nationalism that gave it the needed leverage to emerge as a power to be reckoned with regionally and internationally. The neutralisation of Egypt had always been one of Israel's most cherished strategic aims. Breaking away from the Arab composite not only further weakened the Arab world but it also undermined Egypt's perceived and real strength and diminished its status on the world arena.

True, the Camp David Accords restored the territory Egypt lost to Israel in 1967, but the occupation of Sinai was the consequence, not the cause, of Egypt's conflict with Israel. Egypt's engagement in wars with Israel in 1948 and 1967 emanated from its conviction that Israel was a settler-colonial project that harboured ambitions that went beyond Palestine. Zionist extremists who massacred Palestinians and triggered their exodus were influential in Israel's power hierarchy. Leaders of the powerful Gush Emunim movement, for example, believed that liberating Israel from the Arab 'thieves' was only a first step:

> Rabbi Ariel published an atlas that designated all lands that were Jewish and needed to be liberated. This included all areas west and south of the Euphrates River extending through present-day Kuwait ... Rabbi Aviner [was quoted as saying]: "We must live in this land even at the price of war. Moreover, even if there is peace, we must instigate wars of liberation in order to conquer it [the land]".[6]

What all the interlinked countries of the Middle East, including Egypt and Israel, needed was not piecemeal treaties but a rules-and-justice-based comprehensive and sustainable peace that mobilised the best of human ingenuity, in order not to engage in a futile smoke-and-mirrors game but to extinguish the fire in the pit where it was still burning – in Palestine, not Sinai. Egypt, Palestine and the rest of the Arab world were organically linked. Whatever happened in any of those countries had a direct bearing on the people of the whole region.

III

Writing, Activism and Historical Perspectives

Demonstration in Paris following Israeli invasion of Lebanon, 1982

12

I started my job at the bank in the summer of 1978. BAII was a consortium investment bank owned by thirty-six international banks; 50 per cent of the shareholders were from developed countries, and 50 per cent from developing countries, including some from the Arab world. The biggest shareholder was Banque Nationale de Paris, which owned 6 per cent. This gave it the right to nominate BAII's CEO. The chair of the board of directors had to be from a developing country. One of the bank's main activities was to arrange syndicated loans to developing countries and offer trade finance as well as to provide portfolio management services to several sovereign funds from the Arab countries of the Gulf and North African countries.

With that lucrative banking job the sharp turn in the course of my life was beyond anything I could have imagined only a few months earlier. There I was, a young man with a prestigious position, a decent salary, living in beautiful Paris. The bank's executives were swept up in a wave of enthusiasm and dynamism that left little time for other activities. Although I myself became engrossed in banking and attuned myself to the exigencies of the job, my passion for Palestine and for defending the Palestinian cause were enhanced, not diminished. Meanwhile, I was far from being one-track minded. As a lover of music, art, sports and socialising, it was also unthinkable for me to slip into the rat race routine or become what they charmingly call in French *métro, boulot, dodo* (metro, work, sleep). I was willing to make the necessary mental and physical efforts to keep a balanced lifestyle that revolved around all of these interests, including my professional responsibilities, and was lucky to have the friends and circumstances that helped me achieve that. The personal equilibrium later attained and the contacts made helped deepen my interest in following and trying to improve the fate of my Palestine.

Two of the friends who helped me to settle into Paris life were Henry Scott Stokes and Jérôme Halard – Henry by introducing me to Christo, the sensational modern artist, and Jérôme, thanks to the extensive network of his family, by saving me lots of socialising mileage. Another exquisite social venue I had the privilege to access was the home of the Iranian economist Hossein Mahdavi and Nevine, his highly cultivated Egyptian-Scottish wife, and their wonderful children, Tohra, Khashayar, India, Mariam and Amin. Their delightful company and lavish weekly dinner parties crowded with amazing guests, once relished, were very hard to turn down.

Paris at the time was spilling over with Arab intellectuals, thinkers and dreamers, and I was lucky to call many of them my friends, such as Shukry Bishara, Hail and Firyal al-Fahoum, Ghassan and Serine al-Saleh, Jumana Hussaini, Zohdi and Dalal Ayubi, Rufaida Hamza, Rajai Masri, Omar Massalha, the Shahin family, Ibrahim Souss, Afif Safieh, Christine Abu Filleh and the archaeologist and novelist Dr Yasmin Zahran.

These were the golden days of my social and intellectual life in Paris, with a regular inflow of Palestinian and Arab friends visiting from abroad, including writer Fawaz Turki and Mahmoud Darwish, who was regarded as Palestine's national poet. Edward Said was also a frequent visitor to Paris. Sometimes he stayed with me, as did Ibrahim Abu-Lughod, one of the most articulate Palestinian-American intellectuals. Abu-Lughod worked on establishing a Palestine national open university, to be headquartered in Beirut, and he spent long stretches of time in 1981 and 1982 living in Paris and working on that project with UNESCO.

One element of this transformative period of my life was learning to play the piano. I was fortunate to meet a retired pianist, Marcel Daljan, who had worked at the world-famous Parisian music hall the Moulin Rouge. I arranged to have an hour's lesson every fortnight. After a few sessions he noticed my enthusiasm and satisfactory progress and insisted on at

With Edward Said and Ibrahim Abu-Lughod in Tunis, 1982

least doubling the frequency of my attendance. To achieve that, without telling me, he addressed a letter to the bank's CEO in which he wrote:

> If this pupil does his homework properly, I can promise he will become a very good pianist. With my compliments for his talent which is yearning to be developed.

Monsieur Daljan told me later that it was his habit to write to parents of students he found promising, urging them to discourage their children from watching television and spend time revising their solfeggio and practising their piano exercises instead. He must have thought that I was still at primary school!

Christo and his wife Jeanne-Claude were easy-going, and we soon became friends. They were two of the most outstanding modern artists of the twentieth century. It is not possible to give an exhaustive description of their numerous works – the thoughts they provoke have already filled several volumes. Their *Running Fence* (forty kilometres long and six meters high),

Wrapped Coast (92,900 square metres) and other projects are still subjects of learned debate worldwide. The main characteristic of Christo and Jeanne-Claude's projects was their lack of permanence. *Running Fence*, for example, was exhibited for two weeks before it was taken down. Their projects were like mirages. The only remnants we have of them are to be found in their imprint on our memories or in the many drawings and books they have inspired.

Happily, Christo and Jeanne-Claude had the idea of building one permanent public artwork for generations to see. They were infatuated with the idea of building *The Mastaba*, a modern pyramid with horizontally stacked oil barrels in one of the Arabian desert dominions. In addition to aesthetic beauty and magnificence, they wanted it to symbolise and eternalise the impact of oil and its generated wealth on the twentieth century. After many passionate discussions, the idea was transformed from creating a massive block structure to producing an edifice containing public utilities, such as a museum and a library. I wrote the introduction to a brochure describing the project that I presented to Shaikh Zayed al-Nahyan, president of the United Arab Emirates. Among other things, I argued that sponsoring the arts and innovation was needed more than ever in the Arab world:

> As an Arab, I am aware that some parts of the Arab world are still lacking the most basic amenities. Thus, even to contemplate sponsoring an extravaganza such as *The Mastaba* might border on social heresy. But such reasoning would be similar to arguing that the undernourished should also dress shabbily. We, the Arabs, are no strangers to the development of art and sciences. Some of our ancestors patronised the arts well before Europe had its Medicis and Habsburgs. Some of our writers and scientists were rewarded with their works' weight in gold. For the last five hundred years, adverse circumstances have gradually eroded that great tradition … Now, thanks to the inherent resourcefulness of our people and the natural richness of some parts of the Arab world, we are breaking

away from that stagnation and renewing our contributions to Man's capacity for innovation.

Shaikh Zayed adored the project and gave it to an adviser to follow up. The adviser told me that the project lacked immediate returns. Perhaps that was a euphemism for something I was not willing to understand. I could not divulge my doubts to Christo and Jeanne-Claude for fear of undermining their enthusiasm or offending their artistic sensibilities. I knew that Jeanne-Claude was well connected in France. There was even talk of her being a distant relative of Charles de Gaulle. She was thrilled to hear that their project was discussed at such a high level and accepted my recommendation to initiate a parallel line of intervention. In 2007 Christo and Jeanne-Claude published a book about *The Mastaba* in which my 1982 introduction was reprinted.[1] Despite future attempts by the couple, however, the ambition of erecting *The Mastaba* in the desert near Liwa in Abu Dhabi never materialised, and Christo passed away in 2020. During his lifetime their grandiose plan had been reduced to erecting scaled-down replicas of the original concept of *The Mastaba* in the south of France and in London's Hyde Park, which, like all his projects, were gone with the wind and taken down a few weeks later.

Another futuristic project I tried to get off the ground was the Sunship. My friend Gaby Khoury, who had helped me prepare my banner when I went to welcome King Faisal in London all those years before, had meanwhile completed his studies in physics at Imperial College and stayed on as a professor. While there, in 1978 he conceived a solar-powered airship, which he called the Sunship. Covering its surface with flexible, thin-film solar cells, the Sunship was designed to achieve speeds of about 100 km/h and transport payloads up to 500 tonnes. The solar cells would convert sunlight to electricity to power the motors, while surplus energy would be stored in batteries for flights outside daylight hours. The Sunship's lift would come from lighter-than-air, non-flammable helium contained in its large envelope, while solar electricity provided the forward motion.

The Sunship was a space-age project especially suited for countries lying in the belt spanning North Africa and the Arabian Peninsula. These zones of sub-tropical anticyclones enjoyed sunshine averages of about ten hours a day throughout the year and a wind speed of less than 15 km/h for most of the year. A second major attraction was that for take-off and landing the Sunship did not need costly infrastructure like airports or ports. It could rise and land vertically and transport loads directly from one site to another. Another advantage was the constancy of its weight and thereby the absence of problems related to weight fluctuations due to fuel consumption.

The Sunship was a worthy project. It was ecological, cost effective, safe and practical and was the cover story of the *New Scientist* and the *Crown Agents Quarterly*. It was estimated that a prototype Sunship would cost only £800,000, and yet none of the high-net-worth Middle Eastern individuals contacted to consider investing in the project showed any interest. These people were on the look for 'quick kills', not long-term visionary ventures. In September 2020 I saw an announcement that an Israeli company called Atlas Advanced Technology Ltd was starting to manufacture solar-powered airships! That must have shocked my friend Gaby and left him feeling bitter at the short-sightedness of Arab private and public investors.

✳

On 30 July 1980, less than two years after the Camp David Accords were signed between Egypt and Israel, Menachem Begin's government annexed Jerusalem. Sadat looked the other way so as not to embarrass his new ally. Saddam Hussein was no better. Defying all logic, instead of forging alliances with regional and international powers to counterbalance Israel's robust Western backing, Saddam Hussein expressed his outrage by attacking Iran on 22 September 1980! The rest of the Arab countries unleashed a barrage of impassioned denunciations against Israel's 'cowardly act' of annexation.

As for me in Paris, I broached the idea of an article to André

My desk and Paris apartment, Rue du Paradis, 1976

Fontaine, chief editor of *Le Monde*, and he liked what I suggested. I then submitted my first article written in French, which also became my first article published in *Le Monde*, on 18 November 1980. In it I expressed my frustration with the condition of the Arab world, including lack of vision, disunity, corruption and the lamentable Arab response to Israel's annexation of Jerusalem. I ended my article asking whether I could be blamed if I found our world so small? Once again, I wrote, I take the road, although with a heavy heart, a measure of hope and a determination never to forget.

☀

Meanwhile, after Camp David, the situation in the occupied territories went from bad to worse. Continued settlements, combined with restrictions on all kinds of movements, paralysed the economy. The management of basic daily tasks – such as going to school or hospital, performing standard commercial activities, cultivating land and farming livestock – became a humiliating and exhausting ordeal. The military occupation continued to create intolerable living conditions for the Palestinian civilian population, often with the aim of producing an environment that Israel hoped would cause people to decide to pick up their bags and leave. While the population steadily increased,[2] permits to build new homes or renovate old ones virtually dried up or were cynically used for cultivating *quid pro quo* nepotism favouring the occupation.

To alleviate these conditions, in late 1978 a group of philanthropic Palestinian Americans set up a charity called United Palestinian Appeal (UPA) to raise funds from corporations and individuals of all nationalities, especially those doing business in the Middle East. UPA was modelled on the United Jewish Appeal (UJA). UJA's success in raising funds in the US was inspiring, bringing in up to hundreds of million dollars per annum.[3] Some Jewish groups objected to UPA's creation and it took two years of legal wrangling before it was finally incorporated in New York as a tax-exempt, not-for-profit, charitable organisation.

I was invited to chair its board of trustees. Inspired by the ambition and charitable objectives of UPA, I was delighted to accept. This was an opportunity to bring my expertise as a banker at BAII into the charitable sector in service to the Palestinian people. The first formative years were spent establishing UPA's authenticity as an independent humanitarian charity, a formidable task to achieve in an environment saturated with negative stereotypes and misconceptions of anything Palestinian. Our fund-raising campaigns barely paid for the cost of conducting them. Polemics and political considerations were of no interest to us as a charity. Our paramount concern was how to contribute to improving the social, economic and human condition of ordinary Palestinians, by financing schools and orphanages, offering scholarships, helping the disabled, the aged and the homeless and by aiding peasants and farmers. During the first years the urgency of the Palestinians' condition forced us to channel our meagre resources into relief work. Against our convictions we ended up supplying people with fish instead of teaching them to fish. Military occupation, and reactions to it, made long-term planning a luxury neither donors nor recipients could afford.

Early in 1983 I met two young nephews of Saudi Arabia's King Fahd, and we soon became good friends. They did not correspond in any way to the stereotypical images commonly held about Saudi royals. Their natural humility, innate finesse, open mindedness and sense of humour made a lasting impression on me. The younger one, whom I will call Ahmad, was educated in Saudi Arabia and the United States, while the elder, Majed (for our purposes), was a graduate of a British university.

Ahmad, in particular, was so spontaneous in his feelings of compassion for the weak and vulnerable he would impulsively deprive himself of something that was more needed by someone else. Once, on a freezing evening, we were strolling down Paris's Boulevard Saint-Germain when we passed a homeless man, shivering, trembling hand outstretched, asking for help. Without any hesitation Ahmad took off his cashmere overcoat, handed it graciously to the man and kept on walking, shivering in his turn.

Another time Ahmad overheard me when Mahmoud al-Hibbyeh, director of al-Makassed Hospital, called me from Jerusalem to ask for help. They needed an ECG monitor and other equipment costing US$1.2 million. 'Tell him you will call him back,' he whispered, before taking the phone and calling his uncle. After the standard greetings, I heard him say '*Talabtak*', a polite word for soliciting help without any explanation. Evidently, according to an ancient tradition, his uncle, too, gave a one-word answer, '*A'taytak*' (You have it). Only after that ritual was performed did he give some details and asked for a donation to the impoverished hospital in Jerusalem. His uncle asked for the bill to be sent to the Saudi embassy in Paris and the ECG monitor was bought by the hospital directly from the United States and shipped within a month.

In 1984, when UPA's disbursements were significantly short of our people's needs in the occupied territories, I consulted Ahmad and Majed about the possibility of extending our fund-raising efforts to Saudi Arabia. As Erasmus, the Dutch philosopher and humanist, wrote: 'bashfulness is useless to a man in want'. They were enthused by the idea and promptly set out to make the necessary preparations for a fundraising campaign and banquet. Since many US corporations had vested interests in the Arab world, particularly in Saudi Arabia, it was natural for UPA to assume that US corporations would be sympathetic to an American charity that worked to alleviate the day-to-day hardships of ordinary Palestinians in a region intimately bound up with US national interests.

To convey our message, Dr Sami Jadallah, one of UPA's founders and a member of the board of trustees, gave some interviews to the Arabic and English Saudi newspapers, emphasising that donations from US corporations to UPA were tax-exempt, adding that, except for the word Palestinian, UPA's statutes were almost identical to those of the UJA and how, in 1984 alone, UJA raised US$640 million in tax-deductible funds, about half of which was allocated for projects in Israel.[4]

The fundraising banquet was held in Riyadh on 20 November 1984 under the auspices of Prince Salman bin Abdulaziz, then Riyadh's governor, later king of Saudi Arabia. All US companies working in Saudi Arabia were invited. Many sent no one, but some were represented, as was the US embassy.

Prince Salman told the approximately 200 diners that whatever the legal and historical rights or wrongs, the world should not forget the needs and suffering of the Palestinians, an ancient people worn down by wars and material hardships. I spoke about the humanitarian objectives of UPA and how it was a non-political, private, voluntary organisation, subject to American scrutiny and auditing standards:

> People disagree on how to solve the tragic problem of the Palestinians, but everyone recognises its existence, if not its urgency. The Palestinians had to swallow their tears while new Israeli settlements sprang up on their confiscated land. The anomaly was that US dollars financed the settlements which the whole world, including the US, had condemned. Living under restrictive military occupation, with Israeli products flooding their markets, the Palestinians were unemployed or forced to become

With Prince Salman of Saudi Arabia, 1984

> cheap labour working on land that was confiscated from them. They needed a hand-up, not a handout. They needed concrete help, not rhetoric. The West that is at the heart of their tragic problem, must do whatever it takes to draw the final curtain on this human tragedy. It should not absolve itself from the consequences of a calamity that it itself has created. Help us with ideas and your donations, but whatever you do, for humanity's sake, do not wash your hands and walk away.

To my dismay, many did just that: washed their hands and walked away. Donations and pledges from representatives of US firms in attendance totalled US$4,000, not $4 million. $4,000. No doubt due to the Saudi royal family's sympathy for the Palestinians' plight, but perhaps also as a reaction to the Americans' indifference, King Fahd donated US$1 million and Prince Salman gave US$100,000. Prince Salman also authorised the opening of a UPA office in Riyadh and signed a letter endorsing our fundraising activities in Saudi Arabia.

US corporations working in Saudi Arabia, UPA's main fundraising target, fell out of the conversation. That was a first-hand experience of how the *raison d'état* surpassed all other considerations. As individuals, members of that audience may have been sympathetic to our cause, but their perceived corporate and state interests outweighed anything else. It was thought by some members of the steering committee that at the behest of the Israel lobby in Washington, Saudi officials got a slap on the wrist from the US administration. Mobilising civil society for funding Palestinians, especially through *zakat* (the Muslim duty of almsgiving, a kind of charitable giving via an annual tax amounting to approximately 2.5 per cent of an individual's wealth), had the potential to significantly improve their financial capabilities and political outreach. This, from the perspective of Palestine's adversaries, had to be nipped in the bud. UPA's fundraising banquet in Riyadh was viewed as a dangerous precedent and was never repeated.

Our efforts did not produce enough funds to fully meet our pledge to finance building a nursing college in Jerusalem. We were US$600,000 short. Those results were truly disappointing. Professor Hisham Sharabi, chair of the US charity The Jerusalem Fund, sent a letter stating that they had in hand over US$5 million in requests for scholarships and educational projects and thirty-one nursery schools seeking assistance for the coming school year.

That gross absence of meaningful inter-Arab solidarity brought to mind a memorable encounter I had with a Jewish student in Oxford. My supervisor, Albert Hourani, combined being chair of the board of Oxford's Faculty of Oriental Studies with occasionally being a visiting professor at Harvard's Center for Middle Eastern Studies. He once asked me to receive and advise one of his Harvard graduate students who happened to be Jewish and who was coming to Oxford on his way to London where he planned to spend a few months researching at the Public Records Office.

When I met him in my lodgings in Oxford, he pulled out a long list of names and telephone numbers and asked for permission to use the phone. The ease with which he told his interlocuters that he was calling as friend of a friend of a friend was really extraordinary. Without the slightest embellishment, he said that he would be arriving in London within a few days and needed help in finding accommodation. After half a dozen calls he was all set with suitable accommodation not far from Chancery Lane. When I expressed my admiration at the impressive community spirit I had witnessed first hand, he went on to give me more examples of the all-embracing solidarity within the Jewish community worldwide and of the powerful charities that took care of that community's interests in every walk of life.

For a number of complex reasons, this impressive altruistic community spirit was virtually absent in Arab societies. Internal divisions and rivalry which grew out of the post-Second World War arrangements created by the European powers remain a feature of the Arab world well into the twenty-first century. Distrust between these new nation states undermined deep-rooted social traditions, including the legendary Arab generosity and hospitality as well as religious tenets like *zakat*.

As mentioned earlier, UPA was given permission to open an office in Riyadh for receiving donations from the Saudi public. Strenuous efforts were then made by UPA staff and by several Saudi sympathisers to obtain a *fatwa*, or ruling, from the *ulema*, the religious authorities, declaring UPA eligible to receive *zakat* allocations. Almost two years were spent haggling with clerics and government bureaucrats. Several in both camps reaffirmed their personal consent to that request, while blaming each other for withholding their opinion from the public. In practice, the Saudi state was omnipresent, and the terms of reference for the *fatwa* were deemed to be political, not religious. The same was true in other Arab countries: the stability and survival of each regime would always be paramount, and anything with the potential to arouse the disapproval of a regime's external allies (for example, the US, Israel's protector), even a philanthropic activity, was banned. State phobias had seeped into and impaired the behaviour of private citizens.

Even for Arab immigrants living in faraway places, overcoming these inherent state phobias was a cumbersome and lengthy process. In the late 1980s, for example, UPA wanted to publish a directory listing the names and professions of Arab Americans in order to facilitate and enhance contacts within their community in the US, as well as offering the Arab world access to that network of skills and services. That project never saw the light of day. The community's perception of the state's coercive role and exaggerated outreach – be that state American or Arab – undermined any organised collective action regardless of how benevolent its objectives were. It was not until the twenty-first century that a new generation of Arabs in the US and Europe, who are also much more clued up about the ways and workings of social media, managed to overcome their parents' fears and became vocal about solidarity and open about altruistic work for their communities.

Happily, since 2011, UPA received the highest rating from Charity Navigator, the largest independent charity evaluator in the US. In a letter to UPA in 2018, Michael Thatcher, president and CEO of Charity Navigator, wrote:

> Only 6 percent of the charities we evaluate have received at least 6 consecutive 4-star evaluations, indicating that United Palestinian Appeal outperforms most other charities in America. This exceptional designation from Charity Navigator sets United Palestinian Appeal apart from its peers and demonstrates to the public its trustworthiness.[5]

Since its inception, UPA has attracted several dedicated Palestinians from different walks of life who volunteered to serve on its board of trustees. Over the years, they included, inter alia, Afaf Nasr Ajlouny (publisher), Sami Jadallah (lawyer), Isam Salah (lawyer), George Salem (lawyer), Najat Khelil (scientist), Gaith Musmar (auditor), Frederick Hadeed (financial expert), Ghassan Salameh (engineer) and the late Dr Haidar Abdel-Shafi, the eminent Palestinian physician who headed the Palestinian negotiating team with Israel after the 1991 Madrid Conference sponsored by the United States and the Soviet Union. UPA continues to aid and uplift Palestinian people through its charitable activities, and it remains a humbling example of the power of the Palestinian diaspora when our talents are harnessed and our efforts concentrated.

*

The continued Israeli occupation and the mushrooming of Israeli settlements in what was left of Palestine also gravely affected the cultural dimensions of Palestinian lives.

In March 1981, determined to promote and safeguard Palestinian culture, I joined up with Omar Massalha, then Permanent Observer of Palestine at UNESCO, to establish the Palestinian Cultural Heritage Association (PCHA), a not-for-profit apolitical association focused entirely on protecting and preserving the culture and heritage of Palestine. All PCHA activities were to be financed through private donations, and membership was open to all nationalities provided there was no evidence that they were motivated by anything other than a belief in the general aims of PCHA. Seán MacBride, Nobel Peace Prize winner, Irish politician and human-rights activist, accepted the invitation to be president of PCHA, which boosted our determination to rapidly launch the association and invite like-minded people to become members. As it would turn out, Palestinians and Palestinian cultural heritage would face a series of new tragedies before PCHA could be established.

By the time we finished the groundwork to establish PCHA, Israel had invaded Lebanon, which was embroiled in civil war, and imposed a seven-week siege on Beirut in 1982. Israeli forces raided the Palestine Research Centre and seized the Palestine National Archives. This revived the urgency of preserving and protecting Palestinian cultural heritage, which was supported by numerous UNESCO resolutions. Confiscating the Palestinian archives was followed in September 1982 by the massacres in Sabra and the Shatila refugee camp in West Beirut, when Israel-allied Lebanese Phalange militiamen killed, in cold blood, hundreds, maybe thousands of civilians, most of them Palestinian refugees.[6] In that charged political environment, under the auspices of the Arab League Educational, Cultural and Scientific Organization (ALECSO), itself established in January 1982, it was agreed to transform PCHA into the International Association for the Safeguarding and Enhancement of the Palestinian Cultural Heritage. The great support and commitment that the idea received worldwide was uplifting: 120 eminent figures agreed to become founding members. Their geographical, political, professional and social diversity epitomises the solidarity and sympathy many people felt for the Palestinian predicament, especially after the Sabra and Shatila tragedies.

The first meeting of the association, held in Paris later that month, issued an appeal to the international community. Its simple eloquence warrants being recorded here:

> To the Jews who are unwilling to see their faith or their great intellectual traditions tarnished before the eyes of the entire world by being used to cover at all costs the militarism and the crimes of the Israeli leaders;
>
> To the Christians of the Church of Rome, whom Pope John Paul II has called upon to acknowledge the right of the Palestinian people to a homeland of their own;
>
> To the World Council of Churches, which is striving vigorously against apartheid and all forms of racial discrimination;
>
> To the Muslims, for whom Jerusalem is an essential spiritual reference and whom the Organization of the Islamic Conference has urged to join in active solidarity with the Palestinian people;
>
> To the UN, whose resolutions on Palestine have shown the way to peace;
>
> To UNESCO, which on 15 December 1982 decided to add Jerusalem to the list of World Heritage in Danger;
>
> To ALECSO, that took the initiative of establishing our association for the safeguarding of the Palestinian cultural heritage;
>
> To the International Red Cross and other humanitarian organisations whose assistance is not restricted to the bodies

of the victims but extends to the spirit that is being killed along with the persons concerned and the works that they create;

To the Journalists whose truthful testimony about the massacres [Sabra and Shatila] awakened the conscience of the world;

To the Humanists, whose faith in mankind is outraged by the violations of human rights and human culture, and who see Israel's expansionism at the crossroads of three continents as a threat to world peace;

Let us all preserve hope that in Palestine, we will be able to build there, in peace, a future with a human face.

13

After neutralising Egypt at Camp David in 1978 Israel continued to have free rein all over the Arab Middle East. In June 1981 it bombed Iraq's nuclear reactor at Osirak, and on 5 June 1982 it invaded Lebanon – its main targets being the PLO and the Palestinian refugees settled in the south of the country.

Since the PLO's eviction from Jordan in 1970, Beirut – with its connections to the outside world, sophisticated mass media and well-educated and politically aware middle class – became the home of the organisation and its political, social and educational institutions. It was also in Beirut that the PLO flexed its muscles and sought to build a military infrastructure. Although Israel's strategic planners knew that the PLO's hard power was hugely exaggerated, their overall strategic objective to crush Palestinian nationalism, which the PLO embodied, led them to recommend destroying the PLO's military and political infrastructure in Beirut. Israeli leaders also feared that the PLO might mobilise its soft power against Israel through its research and information institutions and the number of bridges it had built to the Western media, which until then had largely portrayed Israel as a vulnerable victim surrounded by a sea of hostile Arabs and not as the military superpower it actually was. If the PLO could use its soft power to expose the reality of the Israeli occupation and the sordid conditions of Palestinian refugee camps to the international media, this would pose a threat to the sympathy that Israel enjoyed.

The glaring power disparity between the two parties might eventually lead to growing calls for subjecting the two protagonists to the same moral code. Such a sea change in public perception would prove awkward and dangerous for Israel and could even trigger outcries against the unconditional and boundless military support and economic aid it had routinely received from the West since its birth.

With General Ariel Sharon heading the invading army into Lebanon, and with the history of atrocities associated with him against Palestinian civilians, I was fearful for the survival of ordinary Palestinians and Lebanese. There were almost daily demonstrations in Paris and other French cities against the invasion. In that atmosphere I drew a profile of the Palestinian people in an article published in *Le Monde* on 22 June 1982, underlining their humanity as people made of flesh and blood, with children who felt the agony of pain as intensely as they enjoyed the glow of happiness. They had not chosen the circumstances of their birth any more than anyone else. Left alone, they would have chosen to stay in the homes and farms of their ancestors. Instead, they found themselves unwanted strangers in their own homeland, constantly being chased, with no right to protest or to exercise their basic rights as human beings. After their 1948 dispossession, they became the new Wandering Tribe, constantly threatened with extinction wherever they might turn for refuge.

We say in Arabic, *katal el-kateel wa mishi fi janaztoh* – he killed the victim then walked in his funeral procession. That proverb came to mind when I read statements by Henry Kissinger about Israel's invasion of Lebanon, praising the Reagan administration for its statesmanship, notwithstanding its decision to veto a draft Security Council resolution proposed by Spain demanding full Israeli withdrawal,[1] and a draft Security Council resolution proposed by France on a plan for military disengagement in Beirut.[2] I replied to his comments in a letter published in the *International Herald Tribune*, stating that Kissinger was not qualified to talk about the tragic events in Lebanon, for which he was at least partly responsible, as his shuttle diplomacy had concentrated more on excluding the Soviet Union and severing Egypt from the Arab world than on finding a comprehensive peaceful settlement to the Arab–Israeli conflict.[3] In the same letter I pointed out that, although created and nourished by the West, Israel had grown into a Frankenstein's monster, which was now hurting the interests of its masters, as none other than Kissinger had admitted during his involvement as secretary of state in disengagement agreements between Egypt and Israel following the October 1973 war. As he had expressed it, 'I ask Rabin to make concessions, and he says he can't because Israel is weak. So I give him more arms, and then he says he doesn't need to make concessions because Israel is strong.'[4]

On 18 August 1982, France and the United States intervened and forced the parties to sign a ceasefire agreement, stipulating that the PLO would evacuate West Beirut and that the safety of Palestinian civilians left behind would be guaranteed by a multinational force supervised by France and the US. Two weeks later President Reagan launched a peace plan bearing his name. It called for self-government by the Palestinians of the West Bank and Gaza in association with Jordan.

Israel violated the ceasefire agreement and sent its troops to West Beirut. It imposed a siege on Sabra and the Shatila refugee camp, where the ghastly carnage of innocent civilians was performed on 16 September under the benevolent supervision of the Israeli army. After the horrors at Sabra and Shatila, I submitted an op-ed about those atrocities to the *International Herald Tribune*. An editor, who knew me, called and said, 'No way can we print it. You're too angry.' When I went to sleep that night, his words were still hammering in my head like a pneumatic drill. I finally sat down to rewrite my previous day's article, this time without anger. I submitted two slightly different versions of it, in English, to the *Observer* and the *International Herald Tribune*, and a hybrid of the two, in French, to *Le Monde*. The chief editor of *Le Monde* sent me a letter on 6 October expressing doubts about publishing it:

> Dear friend, I found your article on my return from the United States. I will not hide from you that, given the fantastic accumulation of texts that have reached us on this problem, I very much doubt that we will be able to publish it. Believe me, I regret that. Sincerely yours, André Fontaine.

A few days later another letter arrived from *Le Monde* with a typeset version of the article attached, explaining that although they had got it ready to be printed, it had finally been decided not to publish it. The *Observer* did print the piece on 26 September 1982 and the *International Herald Tribune* on 28 September. Here is a synthesis of the three articles:

> Today, while Palestinians everywhere weep in silent rage, they wish that they had been spared the empty gratification of having their worst fears about Zionism confirmed. For more than forty years they have appealed to mankind to forestall the inevitable threat that Zionism posed to their existence. But, like Caesar before the Ides of March, the world heeded none of their warnings. How many massacres, how many more men and women, babies and adolescents, Christian and Muslims, how many more Jews and Palestinians must die before the world awakes from its torpor, regains its senses and finds the courage to say that Zionism is a disastrous doctrine for us as well as for the Jews? How could the world have been duped into believing that this anachronistic ideology could ever succeed in creating an exclusively Jewish state in an already populated land, in the heart of our ancestral homeland, without bloody conflict?
>
> Only in the number of victims do the Sabra and Shatila massacres differ from the tragic litany of those earlier nightmares of Deir Yassin, Kalonia, Qibya, Kafr Qasim, Qalqilya, Nabi Elias, 'Azzum, Khan Yunis, Sammu', Tel al-Za'tar. In April 1948, while the Palestinian village of Deir Yassin on the outskirts of Jerusalem slept, 200 armed members of the Zionist underground terrorist gang, Irgun, attacked, butchering 243 men, women and children. House by house, the inhabitants were pulled into the streets, lined against walls and shot, regardless of age or sex. Homes were dynamited. The attackers raped, tore earrings from women's ears and slaughtered some who were pregnant with carving knives. When day broke, corpses littered the streets. No one was allowed into the village except a Jewish policeman, who reported one

Palestinian had died. It took a persistent Red Cross officer to unearth the truth. The survivors were stripped naked and paraded through a Jewish quarter of Jerusalem, to be mocked and spat upon. The then leader of Irgun, Menachem Begin, is now the prime minister of Israel. Five years later a similar raid on the unsuspecting inhabitants of Qibya, that left seventy-five slaughtered, was led by General Ariel Sharon, now the man who holds the reins of Israel's army. Such mass murder of Palestinians is consistent with the cold logic of Zionism, which dictated the destruction, expulsion or, at best, oppression of our people.

We Palestinians cried out against these crimes from our mosques and our churches, from the playgrounds of our schools and the courtyards of our homes, and, when in your more reflective moments you allowed it, from the columns of your newspapers and the airwaves of your radio and television stations. The world ignored our warnings, refused to read the writing on the wall. Was it apathy? Perhaps. But the main reason was that it was too busy washing its conscience of the stains of shame from the crimes of the Second World War committed against the Jews to listen to our unpleasant bulletins. Now that, thanks to on-the-spot reporting in full newsreel colour under your very nose, will you continue to look the other way? In its implacable campaign against us, Zionist propaganda stopped at nothing to deprive us of what was ours. Our literature (we were depicted as aimlessly roaming Bedouin), our history (Palestine, one of the most ancient nations on Earth, ceased to exist in their historical narratives), our geography (the cradle of human civilisation – we grew fruit trees centuries before Europe, perfected irrigation and plant hybridisation – was presented to the world as strips of desert or malaria-ridden swamp).

Thinking people everywhere should have known better. The world's ancient travellers and artists had testified otherwise, that it was as developed as its peer countries in the eastern Mediterranean. Yet many of you blocked your ears and blindfolded your eyes, preferring not to know – and so, despite the

> inherent dangers of Zionism, Israel was planted as a Western outpost in our midst, robbing us of our homeland. As grim reports of the bloodbaths in Sabra and Shatila flashed in and the flickering screen featured Israeli soldiers rounding up our civilians, I wondered: will anyone now be surprised, if the voices of people who once believed it possible to live side by side with the Israelis are stifled, if there is a rebirth of Palestinian extremism – indeed, if there is an embittered, radicalised insistence that the Israelis have no place at all in our part of the world?[5]

Geula Cohen, a leading Israeli politician and member of the Knesset (for Tehiya, a breakaway party from Likud opposed to the Camp David Accords), answered my outburst in an article headlined 'Too Many Attacks on Jews in Palestine' in the *International Herald Tribune* on 14 October 1982.[6]

In it, she decried my article as 'one-sided and far removed from the historical truth'. She took umbrage with my claim that Palestine had been populated by indigenous Palestinians before the arrival of Zionist settlers and argued that the Zionists 'found the land underpopulated'; that the historical record left by travellers testified to its 'desolation and its lack of population'. If any Arabs were there, she argued that they were 'quite recent immigrants ... from Egypt, Sudan, Syria, Lebanon and other areas' who moved in to take advantage of the 'employment opportunities and the health service' that resulted from Zionist 'enterprises', or descendants of Hijazi tribesmen who 'subjugated most of the land of Israel' in the seventh century.

She wrote that the raid on Deir Yassin was a reaction to attacks on Jews and rejected my narrative of the atrocities there, describing the events as 'a battle' in which a third of the Zionist forces were wounded in the fight against people who Cohen depicted as illegitimate and dishonourable; she claimed that some of the fallen Palestinian combatants were in fact 'Iraqi "volunteers"' and that others were found 'dressed up in women's clothing and hid behind children'. According to Cohen, the casualties at Deir Yassin resulted from villagers either refusing to leave when they were given the chance by Zionist forces or being 'forcibly held there' by their own fighters. For their deaths, in other words, Cohen holds the Zionist forces entirely above responsibility.

Perhaps unsurprisingly at this point, where I saw a parade of prisoners through the streets of Jerusalem, she saw 'the transfer of the rest of the villagers to Arab-held Jerusalem for their own benefit'. In Cohen's telling, Zionism is a triumphant story of Jews finding 'political sovereignty in their ancient homeland' and the Palestinian tragedy a mere fiction.

The editors of the *International Herald Tribune* allowed me the right of rebuttal. In my rebuttal, entitled 'In Palestine: Room for Debate',[7] I reminded Cohen and readers of the historical evidence of the long and rich history of Palestine and its people, and the reality of its population of 700,000 Palestinian Arabs owning 90 per cent of the land at the beginning of the twentieth century and the start of Zionist immigration. I lamented that when Geula Cohen, a member of the Knesset, wrote about Palestine as if its people did not and do not exist, I was forced to question the willingness of Israel to coexist peacefully with Palestinians.

As for Deir Yassin, I challenged Cohen's depiction of it as a 'battle' by drawing on the written record left by investigators, journalists and eyewitnesses, who reported that atrocities and a massacre had occurred at Deir Yassin. I quoted Richard Catling, a member of the British investigating team, who reported that 'Sexual atrocities were committed by the attacking Jews; many young schoolgirls were raped and later slaughtered.'[8] And I recalled the words of Erskine Childers who wrote in *The Spectator* that captured villagers were 'paraded ... through Jewish quarters of Jerusalem to be spat upon: then released ... to tell their kin of the experience'.[9]

The motive for the violence that lay behind the reprehensible acts that took place at Deir Yassin, I argued, wasn't hard to find. The Palestinians had no place in Zionist plans, as the architects of Zionism made clear. David Ben-Gurion said that 'Israel is the country of the Jews and only of the Jews.' Such words were systematically translated into deeds. In 1948, Jewish ownership of Palestine was still only 5.6 per cent. But of the 370 kibbutzim and other settlements established between 1948 and 1953, 350 are on the sites of destroyed Arab villages, including Beit Nattif, my birthplace.

I also took my rebuttal as an opportunity to remind Cohen and our readers that Palestinians today are still living in under the shadow of Deir Yassin, in a world in which Zionist plans still make no place for them. How else to answer that most painful question, the question that is salt in the wound of every Palestinian: why is a Jew from anywhere entitled to Israeli citizenship and residence, when my compatriots and I, the ancestors of whom inhabited Palestine for centuries, cannot share in that fundamental privilege?

I ended my rebuttal to Cohen by reminding her that Palestinians will not simply disappear. For better or for worse, I argued, our destiny has been interlocked with that of the Israelis and peace can be found through real dialogue and using care with language and how we talk about history.

Between them, these articles contain the fundamental arguments of the Israeli and Palestinian narratives and should be helpful for a grasp of our convergence or divergence points and for the need of honest brokers for our two peoples. What was at stake in my epistolary debate with Geula Cohen was both the character of historic Palestine and the nature of the Zionist movement. For Cohen Israel was the ancient homeland of the Jews, a land across which transient Arabs drifted, 'a land without a people'. For me, Palestine was the homeland of Palestinians, some of whom were and had always been Jews, but also who were Muslims and Christians, with a shared rich culture and heritage going back centuries. To Cohen the Zionist project was therefore the righteous return of Jews to a homeland that had been awaiting them and where they could build safety and liberty for the Jewish people. To me the Zionist project was a movement of violent dispossession and ethnic cleansing, a movement that would come to be known as settler colonialism.

*

Although Reagan's 1982 peace plan ruled out the creation of an independent Palestinian state, it offered the prospect for opening political dialogue with the United States. To learn about how that plan was viewed by the PLO leadership, I was encouraged by an editor at the *International Herald Tribune* to interview Yasser Arafat, chair of the PLO, about it. I went to Tunis, where friends had arranged a meeting with him for me. After the eviction from Beirut he had set up the PLO's headquarters there.

I had never met Arafat before nor ever belonged to any political organisation, much less the PLO, but I knew about Arafat's popularity among my fellow Palestinians. Most Israelis regarded him as a terrorist. Some in the West shared that view. Much of the world beyond Western Europe and the United States ranked him among the leading freedom fighters of the century. To most Palestinians he was simply the national leader. Seen face to face in Salwa,[10] that night in December 1982 and on several succeeding nights, he came across like the head of a family whose youngest daughter had been kidnapped: her release was his *raison d'être*. He appeared to be devoid of self-indulgence, an evidently religious man who ate and dressed simply, worked hard and slept little.

This was also the rhythm of life of many of the men, women, and children around him. It struck me as an outsider that these abnormal hours contributed to making the man and his entourage disorganised. I was aware of the negative way Arafat was often projected in the Western media. I was going to ask why he never seemed to be clean shaven or why he insisted on speaking to the Western media in his imperfect English. As we sat down to talk in Arabic, his bearing discouraged me from asking such questions about his image.

He said the Reagan administration had to free itself from the undertakings made to Israel by Henry Kissinger and relentlessly adhered to by his neoconservative disciples in the US administration. Kissinger's 1972 boycott of the PLO, which he dismissed as a Soviet surrogate and labelled as the main cause of instability in the Middle East, was still a cornerstone of US foreign policy. To the Americans the Palestinians were an obstacle in the path of US strategic designs. They simply had to go. Arafat characterised the Reagan plan as 'positive' but compared it to 'a car trying to run on three wheels' – the missing wheel being recognition of the Palestinians' right to self-determination and to having their own state. Commenting on the 1979 Camp David treaty between Egypt and Israel, he said that bilateral treaties alone could lead at best to the forging of diplomatic relations but not normalisation. I thanked him for agreeing to our interviews and flew back to Paris.

As it turned out, the Reagan plan, that vehicle with a missing wheel, made no headway and was soon relegated to the overladen shelves of failed schemes. In the meantime, the Reagan administration elevated Israel to the status of a 'strategic asset', designated it as a 'major non-NATO ally' and even 'gave Israel access to certain forms of intelligence that it denied its closest NATO allies'.[11]

*

In 1984 the brokerage firm Dean Witter Reynolds, a subsidiary of Sears, Roebuck and Co., entered the capital of BAII. We soon discovered that Sears, Roebuck and Co. appeared on the Arab League boycott list. In 1951 member states had voted to establish the Central Boycott Office, based in Damascus. It was designed to sanction foreign companies and individuals dealing with or on behalf of Israel. In the 1970s Israel launched a successful campaign in the United States that led to the introduction of legislations outlawing compliance with that boycott. Sears, Roebuck and Co. was on the boycott list, apparently due to the Boycott Office confusing that company's name with its namesake company, Sears PLC, which had no connection to Sears, Roebuck and Co. In line with US legislation the company was not allowed to contact or negotiate with the Arab League Boycott Office.

As a director of one of the bank's departments, I was appointed by BAII to take charge of the matter. Sears, Roebuck and Co. was one of the biggest players in corporate America, and building a sound relationship with them was valuable. I spoke with Yasser Arafat about it. That was the time when he desperately needed to build bridges with the US establishment. He agreed that everything should be done to help Sears, Roebuck and Co., provided they gave us the documented evidence proving their case that they were distinct from Sears PLC. I passed that message on to their lawyers and was surprised when a few days later I was contacted by the office of the president and CEO of Sears World Trade, the trading arm of Sears, Roebuck and Co. He was Frank Carlucci, ex-deputy director of the CIA, and ex-US defence secretary. He wanted to see me in person in Washington, DC. A few days later I received a return ticket from Paris to Washington via London on the Concorde flight.

It was a great feeling flying at that speed and height – 6,000 metres higher than normal commercial flights. While cruising at 15,250 metres altitude, I remembered that Jericho was 258 metres below sea level. I felt smug thinking that, employing the mode of travel I used from Jericho to Switzerland as a teenager, the Paris–London–Washington journey would have taken 150 days! Now, barely twenty years later and travelling on Concorde, it would take only three hours from London to Washington. The planes we were streaming past below us looked as if they were standing still.

I liked the mission I had been entrusted with and how the boycott, a form of peaceful resistance, was bearing fruit. From that perspective I had the chance to defend our cause through my encounter with Frank Carlucci. I tried to imagine what he looked like, and a string of stereotypical images of detectives paraded in front of my eyes, intermixed with thoughts about the CIA's covert involvement in *coups d'état* in Iran, the Dominican Republic, Lebanon, Panama, Chile and Nicaragua, among others. And now I was off to meet the man whose former organisation had, in my mind, much to answer for.

After three hours of supersonic flight the Concorde was returning to subsonic speed as we approached the runway in Washington. Following a quick passport check I was sitting comfortably at the back of a chauffeur-driven limousine. The driver wanted to know if I'd had a good crossing, and on arrival he accompanied me to the lift. Carlucci's secretary was waiting and walked me to meet her boss.

Frank Carlucci did not look anything like I had imagined high up in the stratosphere. He was a humble and frail-looking man, perhaps five centimetres shorter than me. He invited me to take a seat at a large table covered with a selection of drinks and sandwiches. He reiterated what his group's lawyers had told us, and I repeated what we had told them all along. We would present their case, but the decision would be that of the member states represented at the Boycott Office.

Arafat arranged for me to join the Palestinian delegation at the next Boycott Office session, which was held in Tunis on 7 September 1984, where I presented the Sears, Roebuck and Co. case. The Arab League's bureaucracy was notoriously slow. Once I'd made my statement, the follow-up was left to the bank's legal department. I later heard that Sears World Trade was involved in the arms trade, and that was enough to puncture my enthusiasm. In any case, after the 1993 Oslo Accord between Israel and the Palestinian Authority nine years later there was a de facto end to the boycott.

My despair at hearing claims that Sears World Trade was involved in the arms trade lay in my strong convictions that total disarmament outweighs all other considerations. That had made me a stout admirer of the late John F. Kennedy, not only because he supported the Palestinian refugees' right of return and vigorously opposed Israel's acquisition of nuclear weapons but also because our world today would have been safer, certainly more peaceful, had it heeded his pleas for disarmament. Kennedy, as so often in his policy speeches, was deeply articulate in expressing his commitment to disarmament. His words from the January 1962 State of the Union speech to the joint houses of the US Congress are worth repeating here. They've had a profound impact on me throughout my life:

> World order will be secured only when the whole world has laid down these weapons which seem to offer us present

> security but threaten the future survival of the human race. That armistice day seems very far away. The vast resources on this planet are being devoted more and more to the means of destroying, instead of enriching, human life. But the world was not meant to be a prison in which man awaits his execution … This nation has the will and the faith to make a supreme effort to break the log jam on disarmament and nuclear tests – and we will persist until we prevail, until the rule of law has replaced the ever dangerous use of force.[12]

I saw Carlucci again during my six-month sabbatical in Riyadh when he came to Saudi Arabia on business. We met in his hotel's lobby. As we chatted he looked uneasy and self-conscious and kept touching the right-hand pocket of his jacket, as if to conceal it. I then noticed that it was slightly torn. It looked like it had been caught in the door of an elevator. If you allow me, I have a solution for that, I told him. He looked startled but said, yes. I then got up, walked to the hotel's reception and asked the concierge for a mending kit. We must have looked odd to the other guests filling the lobby, but we continued chatting while I was mending his jacket. He was certainly impressed with my display of skill, learnt during my summer job at Rivoli dry-cleaning and laundry in the early 1960s in Ramallah.

14

In 1982 Abir Dajani, an eminent London-based Palestinian lawyer, introduced me to Michèle Ray-Gavras and her husband the iconic filmmaker Costa-Gavras. They were both what they call in French *des gens engagés*, meaning people who care, interested in what goes on around them and in the world. As a journalist, Michèle sometimes covered events in Vietnam, Bolivia and Uruguay, while Costa-Gavras directed films that dealt with issues about the suppression of freedom by military dictators, corruption and the legacies of colonialism.

Before meeting them I had seen several films directed by Costa-Gavras, including *Z*, *State of Siege* and *Missing*. During our first encounter I started to say something about the justice of the Palestinian cause, when Costa-Gavras interjected with, 'Listen, when I was born, there was a country called Palestine. Now that country is there no more! That says it all.' Not long after that meeting, Israel's invasion of Lebanon in June 1982 sparked popular reactions in France. The demonstrations it provoked grouped French intellectuals and people from different shades of the political spectrum and the Arab community.

Franco Solinas, the screenwriter of *The Battle of Algiers*, reacted to the invasion by writing a scenario for a film based on the Palestinian tragedy. Costa-Gavras was keen to produce that film and managed to get pledges for 50 per cent of the funding from French television, but needed investors to cover the remaining 50 per cent. I called my friend Zain Mayasi, a Palestinian engineer and owner of a construction company in Saudi Arabia, and through him his partner Rafik Hariri. They agreed to chip in what was required without much ado, and the film *Hanna K.* was made and released in spring 1983. One of my family's Ottoman land deeds features in the film.

In France it was largely ignored by the mainstream media and was only shown for three weeks, while in the United States it was virtually boycotted, as Universal revoked its distribution contract with Costa-Gavras.[1] It was also met with hostility by the Israel lobby for its sympathetic portrait of the Palestinian issue. B'nai B'rith circulated a memorandum to its members outlining sets of prepared arguments that they could use against the film.[2] *The New York Times* called it a 'large, soggy dud',[3] while Edward Said wrote in *Village Voice* that 'as a political as well as cinematic intervention *Hanna K.* is a statement of a great and, I believe, lasting significance'.[4] I wrote a review in Arabic in the Lebanese weekly *Al-Mostakbal* encouraging readers to see it.

It was a disappointing experience. The virtual boycott of the film in the US *and* in France, where Costa-Gavras is a household name, confirmed a disavowal for the Palestinians to advance a counter-argument, however modest, against the giant Western film industry that was regularly churning out films with colossal budgets portraying us and all Arabs and Muslims as monsters, as 'others', as aliens bereft of any shared values with Western societies. It was an uphill struggle conceiving anything that challenged those deeply ingrained misconceptions and generalisations. But, having said all that, it is also true that some of the negative reception of the film was based on artistic rather than political judgements. To call the film pro-Palestinian would be an overstatement. But, for me, it had an important symbolic value: a prominent filmmaker turning his camera on the Palestinian tragedy was in itself a refreshing and positive contribution.

Nevertheless, whatever the failings of Palestinians' efforts to press their cause, and however much those efforts may have occasionally misfired, it was clear to all of us seeking to raise awareness of Palestinian lived reality that the Palestine question was interwoven with the image of an Arab and Muslim world that was regularly mocked by Zionist sympathisers such as Bernard Levin of *The Times* and A. M. Rosenthal and William Safire of *The New York Times*. Those negative images significantly affected outsiders' views of our cause.

Within my limited personal outreach as a banker and an

occasional op-ed writer, I tried to sustain the conversation begun in Britain while I was a student and continued in the French and American press. I strove to show that judgements about the 'Muslim world' are as fatuous as judgements about the 'Christian world', which covers both Sweden and Paraguay.

Things were not made easier for those of us trying to achieve some balance when even respected Western journalists advanced absurd quotations and mistaken attributions to the Quran with which to fill their columns. For example, I remember being particularly incensed by an article in the *International Herald Tribune* by David Lamb,[5] which stated that Islam promised Muslim men sexual intercourse seventy-two times a day after death. This, and so much more that was being dished out as 'Islam', was very wide of the mark and often based on inauthentic *hadiths* (sayings of the Prophet Mohammad). The Quran does not go into such specifics about the joys and pleasures of Paradise, either for men or women, noting:

> And whoever does righteous deeds, whether male or female, while being a believer – those will enter Paradise and will not be wronged, [even by as much as] the speck on a date seed.[6]

The rise of Ayatollah Khomeini in 1978 nourished that trend of belittling the Muslim world and led to a wave of new sweeping generalisations about Islam that ignored the diversity of Muslim societies: that Muslims might have European, Asian or African features; live in the wilderness of the Sahara or in cosmopolitan Beirut, Kuala Lumpur or Jakarta; be stylishly dressed women coming out of a cinema in Cairo, beret-wearing farmers tending their lands in the south of France, or wanderers strolling through the souks and bazaars of Fez, Tripoli, Tehran or Istanbul in a loose *jellabiya* or other local attire. The revival of conservative Khomeinism affected all sectors of Iranian society, male and female, and led to a resurgence of old traditions, including the wearing of the veil.

At about the time Christian missionaries were at work in northern Europe fourteen centuries ago, Islam came to the pagan tribes of Arabia as a civilising agent. In the pre-Islamic period, polygamy and the slave trade had flourished, women were considered inferior and worthless and female babies were sometimes even buried alive, while excessive consumption of alcohol was a problem. As a practical religion, Islam addressed itself to all aspects of life. It commended the freeing of slaves. It asked believers to refrain from alcohol and to wash before prayer. It enhanced the status of women compared to their lot in Arabia before the arrival of Islam. A woman, Khawla bint al-Azwar, became an army commander. The Prophet held that learning was a duty for every man and woman. The delegation of seventy notables, which in the seventh century endorsed the union between Mecca and Medina, included twelve women. Islam gave women the right to vote twelve centuries before the UK and the United States.

At one point Arabic works were being translated into Latin and used as textbooks at the universities of Paris, Oxford and Bologna. It was from such heights that the Islamic empire slipped into a decline from which the Arab world, the nerve centre of Islamic civilisation, never completely re-emerged. In several of today's fractious Arab states, suppression of basic freedoms for women and men became the order of the day, with governments, lacking legitimacy, hiding behind distorted versions of Islamic thought. But for the delinquency of such regimes, Islam was no more at fault than was Christianity for fascism in Europe and military despotism in Latin America.

Another favourite theme for sensationalist journalism was the Arabs' oil wealth, which was scorned and resented with a passion. Above all, it was exaggerated. Even at the peak of the boom in the 1970s, the combined annual GNP of Saudi Arabia, Bahrain, the United Arab Emirates, Kuwait and Qatar was only slightly higher than that of Belgium. The aggregate population of those five Arab countries constituted a mere 7 per cent of the population of the Arab world, yet journalists rarely made the distinction and more commonly spoke of oil-rich Arabs and their tales of unfettered shopping sprees. True, to the Arab oil-producing countries, wealth arrived with the suddenness of a winning lottery ticket and some doubtlessly misused this windfall.

But, if Arab oil-producing countries benefited financially during this boom, so, too, did the West. When oil wealth first arrived in the late 1970s, the West was feeling the pinch of its first major post-war recession. With their own economies capable of absorbing only so much of the new wealth, Arab oil-producing countries invested as much as 60 per cent of their surplus cash reserves in the West and a major portion of their imports came from the West. Thus, the bulk of the revenue from oil was recycled, directly or indirectly, generating economic activity back in the industrial countries from which it had been earned. Interest payments may have boosted the 'book value' of those Arab funds, but the real value has ultimately been reaped by the Western banks, financial institutions and economic sectors that housed, borrowed or used those funds.

For an Arab like me living in the West, I did not escape the ramifications of these negative images. Telephone conversations with bureaucrats usually shifted in tone the second I gave my first name or place of birth. My first name conjured up caricatures of an oil-rich shaikh or backward misogynist, while my place of birth prompted dramatic images of the defiant terrorist or the abject refugee. Facing a world in which my identity was so misunderstood, I was desperate for ways to assert the reality of the Palestinian experience. Our reality was far more nuanced, varied and humanly compelling than the stereotypes allowed.

In November 1983, I invited Martha Stuart, an independent American video producer who had a show called *Are You Listening?*, to make a short documentary at my wedding reception in Paris.[7] It was an opportunity to challenge such stereotypes: the guests in attendance formed a mosaic of the Palestinian experience and came from many different backgrounds and from across the diaspora. Some had come to Paris from as far apart as Minnesota and Saudi Arabia.

Martha Stuart and her team attended and filmed our wedding reception and the following day interviewed some of the guests. Their diversity provided Martha with a poignant opportunity to explore the Palestinians' diversity, exile and way of life. People spoke to *Are You Listening?* about the threatened loss of Palestinian national identity, the pain of being denied the right to return to their homeland, the negative publicity and stereotyped portrayal of their struggle for freedom in the Western media, the agony of exile, the grief caused by family separations, the statelessness and the great difficulty in travelling without proper documents. One of the guests, the novelist Fawaz Turki, described his childhood in the refugee camps of Beirut and regretted that Americans he met while living in the US expressed indifference at the massacres of Palestinians. 'When an American comes to me and says "I don't know, I'm an innocent bystander, I have no idea". I say "No, you have an idea. There's no such thing as an innocent bystander. Any man or woman who does not take an interest in politics is giving approval through their silence to the prevailing order of things ... There's no such thing as 'I'm in the middle, I'm not concerned.'"' Another guest, Janet David, said that we are Palestinians no matter what our religion is. 'If you ask my son "What is your religion?" he will answer "I am Palestinian." To reinforce Janet's point, Gaby Khoury said that 'among the Palestinians the way we treat each other is understanding and kindness despite differences in religious background. We are free of inter-religious conflict which shows we have reached a stage above it'. He described how, when as a young boy he went to church, 'my Muslim friends used to come with me as a gesture of goodwill ... and I think this is something which very few people in the world have understood or appreciated of us. We are not homogeneous in a religious sense, yet we are more homogeneous than most, and I think this is our strength.'

In a letter Martha Stuart sent me after the production she wrote that she found the participants 'vibrant in their ordinariness, temperate in their assessments of blame, passionate in their belief that the Palestinians simply have not been heard'.

Part of our struggle to be heard was rooted in the problem not just of negative stereotypes about Arabs and Palestinians but in the problem that when some people heard 'Palestinian', they didn't imagine a real people at all, instead believing that Palestinians are a political hoax. And so I also at times found myself facing a world in which my identity as a Palestinian was reduced to a fraud, a made-up identity of a people who never existed.

In 1969 Golda Meir declared to *The Sunday Times* that there was no such thing as a Palestinian people. In 1984 this belief was alive and well and bolstered by the work of Joan Peters, a Jewish-American journalist, who wrote a book in which she posited that there was an Arab population in Palestine but that it was not indigenous to Palestine.[8] According to her statistical models, the Palestinians were economic migrants who drifted into Palestine from Egypt, Saudi Arabia and Syria in the later nineteenth and early twentieth centuries in search of work and a better life, and since they had no roots in the country, when war broke out in 1948 they fled for their safety and became what is known as 'Palestinian refugees'. The book was widely acclaimed in the United States and went into multiple reprints despite the flawed scholarship on which it was based. Jewish-American political scientist Norman Finkelstein called Peters' findings 'crude and shameless distortions',[9] and wrote that her book was 'among the most spectacular frauds ever published on the Arab–Israeli conflict'.[10] Albert Hourani denounced it as 'ludicrous and worthless',[11] and British Conservative politician Ian Gilmour and his son David, the historian and writer, described it as 'strident, pretentious and preposterous'.[12] The Israeli scholar Yehoshua Porath dismissed the book as sheer rubbish, 'except maybe as a propaganda weapon'.[13]

☀

In the 1980s civil society was virtually absent in most of the Arab countries, and building bridges with the West could only be done through government agencies or personal initiatives. In October 1984, under the auspices of the International Information Relations Committee of the Arab Gulf States, a three-day international press seminar was organised in Paris – with the help of, among others, my friends Dr Issa al-Kawari and Dr

Hamad al-Kawari – to discuss the unfavourable treatment of the Arab world, including the plight of the Palestinians, by the mainstream Western media. Issa al-Kawari was in the vanguard of Qatar's educated elite, being the first Qatari to graduate from the American University of Beirut. Hamad al-Kawari, a gifted polyglot, was Qatar's ambassador to the UN at that time. That conference was attended by around 200 Western and Arab journalists and politicians.[14]

The Arab participants complained about the problem of their negative image in the Western media. A typical Arab was often featured as a terrorist, a monstrous oil-rich shaikh or a grotesque belly dancer. According to Professor Jack Shaheen, on average, six motion pictures incorporating negative Arab stereotypes were produced by Hollywood annually, all with the potential to reach audiences numbering in the millions worldwide through cinema, television channels and home entertainment systems.[15]

Even serious media outlets talked about the Arabs and the Arab world in blanket terms, ignoring the many distinct geographical and cultural differences. It was not rare for leading American politicians to refer to Iran as an Arab country. James Atkins, a retired US ambassador cited the case of an eminent American politician who described the Iran–Iraq war as an 'inter-Arab squabble'. He also told the conference that '[it] is only acceptable and even fashionable to be anti-Semitic if the Semites are Arabs'.[16] Others referred to OPEC as an Arab cartel despite its mixed multinational composition and the fact that it was founded in 1960 at the initiative of the Venezuelan oil minister, Juan Pablo Pérez Alfonzo. Atkins added that misconceptions about Arabs were a major factor in causing the 'oil shock' of the 1970s. If that shock was not foreseen, it was mainly because Western journalists and leaders perceived the Arabs as a quarrelsome lot, not intelligent enough to coordinate or agree on a common policy.

Denis Healey, who was British chancellor of the exchequer from 1974 to 1979, told the participants that the advantages of a physical military presence in the Middle East were very doubtful, while Helmut Schmidt, chancellor of the Federal Republic of Germany from 1974 to 1982, spoke about his role in drafting the Declaration of Venice in June 1980, which recognised the existence and national rights of the Palestinian people. Bruno Kreisky, chancellor of Austria from 1970 to 1983, recalled a heated exchange with Golda Meir at a Socialist International meeting when he disagreed with her denial that the Palestinians are a people. André Fontaine regretted that people often concluded 'that a wrong done to one people (the Jews) was [to be] repaired by a wrong done to another'.[17] Western, particularly British, journalists complained about the inaccessibility of parts of the Arab world, difficulties in obtaining visas and incompetence or inefficiency by government officials in disseminating information, which came about as a result of both lack of foresight and lack of insight. Roger Mathews from the *Financial Times* said that many of these officials were well-meaning and intelligent men and women who had virtually no experience or knowledge of the techniques, structure and requirements of the media. By contrast, in Israel, information, which is often 'suitably tailored', is 'thrust at the visiting journalist'.[18]

At times, however, the discourse of those present at the conference typified the kind of misunderstanding they had gathered to dispel. It was not a problem of crossed wires but of no wires at all. Decidedly, the same words meant different things to each of them. Words, as Descartes explained, are ideas. Arabs complained about Western journalism's failure to put its phenomenal capabilities and talents into accurately reflecting the true aspirations, preoccupations and achievements of Arab people. Mathews pointed out that most people in the West knew about Israel's success in 'making the desert bloom', but hardly anyone was aware that Saudi Arabia had become an exporter of wheat. I raised doubts about whether the core problem came from Western journalists' misunderstanding or rather from suppression of the Arab viewpoint. Andrew Neil, editor of *The Sunday Times*, acknowledged that they had 'to operate within market constraints' while, quoting the nineteenth-century philosopher John Stuart Mill, Professor Jack Shaheen signalled the danger of not presenting 'both sides' of the truth. 'Not the violent conflict between parts of the truth,' Mill wrote, 'but the quiet suppression of half of it, is the formidable evil: there is always hope when people are forced to listen to both sides; it is when they attend only to one that errors harden into prejudices, and truth itself ceases to have the effect of truth, by being exaggerated into falsehood.'[19]

Inbuilt prejudices and hangovers no doubt existed on both sides: the Crusades, a history of harsh colonial rule and, the elephant in the room, the insertion of Israel in the Arab midst as well as the dispossession of the Palestinian people. To bridge the divide many Arabs worked hard and made the effort to learn European languages and to read classical works of Western literature, philosophy and history. Admittedly they had an easier time bridging the divide than their Western counterparts, given the tsunami of Western cultural influences in the Arab world that was driven by Western economic and political power – of which the Arab world had no equivalent in the West. Even Western intellectuals and journalists who made the effort to understand Arab history and culture were largely ignored by the mainstream media, and to get their points of view across required extraordinary determination and effort.

☀

In January 1985 André Fontaine was named director-general of *Le Monde*. He was such a dignified and conscientious man. *Le Monde* was his whole life. One day, shortly after taking on his new role, he told me that the paper was facing serious financial difficulties and he wanted my opinion as 'a financial expert', adding that he would never consider any proposal which would compromise the total independence and integrity of the paper's editorial policy.

Since its foundation in 1944, *Le Monde* had been owned 44 per cent by its founding shareholders, 40 per cent by its journalists, 5 per cent by its administrative staff and 11 per cent by its director-general. It was considered the most reliable evening paper in the world. Nevertheless, its daily sales were never as high as tabloid papers. Together with subscriptions, circulation hovered around 400,000.

Fontaine wanted to address *Le Monde*'s precarious financial health and asked a reputable Paris consultancy firm to investigate these problems and suggest solutions. They estimated that to stay afloat, the paper needed to raise 150 million francs (at that time approximately US$40–45 million). Their solutions included selling *Le Monde*'s Paris premises at Boulevard des Italiens and, more controversially, laying off 20 per cent of its staff. He wondered if there were miraculous alternatives that could spare him taking such painful decisions.

I knew that *Le Monde* was well fortified, its absolute independence well shielded. The funds required represented only around 12 per cent of its overall capitalisation. Fontaine needed an injection of capital increase to consolidate, not compromise, the company's autonomy and ensure its development and growth.

With such assurances in mind, and given my respect for the integrity of Fontaine, who had always shown real interest in the nuances of events in the Middle East, I thought of Prince Salman bin Abdulaziz. He was a known investor in the media, having placed colossal amounts in that sector in London since 1978. I had an executive summary of a proposal delivered to him personally, outlining my reasonings as an investment adviser, adding that investing in such a prestigious newspaper would be a good deed and a source of pride, a way to support real journalism and to counterbalance the image of rich Arabs frittering their wealth away on petty materialistic investments.

But it never happened. An adviser to the prince called a few days after my proposal, dismissing it for its 'low returns on investment'. Perhaps he was taking the initiative off his own bat, like Shaikh Zayed's adviser who had expressed a similar opinion about Christo's *The Mastaba* project, or the cultural attaché at the Saudi embassy in London who scuppered my scholarship application to King Faisal, both without the knowledge of their bosses. Perhaps not. I never found out.

*

The fragmentation of the Arab world, which had such a negative impact on the Palestinian cause, was at once a cause and effect of its negative image, especially in the West. It was a lethal combination of faulty policies at home and a lack of Western news outlets ready to engage in balanced news coverage in their countries. But the Arab world had the talent and resources to work on changing that image. That is why in 1986, partly to follow up on fund-raising efforts for UPA but mainly to work on establishing an effective Washington-based Arab lobby – which I hoped would also help to create a climate in which the plight of the Palestinian people might get a fairer hearing in the United States – I took a six-month sabbatical from my work at BAII and moved to Riyadh. The lobby idea was greeted with enthusiasm. A steering committee was set up and supported by Arab expatriates and the Saudi elite, including a member of the Saudi royal family.

The estimated US$10 million annual budget to create the lobby was relatively modest. Any of the high-net-worth individuals who supported the concept – such as Abdul-Rahman al-Zamel, Omar al-Akkad or Shaikh Sulaiman Olayan – could have underwritten that amount by themselves without appreciably compromising their lifestyles. After six months of intensive research and weekly meetings, I summed up my recommendations in a memorandum, written in no-beating-around-the-bush language.

> Without the support of public opinion (which matters in the West), we cannot expect any ambitious politician to take up our cause when rarely a book, or an entertainment programme, or a film, or a newspaper article fails to portray us as the 'other'. More than financial support, what a Western politician needs is a supportive constituency or a guaranteed influence over one. Without that cushion he/she will retreat at the first public outcry.
>
> Westerners read, but we Arabs do not write. Even those

> Arabs who have written or produced worthy works are not properly promoted internationally. Image-building abroad will never succeed unless it is accompanied by many improvements at home. We will never have a strong case against the degrading treatment of the Arabs by the Western media when Arab ministries of information treat their publics as if they were fools. Most foreigners interested in our part of the world are aware of the virtual absence of intelligent public debate in our mass media and of how it is dominated by mercenaries. The state of our media must suggest our shallowness and confirm our 'otherness' to outsiders. Given this perspective, dehumanising the Arabs and featuring them as pigs (as the *Sun* newspaper has done recently) will never provoke a public outcry in the West.
>
> The above considerations are some of the reasons which lead me to conclude that the lack of an effective Arab lobby in the United States is highly detrimental. What is being spent on keeping bureaucracies alive could have financed a serious process for better informing and assisting opinion-makers, and once we have such voices in the West, converting politicians to our cause will be easy or even unnecessary.

The chair of the committee was Shaikh Sulaiman Olayan, a self-made, well-respected, indomitable man, who was probably the most successful businessman in Saudi Arabia. He expressed his appreciation for my memorandum and, with his drive and support, I felt confident that we would succeed in getting our project off the ground.

But it was not to be. When push came to shove, all our deliberations came to nothing. Our ambitions for the creation of a well-funded and effective Arab lobby were met, for largely the same reasons, with a similar fate as UPA's 1984 endeavours to obtain donations from US companies working in Saudi Arabia – not for lack of financial means but of political will. The committee approved only a mere – and very underwhelming – US$1 million annual budget, paid entirely by committee members with no institutional support whatsoever. That resulted in producing only a modest structure – three Arab–American organisations – that spent valuable time and energy worrying about meeting their end-of-the-month expenses rather than working out effective strategies to promote the Arab narrative. Certainly, an independent, well-funded Arab lobby could have made a difference worldwide, particularly in the case of the Arab–Israeli conflict and the matter of Palestine, by spreading objective, well-documented facts about Arab history and culture and countering the myths about Palestine as well as hostility towards and ignorance of the Arab world.

Later, from the early 1990s onwards, instead of forming an effective lobby to disseminate accurate information and play a role in defending the common interests of the Arab people, narcissistic and ruthless Arab dictators overlooked the people's interests and instead formulated narrowly self-interested policies which paved the way for foreign military campaigns into their countries that undermined whatever fragile unity existed between member states of the Arab League. They subverted the real interests of the Arab world, leaving it with largely destroyed infrastructures and armies, hundreds of thousands killed, ruined economies and a completely disoriented polity. The ramifications on the Palestine question were ever-present.

I was encouraged when, in 1986, a collection of my articles, published in a book entitled *Reflections of a Palestinian*, received endorsements from three eminent American personalities: Noam Chomsky (linguistics and philosophy professor at MIT), George McGovern (US presidential nominee in 1972) and Howard C. Nielson (US congressman). This showed me that American audiences were becoming increasingly receptive to Palestinian voices.

15

With the failure of the 1982 Reagan plan, and with the continued Israeli occupation and control over Palestinian lives, the first Palestinian popular uprising, which would come to be known as the First Intifada, broke out on 9 December 1987 and within a few days spread to most parts of the Gaza Strip and the West Bank, with protesters expressing opposition to the occupation by pelting Israeli soldiers with stones. Progressively, these demonstrations were combined with civil disobedience, including a refusal to pay taxes alongside strikes and the boycotting of Israeli goods. Those predominately peaceful manifestations of civil disobedience were later described by Professor Avraham Sela of the Hebrew University as the 'Palestinians' finest hour'.[1] They demonstrated a revolutionary spirit whereby Palestinians expressed their refusal to be subjugated by occupation.

The intifada came as a surprise to Israeli leaders as well as to the general public. Ten years of strict military control of the Gaza Strip and the West Bank had created a sense of complacency among the Israeli public, whose crossings into those areas had become more frequent, attracted by lower prices for shopping as well as for outings. After the outbreak of the intifada, although the demonstrations were confined to the occupied territories, the intifada was perceived as a threat to Israel's national security.

Israel reacted with the tools it knew best: curfews, detention without trial of thousands of people, demolition of homes, closure of schools, uprooting of trees, confiscation of land and violent suppression of these popular demonstrations first with gravel throwers and rubber bullets then soon upgrading to live rounds. The number of Israeli troops controlling the occupied territories increased from 12,000 to 80,000. According to the Israeli human-rights NGO B'Tselem, more than 1,200 Palestinians, including 254 children, were killed by Israelis during the nearly six years of the First Intifada. 179 Israelis were killed, including five children, often by militants beyond the control of the intifada's leadership, the Unified National Leadership of the Uprising.[2] Yitzhak Rabin, at that time Israel's defence minister, was caught on camera urging soldiers to break the bones of protesters.[3]

On 24 February 1988 Israeli troops did just that. A CBS news crew captured footage of two Israeli soldiers, one holding the arm of seventeen-year-old Wael Joudeh, while the other soldier dealt incessant heavy blows to the teenager's outstretched arm with a rock. The footage was seen on television screens all over the world. Some viewers – Henry Kissinger being one – expressed outrage at being *shown* such events rather than the events themselves!

An article published in *The New York Time*s on 8 March 1988 claimed that Kissinger reacted by urging Israel to bar television cameras from the occupied territories. The article was based on a confidential memorandum written by Julius Berman, the former chair of the Conference of Presidents of Major American Jewish Organisations, which was leaked to that paper and other publications, later published in full in *Harper's Magazine*, and which summarises what Kissinger told a group of prominent Jewish community leaders in New York:

> 1. Now is *not* the time for Jewish community leaders to publicly attack Israel or its policies with respect to the Palestinians;
> 2. Israel should bar the media from entry into the territories involved in the present demonstrations, accept the short-term criticism of the world press for such conduct, and put down the insurrection as quickly as possible – overwhelmingly, brutally, and rapidly;
> 3. The proposed international peace conference, as presently conceived by Foreign Minister Peres, may lead to a 'disaster' for Israel.[4]

According to the memorandum, Kissinger started his talk by making it clear that 'he wanted to be perceived by the American public as an American leader and not as a representative of the Jewish community, but that … he would never participate in anything that would negatively affect the security of Israel'. Focusing on Israel's handling of the intifada, he noted that Israel's public relations were terrible. His assessment consisted of the following points:

> Israel made two major mistakes. First, it did not throw all of the media out of the relevant territories … Second, it announced that it would 'beat' the participants [in the violence] (and not shoot them). Israel may have felt that that approach was more humane, but it overlooked the fact that when you 'beat' someone it means you already have control of that person and can no longer claim self-defense …

The memorandum added that Kissinger:

> 'really thinks that Jewish leaders should not yell at Israel now and make them [Israelis] even more paranoid'. We must close ranks and not let the enemy utilize quotations from Jewish leaders as evidence to support [his] position. Kissinger then turned to the international peace conference which has been proposed by Foreign Minister Peres … He feels that if the United States and Israel do not have a prearranged agreement as to what positions will be taken at the conference, it may lead to a disaster. … Kissinger noted that, other than Israel, there is no state attending the conference that does not favor Israel's return to the 1967 borders … In general, Kissinger feels that the issue of a peace treaty is overblown. It is not the be-all and end-all of peace in the Mideast … In terms of an ultimate solution, Kissinger feels that Israel should negotiate with America and work out a unified position …

Alas for Palestinians and Israelis and for world peace, Kissinger's declarations and recommendations were taken as gospel by

Israeli politicians like Yitzhak Shamir, Ariel Sharon and Benjamin Netanyahu and were thereafter used as a compass by successive US administrations on both sides of the aisle.

But even when atrocities carried out by Israel have appeared in the media, such as the footage of the soldiers breaking Wael's arm, public expressions of shock and outrage rarely led to greater accountability. The two soldiers seen breaking the arm of the Palestinian teenager were quickly released. That lack of accountability did not surprise anyone familiar with Israel's history. Terrorising Palestinians did not prevent Israelis such as Menachem Begin, Yitzhak Shamir and Ariel Sharon from making it to the highest echelons of society and government.

That kind of impunity in Israel's legal system has been rampant throughout the country's history. After the killing of forty-eight civilians, including fifteen women and eleven children, by Israeli soldiers at the village of Kafr Qasim on 29 October 1956, and attempts to cover up the massacre failed, those accused of the murders appeared before a military court for 'carrying out an illegal order'. The maximum sentence passed was seventeen years in prison. Appeals were filed, and ultimately, all of the officers' sentences were reduced, with the result that the longest sentence served was three and a half years. The brigade commander in charge at the time of the massacre, Yshishkar Shadmi, was sentenced to pay a fine of 10 Israeli cents. Following his release in September 1960, Lieutenant Gabriel Dahan, who was imprisoned for his leading role in the killings, was promoted and given responsibility for Arab affairs in the city of Ramla.

Where crimes can be carried out without fear of lasting punishment and when brutality is rewarded, extremism flourishes. Professor Israel Shahak, the Israeli scientist who became prominent as a civil rights activist, wrote about Israeli military commando Meir Har-Zion:

> In his diaries and in the many interviews with him in the Israeli press, that man revealed not only what an assassin he was, but also how much he ... enjoys killing an Arab, particularly with a knife, because he can then feel that he is a 'male'

> … He asks his commander the permission to kill an unarmed Arab shepherd, precisely with a knife, and then describes with sadistic enjoyment the way his comrade holds him, while Har-Zion plunges the knife in his back 'and the blood splashes from the wound' … Har-Zion, with a group of terrorists like him, went across the borders of Israel, got a hold of six Arabs, and killed, with a knife, five of them. He felled them one after the other, while the others watched; he left the sixth one alive so that he could tell … That man is considered a national hero by the majority of Israeli Jews. That man was praised and was presented as a model to the youth by the defense minister of Israel and the generals in charge of the southern command (Moshe Dayan and [Ariel] Sharon).[5]

Shahak also writes about *Intifada Responses*, the book written by the ultranationalist, rightist Gush Emunim rabbi Shlomo Aviner, prescribing rules of engagement for dealing with Palestinian protesters, including children:

> [Rabbi Aviner] explained … that if a non-Jewish child intended to commit murder, for example, by throwing a stone at a passing car, that the non-Jewish child should be considered a 'persecutor of the Jews' and should be killed.[6]

Given the violence and brutality endorsed by the Israeli state, the actions of the Israeli soldiers breaking Wael's arm in front of television cameras seem, while never understandable or acceptable, to be the tragic and almost inevitable outcome of allowing such extremism to flourish.

Unbridled ideological fervour, from whomever it may come, produces the same reprehensible outcomes, and all acts of terrorism must be unequivocally condemned, regardless of the proclaimed faith of those committing them and irrespective of whether the perpetrator is an individual or a state. This is no different for heavily committed Zionists than it is for heavily committed Islamists or other extremists. Yet, and here Kissinger would be pleased, manifestations of Zionist extremism or terrorism rarely made the headlines in the West, while Western media readily reported and analysed Christian and Islamist fundamentalist movements. It seemed that from the perspective of mainstream Western media, when the actor was Israel, the substance of what had been said or done no longer mattered. What mattered was the identity of the actor, not the act itself.

I have listed horrific details of the crimes committed against the Palestinian people not in order to demonise any group but to bring a measure of balance to the conversation in the West, where Israel continues to be treated as an exception, and to underline the urgent need for finding a peaceful, just and sustainable solution to a long-standing tragedy.

I am sure that a day will come when most Jews will view Zionism for the dehumanising doctrine that it has been not only to its victims but also to many of its followers. I recall reading about the following episode that took place in the context of a meeting held in 1962 between Martin Buber and Avraham Aderet, a specialist in rabbinical literature, workers' Zionism and Zionist youth movements and professor at Oranim Academic College, Tiv'on, Israel:

> Aderet is extolling the [Israeli] army as a character-building experience for young men, and uses as an instance an episode during the 1956 war with Egypt when an officer ordered a group of soldiers simply to kill 'many Egyptians prisoners of war … who were in our hands'. A number of volunteers then step forward and the prisoners are duly shot, although one of the volunteers avers that 'he closed his eyes when he shot'. At this point Aderet says: 'There is no doubt that this test can bring a confusion to every man of conscience and of experience of life, and even more so to young boys who stand at the beginning of their lives. The bad thing which happened is not the confusions in which those young men were during the time of the deed, but in the internal undermining which took place in them afterwards'. To this edifying interpretation, Buber – moral philosopher, humane thinker, former binationalist – can say only: 'This is a great and true story, you should

> write it down'. Not one word about the story's horror, or of the situation making it possible.[7]

Martinican poet and politician Aimé Césaire wrote about how, by dehumanising the natives, colonisers also end up dehumanising themselves:

> If I have recalled a few details of these hideous butcheries, it is by no means because I take a morbid delight in them, but because ... they prove that colonisation, I repeat, dehumanises even the most civilised man; that colonial activity, colonial enterprise, colonial conquest, which is based on contempt of the native and justified by that contempt, inevitably tends to change him who undertakes it; that the coloniser, who in order to ease his conscience gets into the habit of seeing the other man as an animal, accustoms himself to treating him like an animal, and tends objectively to transform himself into an animal.[8]

☀

In 1988 the Palestinian uprising continued to acquire momentum and attract the attention of the world media, while 'democratic' Israel and its disproportionately repressive measures became an embarrassment to its Western allies. Even the Reagan administration started making conciliatory overtures suggesting its willingness to open dialogue with the PLO if only it would modify its National Charter and recognise the State of Israel.

The charter as a stumbling block was an ever-ready pretext, invariably quoted out of context. There have been three Palestinian charters reflecting Palestinians' aspirations to independence and their opposition to Zionism as a colonial project aimed at dispossessing Palestinians and denying them their fundamental rights. Each successive charter was a reaction to a setback and therefore progressively less assertive. The first was adopted in 1919 by the First Arab Palestinian Congress sitting in Jerusalem in response to the Balfour Declaration. The second, drafted in

Gaza five months after the proclamation of the State of Israel, reiterated the Palestinians' right to independence. The third was drafted in Jerusalem in 1964 by the PLO's constituent assembly and amended at a National Council session held in Cairo in July 1968 after Israel occupied the rest of Palestine.

Among the articles then incorporated, Articles 6 and 15 were frequently singled out for criticism. Article 6 states that 'The Jews who had normally resided in Palestine until the beginning of the Zionist invasion will be considered Palestinians.' Article 15 declared 'liberation of Palestine' to be a 'national duty' and called for repelling 'the Zionist and imperialist aggression against the Arab homeland' and 'elimination of Zionism in Palestine'. These articles were, in any case, superseded by the Palestine National Council in September 1969, which resolved to work towards the setting up of a 'popular democratic Palestinian state for Arabs and Jews alike' and buried deeper by a resolution calling for a two-state solution, which was adopted by the Council in 1988 in Algiers after massive pressure from the US and European states. In the meantime, one wonders why the Reagan administration did not find it useful to demand the revocation of provocative provisions in the 1977 founding charter of Israel's Likud party, including the assertion that 'Between the sea and the Jordan [all of historic Palestine] there will only be Israeli sovereignty', or why he was not offended by the decades-long direct denial both in words and in deeds of the existence of the Palestinian people by Zionist and Israeli forces.

That 1988 resolution and the PLO's historic compromise to recognise Israel on 78 per cent of historic Palestine, leaving Palestinians with 22 per cent – even less than what had been designated for them under the UN Partition Plan – was a signal of Arafat's commitment to finding a peaceful solution with Israel, and it was now up to Israel to reciprocate by recognising Palestine on those remaining 22 per cent. It never did, nor did the Americans or Europeans put pressure on it to do so. Albert Einstein had written many years before that it was worth taking risks for peaceful coexistence between Israel and the Palestinian Arabs. He went further and wrote that he would 'much rather see reasonable agreement with the Arabs on the basis of living together in peace than the creation of a Jewish state'.

As discussions over a two-state solution reached a fever pitch, I imagined a lasting, sustainable peace that could be brought about if the Jews and the Arabs of Israel and Palestine could come together under one republic rather than as two separate states for two separate people. On 23 August 1986 I wrote an article[9] calling for the establishment of a Semitic republic that would challenge existing stereotypes and industries that have profited from portraying Jews and Arabs as antagonistic.[10] This article presented a natural riposte to Zionists' persistent claims that enmity between Jews and Arabs, those two Semitic peoples, is inherent and their efforts to place the Israel–Palestine problem in a religious framework with a view to squeezing an anti-Semitism angle out of Palestinian attempts to defend their lands, their property and their right not to be thrown out of their country and be deprived of their identity. No, the Palestinians are not against the Zionists because they are Jewish; they would have resisted the occupation of their lands and violation of their rights regardless of whether the occupiers had been Jewish, Muslim, Christian, Buddhist, Hindu, agnostic, atheist, or of any other conviction. The religion or ethnicity of adherents of the Zionist movement were and will always remain irrelevant. Palestinian resistance to it should only be seen through the prism of the national independence, anti-colonial and liberation movements of the twentieth century.

Several readers reacted favourably to my article. One of them was André Azoulay. Resourceful, gifted and respected, André Azoulay was then a director at the French bank Paribas and co-president of the committee of the International Centre for Peace in the Middle East. He was genuinely concerned about the deteriorating relationship between Jews and Arabs and the horrors of Lebanon's invasion by Israel was still on both our minds when we met. He expressed that concern by tirelessly participating in or organising diverse forums in search for peace between Israelis and Palestinians. One such conference we both attended was held in Brussels on 18 and 19 March 1988, four months after the outbreak of the First Intifada. It was organised by the Centre Communautaire Laïc Juif, and attended by, among others, Abba Eban, Claude Cheysson, Teddy Kollek, Marie-Claire Mendès France, Giorgio Napolitano and Shulamit Aloni.

Despite Arafat's acceptance of the two-state formula, his public declaration that the charter was *caduque* (no longer valid) and the acceptance of the US power-based diktats – that is, the US refusal to talk to the PLO unless Articles 6 and 15 were formally revoked – the PLO was only rewarded with half-hearted talks that dragged on for about eighteen months before reaching a dead end in July 1990.

For most Palestinians the insistence by Israel and the US that their National Charter be revoked was only a ploy. A PLO revocation of the charter would weaken the intifada and lead to further disunity, while a refusal to revoke it would be a useful propaganda tool against the PLO. Revoking the charter, when it eventually happened in 1988, changed nothing. Israel continued to tighten its hold on the occupied territories and to accelerate the construction of settlements. In summer 1990, with peace efforts stalled, both the Palestinian intifada and the Israeli army's repressive measures against it continued unabated.

*

As they say in French, *même les bonnes choses ont une fin* (even good things come to an end – a little gentler and more nuanced than the English equivalent: all good things must come to an end). After more than ten years of a fulfilling personal and professional life in Paris, it was time to move. I had received the offer of a senior position at Deutsche Bank, Suisse, whose parent company was one of the few AAA rated banks in the world. Perhaps it was middle age knocking, but the idea of returning to Switzerland with its calm and tuned-down rhythm of life appealed to me. What I liked most about the Swiss was their instinctive attentiveness in conversations with others: listen and understand, then answer.

And so, in 1988, I moved to Geneva. I stayed at Deutsche Bank for eighteen years before moving to UBS, the third largest bank in Europe and the first wealth manager in the world, where I worked as managing director and senior adviser until my retirement.

16

After eight years of gruesome fighting with over a million casualties, Saddam Hussein's war against Iran ran out of cash and a ceasefire was signed in July 1988. Cost to the region was estimated at US$238 billion spent on armament, US$400 billion damage to infrastructure and, I estimate, an opportunity cost to Iraq's economy exceeding a trillion dollars. Before invading Iran in 1980, Iraq enjoyed a strong economy. When the war ended its annual deficit amounted to US$80 billion.

It took two more years of haggling before the two exhausted parties finally signed a formal peace agreement in summer 1990. During that time rumours circulated about Iraq's refusal to reimburse the US$30 billion in loans it owed to its partners in the war, Kuwait and Saudi Arabia. Since the United States was a cheerleader in that conflict and principal seller of arms to Iraq, Saddam Hussein lamented the situation to the US ambassador, who then assured him that her government would consider his handling of that wrangle with his Arab partners as an internal Arab–Arab affair. Such statements were welcomed by Saddam Hussein, who already had territorial ambitions regarding Kuwait, which he viewed as a state carved out of Iraq by imperial Britain after the First World War, in line with the Sykes–Picot Agreement and the divide-and-rule practices of Britain and France. It was also rumoured that the US had encouraged Kuwait to reduce oil prices while encouraging it to insist on immediate reimbursement of huge loans owed to it by an Iraq heavily indebted after the eight-year war.

With that American light seeming to flash green, on 2 August 1990 Saddam Hussein sent his troops into Kuwait – another impulsive move showing that eight years of human and material apocalypse were not enough for him to repair the compass he used when invading Iran. That move came like a lightning strike to those who cared about Arab solidarity, let alone unity, and was naturally applauded by the Arab world's adversaries. It shifted the world's attention from the Palestinian intifada, which was progressively gaining worldwide sympathy. None of the Arab League's member states had the intrinsic strength to repel that aggression on its own and most of them had different and opposing alliances, making the idea of creating a united front little more than a pipe dream.

A Security Council resolution was passed on 29 November 1990 calling for unconditional Iraqi withdrawal before 15 January 1991 and empowering states to use 'all necessary means' to force Iraq out of Kuwait after that deadline. The United States, supported by its NATO allies, reiterated that ultimatum while mobilising an international diplomatic and military force against Iraq, the size of which had not been seen since the Second World War. I was completely against a military solution to the Iraqi invasion. My principal concern was to avoid a war that would more extensively polarise an already fragile and explosive region.

Saddam Hussein stayed put. He saw his invasion as correcting a legacy of the imperial past when Kuwait was hived off from a greater Ottoman-ruled Iraq. The Arab League rejected that reasoning because accepting it would have invalidated all the Sykes–Picot frontiers of member states. Saddam Hussein then shifted his focus onto the double standards displayed in asking Iraq to promptly comply with a Security Council resolution when Israel had snubbed such resolutions without ever being sanctioned since it came into existence in 1948. He would withdraw from Kuwait, he declared, if Israel withdrew from the Arab territories it had occupied since 1967. These declarations received applause from Arab nationalists but were scorned by Israel and its allies. They were met with complete rejection by the US administration, Israel's foremost ally. It was clear that both the Israeli and US governments uncompromisingly adhered to Kissinger's February 1988 recommendation calling for perpetual

Israeli dominance of the Arab world through maintaining a favourable balance of power. An invasion of Iraq and a destruction of its military capabilities were in Israel's strategic interest. After Israel's Camp David agreement with Egypt, Iraq was the only Arab country with a force that could rival Israel's military might, at least in theory. Exaggerated reports about Iraq's secret weapons of mass destruction weren't true but still added fuel to the fire. At the same time, Saddam Hussein's megalomania and invasion of Kuwait were viewed as a threat to the whole Gulf region, especially Saudi Arabia. An unspoken, unwritten and unacknowledged de facto alliance was forged between that part of the Arab world and Israel. All of this, and the ramifications of a new war projected to cost US$500 million a day, would further divide an already fragmented Arab world and lead to colossal human and economic losses.

Such arguments proved futile. The drumbeats of war were sounding loud and clear, drowning out European calls for restraint and a mobilisation of conventional wisdom. The inevitable happened on 16 January 1991 when the United States and several Arab countries declared war on Iraq. Iraq responded by launching Scud missiles at Israel and Saudi Arabia. Within five weeks, Saddam Hussein's army was swiftly defeated, forced to withdraw from Kuwait and chased out of southern Iraq. Effectively, Iraq was divided, and whatever remained of Saddam Hussein's meagre and shattered sovereignty was confined to Baghdad and its suburbs. After forty-two days of warfare the United States presented a bill of around US$32 billion to Kuwait and Saudi Arabia.

Before the Iraqi invasion of Kuwait, Palestinians formed the largest expatriate community in Kuwait. Their relationship with the indigenous population was characterised by mutual respect. Arafat had lived and worked in Kuwait in the early 1950s, and it was where he and his comrades had founded Palestinian Liberation Movement Fatah. Moreover, since the 1948 *Nakba*, the wider Palestinian society that either lived under occupation or in exile, knew too well how Kuwaitis felt after their country's occupation.

Saddam Hussein told the Palestinians that their humiliating diplomatic haggling for a state on 22 per cent of historic Palestine was doomed. Even if that sought-after state were ever to see the light of day, American midwifery would ensure that it would be born weak, a state that could never restore Palestinians' most elementary rights, especially the refugees' right of return. At the same time his words and his insistence on a global solution to the region's outstanding issues cornered the PLO's leadership. There was a split between those who thought that, despite Saddam Hussein's rhetoric, they should not side with him against Kuwait and others who believed they could not support a war against Iraq. That was the dilemma Arafat found himself in. His clumsy attempt to find some middle way worsened the situation, and the Palestinians were wrongly perceived as condoning Kuwait's occupation.

After the 1991 Kuwait–Iraq war, Saddam Hussein's hold on whatever remained of Iraq continued, but with more oppression, poverty, economic sanctions and stifling political isolation, paving the way for a more ruthless war twelve years later in 2003.

*

On 11 September 2001 the world changed. The terrorist attacks waged against civilian targets in New York and Washington left about 3,000 people dead and 6,000 injured. They sent tremors around the globe. The ramifications on US foreign policy, US public opinion and the rest of the world has had lasting effects. On 7 October 2001 the United States declared war on an opaque enemy, branded Global Terror. The speed with which a decision was taken to wage this open-ended war was remarkable. According to the Costs of War project at Brown University, by 1 September 2021 the US post-9/11 wars – including in Afghanistan, Pakistan, Iraq, Syria and Yemen – had caused the deaths of more than 929,000 people, and several times as many people had been killed indirectly through the wars' reverberating effects, including infrastructural damage, water loss and disease.[1] To these astronomical numbers of casualties should be added the thirty-eight million people displaced as a result of the wars. The total cost of these wars to American taxpayers has been estimated at over US$8 trillion – mostly paid to US arms manufactures and contractors.

The attacks of 9/11 opened a new chapter in aggressive propaganda against Arabs, and Muslims more generally. The official American discourse mixed the chatter with the matter, and a whole civilisation was demonised. A Manichaean view of the world prevailed. Soon, a criminal terrorist act was perceived as a declaration of war by nameless, faceless 'others' against the whole 'American way of life'. Hundreds of millions of people were neatly classified into distinct categories – civilised or barbarian, with us or against us – while calls for revenge and redemptive violence became widespread. (Here it is worth remembering that, while Muslims worldwide were now perceived as violent perpetrators, the overwhelming majority of victims of Islamist terrorism between 1979 and 2019 have been Muslims.)

The first target of the Global War on Terrorism was Afghanistan, where al-Qaeda leader Osama bin Laden was based. Afghanistan was a country which had become labelled as the 'Graveyard of Empires' for its resilience against foreign invaders like the British during the nineteenth century. With all the hype that went into preparing American public opinion for revenge, the US establishment needed a spectacular and decisive victory, and when that did not happen in Afghanistan it shifted its focus to its next target, Iraq, a country with no proven links to the 9/11 attacks.

Twelve years after the 1991 Kuwait debacle, Iraq's economy was in freefall,[2] oil production was managed by outside powers and education and health suffered from shrinking budgets and sanctions. The only things flourishing were runaway inflation and Saddam Hussein's ego and narcissism. His megalomania blinded him from seeing the deteriorating state of Iraq and its people; only his private estate encompassing his lavish palaces and his own civil servants were untouched by the widespread misery. Millions of people were demonstrating worldwide against the pending war on Iraq and its people in 2003. The (by this time) delusional Saddam Hussein saw them as his fans. His understanding of realpolitik and international relations was at a low ebb. The retro-imperialist instincts and power arrogance of the new White House and Pentagon tenants were glaring for all to see except Saddam Hussein and his acolytes. His well-fortified palaces insulated him from the hardships his people were experiencing, while Iraq's frontiers were porous and left open to outside invaders.

There was no understanding in Baghdad of the missionary zeal of the Bush administration. In interviews with the French journalist Jean-Claude Maurice, French president Jacques Chirac recalled how President George W. Bush told him that God willed confrontation in the Middle East and that Gog and Magog were at work fulfilling the biblical prophecies.[3] Astounded, Chirac and his bemused advisers, on later hearing Bush repeating his apocalyptic Gog and Magog allusion at a press conference, sought an opinion from Thomas Römer, professor of Biblical Hebrew at the University of Lausanne. He confirmed that Gog, Prince of Magog, signifies Apocalypse and a prophecy in the two most opaque chapters of Ezekiel pertaining to a final battle in the Holy Land as a prerequisite for a new age to dawn. Chirac rejected the holy war idea assessing that nothing could be worse than imperialism save religious imperialism.

Apart from his personal convictions, Bush was surrounded by hard neoconservative advisers – including Deputy Defense Secretary Paul Wolfowitz, chair of the Defense Policy Board Advisory Committee Richard Perle and foreign-policy specialists Elliott Abrams and Paul Bremer – all with complex sets of agendas. These went from literal interpretations of scriptures to clash-of-civilisations doctrines, from oil and arms sales to reinforcing Israel's power in the Middle East. They chose to see the West's political differences with some Muslim countries as religious or ideological when, in fact, the situation was one of straightforward economic interests and power games. When Iraq and Iran were locked in a bloody war in the 1980s, directly or indirectly and with Israel's help, as the Iran–Contra scandal revealed, the US and Israel were happy to sell arms to both sides.

The driving force behind the US-led invasion of Iraq was a policy to create a so-called 'democratic' Iraq in the region. This US-friendly Iraq would function as a buffer against a US-hostile Iran and would also provide some measure of US influence over Iraq's oil policies. Meanwhile, rather than pulling the carpet from under their feet by resigning and thereby nipping their whole strategy in the bud and sparing Iraq and its people from impending disaster, Saddam Hussein persisted in playing games with the Americans, making deliberately equivocal denials about Iraq's possession of weapons of mass destruction (WMDs). In his calculation, an attack on Iraq could be prevented if he could deter the Americans with apparently false denials. In fact, Saddam's WMD impotence was already known to the CIA and the White House, who were willing to play along with Saddam in the pretence that he did actually possess WMDs. What better pretext for an attack?

According to the Treasury secretary Paul O'Neill, attacking Iraq was already planned nine months before the 9/11 events.[4] It was also reported that on 9/11 Defense secretary Donald Rumsfeld ordered the Pentagon to prepare plans for attacking Iraq.[5] George W. Bush went to extremes to try to rally America's NATO allies to join his war efforts.

It is beyond the scope of this book to detail and document the reasons and intricacies that then and since caused the outbreak of inter-state wars, proxy wars or civil strife in Iraq, Syria, Lebanon, Libya, Yemen, and Sudan. Suffice it to say that, in terms of its proclaimed goals – namely to bring democracy, freedom and stability to Iraq and to lay the groundwork for similar outcomes in other parts of the Middle East – the 2003 Anglo-American invasion of Iraq was a dismal failure. While Saddam Hussein was indeed removed and hanged, the tribal, sectarian and ethnic antagonisms unleashed in Iraq – not to mention its economy, military and much of its cultural heritage left in ruins – have made the future of that country uncertain and unpredictable. Above all, the Iraqi people were left humiliated, their noses rubbed in dirt. The atrocities committed at Abu Ghraib and elsewhere against Iraqi prisoners, men and women, by American prison guards speak for themselves. None of these atrocities, corroborated by Amnesty International and other human-rights organisations and journalists, was deemed shameful enough to turn down the jarring rhetoric emitted repeatedly from the White House and Downing Street praising their Crusade for Democracy and Freedom in Iraq.

The regime in Iran next door, far from being weakened by that Western intervention in Iraq, became more firmly entrenched and, although domestically highly unpopular and saddled with crippling economic sanctions, did not succumb to any temptation towards an American embrace. Syria and Lebanon in their different ways descended into a far more precarious state than in 2003 and before – not least because of the muscular influence of Iran's proxy, Hezbollah. Egypt, following a promising start in early 2011 towards some form of radical reformism, reverted to its deep-seated habit of settling into a new military dictatorship. In Saudi Arabia and the Gulf mini-monarchies, everything has changed (the accumulation of massive amounts of wealth and some social shifting) and nothing has changed (the same autocracies, the same destabilising reliance on migrant labour and the same excessive dependence on oil revenues). And, as for Palestine–Israel, things only deteriorated further: a more entrenched Israeli military occupation with more Palestinian land appropriated for the construction of settlements, checkpoints and the wall, a growing number of uprooted and displaced Palestinians, the imposition of an illegal blockade on Gaza, heightened Israeli military hegemony, an increasingly unpopular and incompetent Palestinian leadership, a greater disparity in power resulting from a weaker and even less united Arab world and continued international inaction, with the same closed minds in much of the West, whether it be among the public, the media or the political elite.

And so, the same miserable prospects for my Palestine.

17

After the liberation of Kuwait and the subsequent invasion of Iraq in January 1991, in what appeared as an afterthought concession to Saddam Hussein's pre-war demands, under the auspices of the US and the Soviet Union, a peace conference was held in Madrid in October 1991, with, among other attendees, the participation of Israel and Palestinian representatives from the occupied territories and the diaspora. The Palestinian delegation was headed by Dr Haidar Abdel-Shafi, a highly respected surgeon from the Gaza Strip, and included articulate professionals such as Hanan Ashrawi. The conference was followed by the opening of bilateral negotiations in Washington, which, it soon became clear, were doomed to failure because Israel refused to put a halt to its settlement construction and expansionist activities. Pressure exerted by President George H. W. Bush on Yitzhak Shamir, Israel's extremist prime minster, was to no avail. In 1992, Shamir admitted that he would have dragged peace talks for ten years, with a view to meanwhile multiplying the Israeli settler population in the occupied territories by a factor of five.

In July 1992 Shamir was replaced by Yitzhak Rabin, who promised a partial freeze on settlement construction but reneged on that promise as soon as President Bush was replaced by Bill Clinton in January 1993. By that time the Soviet Union had ceased to exist and the United States became the sole referee of international affairs. At the same time, in the aftermath of the First Gulf War, the Arab world was in tatters and the PLO in a state of bankruptcy. Inter-Arab state cooperation, although minimal, was replaced by anarchy, and Israel was able to take advantage of that disarray. In such a situation, only a tyrannically honest broker could redress the situation and, for the common good, endeavour to enforce solutions based on the rule of law and principles of justice and fairness. The Madrid Conference and the ensuing talks in Washington and Moscow could have been a forum for all that to happen. But, again, it was not to be. First, because still faithful to Kissinger's 1988 recommendation and the American policy that gave primacy to Israel's interests, the United States was a party to the conflict. Second, after its direct military engagement in Iraq and its universal status as the only superpower, any moderating influence by Europe, Russia, China, Japan or the UN receded into insignificance.

In that lopsided situation the PLO was left to face Israel alone. The First Gulf War proved catastrophic for the PLO and Palestinians as a whole. Yasser Arafat's sources of finance consisted of official donations from Arab governments and levies on Palestinian expatriates working in the Arabian Peninsula, especially Saudi Arabia. After the war all these sources dried up. Arafat had no financial reserves, notwithstanding all the myths built around his billions, and had no means to cover the running costs of the PLO. It was during his desperate search for solutions that he sent Faisal al-Husseini, one of his most respected advisers, to me. Al-Husseini wanted to know if there was a way to get a three-to-five-year bank loan. I told him that it would be possible only if a friendly government, using its deposits with a bank as collateral, would agree to guarantee such a loan. The PLO could then withdraw the loan amount and pay the interest due upfront, and in that way it could have some relief until the loan's maturity. The conversation came to nothing, and the world's press continued to report on the PLO's inability to pay its staff salaries.

The PLO's bankruptcy, combined with the appearance of credible alternative leaders from the occupied territories during the Madrid Conference, helps to explain Arafat's desperate determination to stay in power at any cost. According to Edward Said, when the Washington negotiations became deadlocked, secretary of state James Baker asked a group of Palestinians that included him, Hanan Ashrawi, Faisal al-Husseini and Nabil Shaath to set out the Palestinians' minimum requirements. They told him that the ultimate goal of negotiations, an end to the occupation of the West Bank (including East Jerusalem) and Gaza, in addition to ending the building of settlements, were the absolute minimum requirements. Edward Said later heard that, not wanting these talks to end, Arafat contradicted all of them and cancelled these minimum conditions. The PLO seemed to be on its knees.[1]

As for Israel, five years of Palestinian intifada had brought chaos to its economy. Since 1967 Israel had counted on a cost-effective occupation compensated by cheap labour and a captive market for its products and services. Already in 1967, to maintain its low-cost control of the occupied Palestinian territories, it had considered subcontracting the security issues to Jordan by inviting its forces back to the West Bank. When Jordan snubbed that option, Israel created the Village Leagues, comprised of Palestinians who collaborated with the Israeli army in maintaining internal security, thereby enabling it to streamline its dense physical presence in the territories. After the intifada the Village Leagues vanished, and Israel's human and economic cost of maintaining control over the occupied territories became too high. Israel was desperate to find a way for the intifada to be put to an end.

Arafat's financial crisis after the First Gulf War, and his eagerness to reach an agreement with Israel, were clear to Israel and its allies. When Rabin became prime minister in 1993, Arafat, who came from a political culture that made use of personality cults, laid all his bets on Rabin and truly believed in the metamorphosis of General Rabin from the advocate of crushing Palestinian bones into a peacemaker, completely ignoring Israel's complex political power structure. This led to a Kafkaesque situation where, at the Washington negotiations, the Israeli team was engaged in a chess match while Arafat was hoping for a lucky break.

With US backing, the Israelis, who had never renounced their territorial ambitions, had no reason or incentive to cooperate. They just kept the process of negotiations running while continuing to consolidate their settlement enterprise. Declaring deadlock could have provoked media coverage harmful to their image and reactions from other international players that might be genuinely interested in a peace settlement, and embarrass the US administration. So the Israelis refused to budge on anything, and then they lured the PLO to Oslo where it fell into their trap.

☀

Not long after the 1988 Brussels conference, André Azoulay had returned to Morocco, where he became senior adviser to King Hassan II. He continued his work for reconciliation between Jews and Arabs. Shortly after the 1991 Madrid Conference he wanted to know who among the PLO Executive Committee was best qualified to lead negotiations with the Israelis. The ideal candidate should not have a military profile, he said. I did not know many people on that committee but had dealings with Dr Nabil Shaath, mainly in his capacity as president of Team International, a top-of-the-line Arab consulting firm, and Ahmad Qurei, president of Samed, the PLO-funded Palestinian charity that supported education and health programmes in Palestinian refugee camps, so suggested them to Azoulay. He did not tell me, and I did not ask, the identity of the party asking for that recommendation, but I guessed that it was related to Shimon Peres's visits to Morocco and his meetings with King Hassan II. Later, on hearing the news about the secret Oslo negotiations, I realised that I may have inadvertently participated in nominating Ahmad Qurei to undertake an arduous task, requiring well-prepared experts with access to a network of high-powered technocrats, which the PLO did not have.

They were no match for the Israelis. Since its emergence as a state in 1948 Israel had benefited to the full from a deep-rooted affiliation of its ruling class with the West. Israel was a Western by-product. Many of its citizens were graduates of Western universities, had the right training and experience as well as the connections. A significant number of Israelis also had dual nationality, ranging from American, Australian, Austrian, British, French, German to Soviet and, later, Russian. Add the backing the Israelis received financially, intellectually and politically from Jewish communities worldwide, and it becomes clear that there was no way for any PLO negotiating team to match the skills and outreach of their Israeli counterpart. The asymmetry was too large a gap to bridge. But, instead of compensating for some of these shortcomings by mobilising the considerable skills of the Palestinian and Arab diaspora and their wide access to a pool of international experts, the PLO marched to Oslo single-handed, equipped with lots of hope but scant knowledge of the rigour and perseverance required at that turning point in Palestinian history.

*

In July 1993 Birzeit University in the West Bank, jointly with the Association of Arab American University Graduates, held a three-day international conference on Palestine, the Arab world and the emerging international system. I was invited to chair the session on Palestinian–Israeli economic interdependency. As usual with such gatherings, the invigorating part often takes place outside the lecture halls. I was particularly happy to see Lord Ian Gilmour and delighted when he remembered our encounter at his son David's wedding about twenty years earlier. Although we had not seen much of each other while at Oxford, I had the highest regard for David, a brilliant scholar and a fine, perceptive writer.

Also attending the conference were Ibrahim Abu-Lughod and Edward Said. After an outstanding thirty-five-year academic career in the US, Ibrahim Abu-Lughod had returned to live and work in the occupied West Bank, where he became vice-president of Birzeit University. He was eighteen years old when he and his family left Jaffa and became refugees in 1948. As someone who knew Palestine before and after the *Nakba*, fortified by his encyclopaedic knowledge of Palestine's history and with his exceptional eloquence and spontaneous sense of humour, he was a Godsend guide for touring Palestine.

We all agreed that this was an opportunity for which it was

Berzeit, 1993. From left to right: Mohammad Miari, myself, Hanna Nasir, Ahmad Harb, Suheil Miari, Edward Said, Ibrahim Abu-Lughod, Ziad Amr, Abdul Salam Abdul Ghani

worth extending our stay in the West Bank. I would be the driver, and with Ibrahim Abu-Lughod as a guide and Ian Gilmour and Edward Said as back-seat cross-examiners. We took to the road, starting at Jaffa, Ibrahim's birthplace, then Haifa and Acre, returning to Jerusalem late at night. Both the virtual and the real of what we heard or saw were heartrending. The virtual – houses, gardens, playgrounds, all part of Ibrahim's childhood that he could only describe – were there no more, and the real – Palestinian homes inhabited by others, sometimes with the same furniture, or turned into public utilities used by anyone except their original owners. In Acre we saw beautiful Ottoman houses crumbling from lack of maintenance due to official Israeli policy that outlawed essential renovations as an inducement for the Arab inhabitants to give up and leave.

The real shock awaited us the following day on visiting Gaza. With our rented Israeli number plates we crossed without much difficulty, but for Palestinians from the occupied territories leaving or entering Gaza, the multiple physical impediments or barriers they encountered – ostensibly designed as 'security measures' – left those making the crossing feeling humiliated and degraded. In later years Israel further fortified these bottlenecks with turnstiles leading to narrow tracks and single-lane metal detectors, not fit even for a cattle crossing. We were told that daily workers providing Israel with cheap labour had to spend an extra two-to-four hours a day just to cross into Israel and later go back home.

Our host, Dr Haidar Abdel-Shafi, showed us the living conditions inside Gaza City and its surrounding refugee camps. We were appalled. Approximately 70 per cent of those living in the Gaza Strip were refugees who had fled or been evicted from surrounding villages and farms in 1948. As head of the Palestinian delegation negotiating with the Israelis after the Madrid Conference, an embittered Abdel-Shafi told us how disappointed he was by the Washington talks and that he and highly respected lawyer Raja Shehadeh had resigned from the negotiating team in protest at the secret negotiations at Oslo that the PLO had entered behind his back, the flaws of which he clearly recognised. We finished the day by visiting the al-Shifa Hospital. The spirit shown by the staff was astonishing as they found ways to cope with their conditions and the desperate shortages of drugs and equipment resulting from Israeli restrictions. I told Abdel-Shafi that UPA's board of trustees had authorised me to invite him to become president of the association. He accepted, and we promptly decided to schedule a fundraising tour together in the near future.

We spent the third day visiting Jericho and other parts of the West Bank, dotted with permanent Israeli army checkpoints. In addition to these, we were told that there were also 'flying' barriers. Without notice – which helped shield them from any observation by NGOs or journalists – Israeli soldiers would stop their jeep, block a road and close it for however long they saw fit. Remarkably, all these roadblocks and checkpoints were there as impediments to Palestinians travelling within the West Bank and not on the Israeli–West Bank frontier. We could only conclude that they were intended to fragment the West Bank into separate enclaves, to subjugate the Palestinians and to protect Israelis living in illegally built settlements on confiscated Palestinian land, making all prospects of a contiguous 'state' even further off.

*

Less than two months later the 1993 Oslo Accord, also known as 'Oslo I', was acclaimed worldwide. For all people hoping for a genuine peaceful settlement, it was a failure. It offered Israel another mechanism that replaced the costly intifada, which came to an end as a result of Oslo, with a low-cost extension of the occupation with no real concessions. Edward Said described it as the Palestinians' Treaty of Versailles, incompetently negotiated from a position of weakness. Power-based treaties produce lulls in hostilities but not durable solutions to conflicts. Arafat was cajoled into signing an agreement that deferred the key issues, such as Israeli settlements, the right of return for refugees, Jerusalem and the setting of borders, and that made no provision for Palestinian sovereignty anywhere. To paraphrase Winston Churchill, no one can leap a chasm in several jumps. A serious agreement should have covered all major issues and included a precise timetable for implementation.

True, the Oslo Accord offered recognition of the PLO as the representative of the Palestinian people, enabled around one hundred thousand Palestinians in exile to return, and allowed for the creation of the Palestinian Authority (PA), but, as it turned out, the PA never had any real authority, let alone sovereignty. More crucially, these recognitions were viewed by most Palestinians as mere window dressing. They did not lead to any significant change in the harsh occupation and its ramifications on their daily lives as Israel maintained absolute control over 82 per cent of the West Bank. Like Sadat before him, Arafat naively thought that by the time fundamental questions would come to be negotiated the balance of power would have changed in his favour. In my opinion, his speech on the White House lawn was a disgrace, a humiliation masked by smiles. He reversed the roles: the victim whose people had been dispossessed, their homes destroyed and land confiscated, was now almost apologising for the inconvenience that his presence and that of his people had caused. He stopped just short of saying to Rabin, 'Sorry for the agony we put you and your brave soldiers through!' He was hoping that the Oslo agreement would pave the way to 'resolve all the issues of Jerusalem, the settlements, the refugees and the boundaries … Thank you. Mr President, thank you, thank you, thank you.'[2] Oslo was a capitulation where Arafat and his inexperienced team accepted Israel's drive to obtain concessions while consolidating its settlement enterprise and hold on the occupied territories.

The Oslo I Accord signed between the PLO and Israel in Washington, DC in 1993 was followed in 1995 by the signing of the Oslo II Accord in Taba, Egypt. These are commonly referred to as the Oslo Accords. Yossi Beilin, one of the main architects of the Oslo Accords, was clear about Israel's strategic aims at Oslo:

> The agreement [Oslo II] was delayed for months in order to guarantee that all the settlements would remain intact and that the settlers would have maximum security … The situation in the settlements was never better than that which was created following the Oslo II agreement.[3]

In 1997, Beilin was more explicit:

> I am in favour of building everywhere in Jerusalem, including the building of Har Homa [a settlement], since this is our right; the question is one of timing and clever tactics. We [the Rabin government] increased settlements by 50 per cent … but we did it quietly and with wisdom.[4]

*

A few months after the Oslo Accord, in January 1994, President Arafat was invited by the World Economic Forum to Davos followed by an official visit to Bern. Perhaps as a concession to the many critics who complained about lack of expertise at Oslo, he asked me to accompany him on those visits and be an ad hoc head of the Palestinian financial delegation.

I had known Arafat since I first interviewed him in 1983. I saw him four or five times after that, about Sears, Roebuck and Co. and at two brainstorming sessions, mainly along with academics such as Edward Said, Ibrahim Abu-Lughod and businessmen or bankers like Hasib Sabbagh and Abdul-Majid Shoman. My impression was that Arafat was a brilliant short-term tactician but a vacillating strategist. His time-consuming insistence on micromanagement of the PLO rendered him shambolic. Once, in 1985, a news item in *Asharq Al-Awsat* newspaper spoke of my nomination to the Palestine National Fund's board. When I called Arafat for an explanation, he said there was a sudden vacancy and he needed a quick solution, without thinking about the implication or the professional harm such an impulsive decision could have. Of course, I declined that nomination, and he withdrew it.

As for Davos and Bern, I knew that the Swiss president was an ex-banker and that I could be useful at Arafat's meeting with him. I answered him to accept, subject to my employer's agreement, but I needed a detailed agenda for the visit. His answer to my follow-up messages was that he was arriving in Davos the day before the meeting and that we could have a discussion then. He arrived in Davos early evening on 29 January 1994. I said that I was an early bird and would like to start working on what I was there for immediately. 'There is nothing to prepare for Davos, just come to the plenary session, and tomorrow afternoon we will talk about the Bern visit,' he said. I heard someone come into my room just before dawn. It was Dr Nabil Shaath. He had just finished a meeting with Arafat and was directed to my room as it had an extra bed and all the hotels in Davos were full.

The following morning I was seated in the front row with the Palestinian delegation. On the podium were Yasser Arafat, Amr Musa (Egypt's foreign minister), Klaus Schwab (the Forum's president) and Shimon Peres (Israel's foreign minister). After an

Translating Arafat's speech on a panel
with Shimon Peres, Davos, 1994

introduction by Schwab, Arafat pulled a piece of paper from his pocket, unfolded it and started to read out his speech in Arabic. We heard mumbling in the hall, and Schwab panicked. He stood up and apologised that they had not arranged for simultaneous interpretation into English. 'No problem,' Arafat said with a big smile, adding, pointing at me, 'Come up, yes you, Mohammad.' Reluctantly, I mounted the stage to act as emergency interpreter.

After Arafat's disjointed speech, degraded further by my unprepared translation, it was frustrating listening to Shimon Peres's discourse delivered in fluent English and peppered with quotes from Thomas Mann's *The Magic Mountain*. As soon as the session was over I slipped quietly out of the hall and wandered down the street adjacent to the conference centre. It was sunny, and people were sitting outside. I saw Raymond Barre, the ex-premier of France, sitting alone outside a small café. I looked in his direction – recalling André Fontaine's description of him as the most cultivated person he knew – when our eyes met.

'*Bonjour*, Professeur Barre,' I said casually.

'Ah, the interpreter. *Bonjour*.'

'Interpreter by decree, not by choice, to be precise,' I said.

'It's important to have the skills and tools to put your message across. You have a just cause.'

Before I could answer, my mobile rang. It was Ahmad Qurei telling me that Arafat was looking for me. 'Another translation?' I enquired. 'No, no, he wants you to accompany him somewhere. He seems unhappy about having cornered you like this.'

Arafat took me in his arms when I arrived a few minutes later and mumbled something about not being as organised as he would wish.

'Last night I would have had plenty of time to translate your speech,' I said as we were rushing out.

Pakistan's prime minister, Benazir Bhutto, was holding a luncheon in his honour, and he wanted to introduce me to her. Not to deflate his enthusiasm, I did not tell him that she had been my contemporary at St Catherine's College and had had the same college tutor as me.

That afternoon we left by helicopter for Bern. Arafat insisted that I sat next to him, although with our headsets and the engines' noise it was impossible to hold a conversation. He was leaning over backwards to make me forget about the interpreting episode. In the evening, there was a state dinner hosted by Otto Stich, the president of the Swiss Confederation. During the reception preceding the dinner, Arafat introduced me to Stich. On greeting the president he wanted to know where I learnt my German.

'In a tiny Swiss village. I don't think many people will have heard of it,' I said.

'Try me,' he answered, in a matter-of-fact manner.

On telling him that it was Dornach, he gave me a big smile, before adding, 'I am from Dornach!' That opened the door to a new world in which our human bond transcended everything else. Arafat was instinctively clever, and, without understanding the words, his eyes lit with excitement and his facial expression signalled his involvement in our exhilaration. My time at the Goetheanum took over as the subject of our conversation. I discovered

With Swiss president Otto Stich, 1994

that my Godsend Herr Estermann, the general manager there, was godfather to the president's son. We continued the conversation at dinner. I whispered in Arafat's ear that I still did not know what he wanted me to prepare for the official meeting the next day.

Our meeting with the Swiss government started at ten o'clock the following morning. After short speeches by the two presidents, Stich asked Arafat about his precise expectations from the Swiss government. 'We need your support,' Arafat said. He then turned to me and asked me to elaborate. In doing so, his gesture inadvertently contained the answer we needed to give to the Swiss government. I realised that, despite all the fanfare, Arafat and his team had not switched from revolutionary to state-building mode. Answering the Swiss president's question, I said that the Palestinian Authority was striving to build state institutions from a *tabula rasa*. I continued by explaining that institution-building required, first, funding, second, a strong banking sector to manage and channel capital to productive sectors of the economy, and, third, a well-trained cadre. Switzerland was well placed to help in all these areas – especially by offering training programmes and giving our young cadres exposure to their wealth of knowledge and experience in financial management and other fields. That triggered a discussion as to how these objectives could be achieved. I was later told that the Swiss government gave sixty million Swiss francs in aid to the PA. That first meeting with President Stich was followed by others in Geneva.

*

A year after the Oslo Accord and the Washington signing ceremony, at the invitation of King Hassan II of Morocco the festivities continued in Casablanca, attended by presidents Bill Clinton, Boris Yeltsin and other world leaders, including Shimon Peres and Yasser Arafat. Also present were over a thousand entrepreneurs, bankers and journalists. President Yeltsin looked doleful while President Clinton basked in his role as peacemaker and leader of the world's only superpower. Shimon Peres talked about the dawning of a new prosperous Middle East. Representatives of the Gulf Cooperation Council (GCC) declared an end to GCC member states' participation in the Arab boycott of Israel. (The cost of that boycott to Israel's economy from 1952 to 1992 had been estimated at US$45 billion.[5]) I skipped several talks, went for a stroll in Casablanca's old souk and was not surprised to see other delegates there.

Apart from a natural concentration of Moroccan entrepreneurs at the conference, the Arab business community was virtually absent. In large measure this was due to an old habit of Western and Israeli policy toward the Arab world, namely reaching out to Arab governments but rarely to Arab people. Despite the signing of a peace treaty by Israel and Egypt fifteen years earlier, the volume of trade between the two countries was only around US$40 million, which represented an annual exchange of goods and services of less than one dollar per person. That spontaneous expression of 'souk democracy' was as good an indicator as any of consumers' preferences and their indirect disapproval of official policy.

☀

Away from the glamour of the Casablanca conference, in Palestine the 1993 Oslo Accord fell short of even the most pessimistic expectations. It was like a firework display; the illumination was as glittery as it was ephemeral and soon gave way to even deeper darkness. Israeli troops maintained their tight grip on all aspects of Palestinian life and Israel only symbolically complied with Oslo-agreed withdrawal schedules. The international press was filled with reports about Palestinians' agricultural produce perishing as they waited for their trucks to be unloaded and loaded back to back while waiting for Israeli customs clearance. Pledged international aid came in trickles and was insufficient to jump-start an economy that had been paralysed by a brutal occupation since 1967.

It is true that to most Palestinians peace had never been about the simple filling of stomachs. No aid, no matter how extensive, could eliminate the deep-rooted feelings of injustice felt by Palestinians everywhere. But the long tales of expropriation of Palestinian land and water resources, the frequent demolition of Palestinian homes and the severe restrictions on the

With Haidar Abdel-Shafi and Robert Donahue, editorial page editor at the *International Herald Tribune*, c. 1998

movement of Palestinian products and labour all created a direct correlation between the loss of Palestine and economic hardship. Any economic prosperity was bound to be seen not only as compensation but also as a correction of an injustice.

In the West Bank and Gaza there was a huge reserve of human potential that was left untapped. No jobs, no capital investments, no hope. They were victims of calculated schemes to drive them into despair and, ultimately, depart from their lands. That reservoir of talent and educated youth, humbled by years of military occupation and repression, was dreaming of a production machine to switch on, an office computer keyboard to type on, a plot of land to tend or a herd of cattle to breed.

Since its founding in 1980 UPA was struggling to extend a hand to those people. Over the years UPA's grassroots support grew, but it still lacked corporate and high-net-worth donors. That was why, in April 1995, Dr Haidar Abdel-Shafi, then president of UPA, and I, chair of UPA's board of trustees, organised a fund-raising tour to the UAE under the patronage of Dr Ahmad

Khalifa al-Suwaidi, the country's foremost international-relations architect and former foreign minister.

Shaikh Zayed, the UAE's president, was out of the country when our visit commenced in early April, but we were able to see the ruler of Sharjah, Shaikh Sultan al-Qasimi, some UAE cabinet ministers and several civil and cultural associations. Throughout the visit Abdel-Shafi attributed his resignation from the Palestinian Madrid–Washington negotiating team with Israel to the latter's intransigence and continued settlement building. He also underlined the occupied territories' need for a welfare state to meet the Palestinian people's acute necessities. Our pleas were met with sympathy and enthusiasm that alas, were not translated into action. Donations received during that visit totalled only US$250,000! Together with my colleagues on UPA's board of trustees, we decided to donate that whole amount to the Palestinian Red Crescent Society in the Gaza Strip.

*

Back in Geneva I was to witness first-hand that Palestinians of all classes aspired to a sovereign state, not just a welfare state. The setting was a banquet held in early May 1996 to celebrate the thirteenth anniversary of the Palestinian Welfare Association. That feast could have passed like any other convivial event, opening with a prayer and ending with a song, had it not been for the fact that the 200 or so mainly Palestinian guests represented the cream of the Palestinian elite with significant influence on Palestinian society worldwide.

The Welfare Association is a Palestinian charity that was established in Geneva by Palestinian business leaders and intellectuals in the wake of the 1982 Israeli invasion of Lebanon. In previous years the organisers of these functions focused mainly on the urgent humanitarian needs of people back home in the occupied territories, and schemes were put forward to help them. That year, the dining hall was buzzing with patriotic fervour. The guests, who included representatives of the canton of Geneva, were first treated to a piano recital of international standing played by a twenty-year-old Palestinian prodigy called Saleem Abboud Ashkar. Listening to him I was reminded of a remark made by Haydn on looking at Beethoven's early compositions for variations. The only theme which should never vary is you, he is reported to have advised the twenty-three-year-old Beethoven.

The novelty came at the end when all those present stood up and with visible emotion, together sang 'Mawtini', a Palestinian song that at the time served as the country's de facto national anthem. This was no gathering of hot-headed militants. Among the guests there was a high proportion of leading academics and Oxbridge and Ivy League graduates, and many of those present were businesspeople who boasted résumés that made them a match for any leaders of corporate America. Although not representing an organised political party, that constituency-in-exile collectively employed or taught thousands of people. Perhaps drawing on the French saying that everything finishes with a song (*tout finit par des chansons*), they all stood up and chanted their aspirations loud and clear, sending a message to the world outside, namely that the emergence of a Palestinian state is ineluctable.

☀

In the late 1990s, with the continuing relentless construction of illegal settlements in the occupied territories, Oslo's accumulated failures for Palestinians became too gross to hide. An international consensus was building that those settlements were an obstacle to peace and I published an article to that effect in the *International Herald Tribune*,[6] which triggered a passionate debate, the main arguments of which remained relevant long afterwards. The impassioned responses to the article were another indication that Israelis wanted to have both the occupation, with its settlement enterprise, and peace and that those tropes about making the desert bloom were still very much alive. Haidar Abdel-Shafi told me that Israel's negotiating team had been on the same fixed track during the negotiations in Washington that had followed the Madrid Conference. They stuck to their pre-prepared texts with no regard as to what we said or what genuine and difficult-to-negate grievances we expressed.

I hope that readers will indulge me and allow me to illustrate this with quotes from my original *IHT* article and some of the responses it generated:

> While recently driving around Israel and the occupied territories of the West Bank, I felt like a character out of Alain Renais's latest film, 'On Connait la Chanson'. 'Look what they've done to my land,' I wanted to sing.
>
> But my voice, feeble at the best of times, is stifled by a cocktail of anger and sorrow. I pull off the small Bethlehem–Tarqumya road and sit for hours contemplating the scene.
>
> It must have been one of those gentle hills I am now facing which Arthur Stanley, canon of Canterbury and Professor of Ecclesiastical History at Oxford, described in 1858:
>
> 'The hills, except where occupied by vineyards and olive groves, are covered with disjointed rocks and grass, such as brought back dim visions of Wales. I am struck by what is ... almost the English character of the scenery ... Cultivated valleys, except by their olives, are hardly distinguishable from the general features of a rich valley in Yorkshire or Derbyshire.'
>
> Nature has certainly been generous in this part of the earth. Aromatic shrubs of thyme, sage and chamomile: scarlet flowers of all kinds; daisies, anemones, poppies, clover, prickly pears, fennel, irises, rock cyclamens – all seemed to dance against a background of a lush green grass that looked as if freshly painted.
>
> I see a parterre of colorful trees – almond, carob, fig – along with cactus and a particular type of olive tree named *Romani* (Arabic for Roman) ...
>
> Having lived in the West for the last 34 years, even I, a Palestinian of many generations, was somewhat conditioned by the systematic barrage of meticulously produced propaganda claiming that, before the arrival of Zionist immigrants in the

1930s, Palestine was a strip of desert later made to bloom by the Israelis.

The perfect orchestration of that falsehood led even indigenous Palestinians like me to doubt whether Palestine and its natural beauty were not products of our imaginations. With Golda Meir denying our very existence, and with Zionist films and literature featuring us as a handful of roaming Bedouins, we, too, were vulnerable to falling into a state of muddle and self-doubt …

[The] settlements are obstructing the peace process and tearing apart the harmony of the landscape. The Holy Land, which ought to be preserved as a unique country, is quickly becoming yet another conglomeration of urban centers in a world not at all lacking in such ugly creations …

Given their exclusive roads and strategic locations, the settlements are perceived by the Palestinian population as military barracks.

For the peace process to really take off, these colonies must go the way of the Berlin Wall and Lenin's monuments. They should be razed to the ground. Armies dismantle their encampments when they leave.

In their place, a million olive trees, preferably Romani, should be planted – a million permanent symbols of peace.

Akiva Eldar, an Israeli journalist from the highly respected *Haaretz* newspaper, did not agree with my article. He responded in the *IHT*:

Israel's jubilee has provided both Jews and Arabs, Zionists and non-Zionists, an opportunity to portray reality using pink or black. For instance, Mohammad Tarbush (*IHT Opinion, April 27*), selected a very romantic description of the occupied West Bank.

The description is from 1858, the impressions of Arthur Stanley, canon of Canterbury, who was struck by the lush scenery he found on the hills of Bethlehem.

Another traveler, Mark Twain, described his visit to the

Holy Land differently 11 years later: 'The hills are barren, they are dull of color, they are un-picturesque in shape. The valleys are unsightly deserts fringed with a feeble vegetation that has an expression about it of being sorrowful and despondent.'

Twain concludes that it is 'a hopeless, dreary, heartbroken land'.

Mr Tarbush's travelogue is meant to dismiss the old Zionist claim that before the Jewish immigration Palestine was a strip of desert. This leads him to the observation that since Israel occupied those territories, including East Jerusalem, it has been tearing apart the harmony of the landscape of the Holy Land.

These descriptions add some extra flavor to the smell of gunpowder in the writer's suggestion to destroy every single house that Israelis have planted in the West Bank, which is his essential prescription for building peace between Israel and Palestine.

I have met Mr Tarbush and enjoyed the opportunity to share with him my views on the negative role that the Netanyahu government is playing in the so-called peace process. Like many other Israelis, I believe that most of the settlements were built to obstruct any option of territorial compromise between Israel and a future Palestinian state.

However, there is a vast difference between his rosy picture of the past and reality, as well as a huge gap between his somber solution of a bitter conflict and any constructive political settlement.

Both Palestinians and Israelis have no reason to look back with nostalgia.

In 1947, the Palestinian leadership rejected the United Nations' partition plan and thus missed the opportunity to establish their own state in the hills of Bethlehem and other parts of the Holy Land. Until June 1967, the Palestinians were second-class citizens of the Hashemite Kingdom [of Jordan], and were not allowed even to dream loudly of an independent state. In 1978, the PLO missed another chance, offered to them in Camp David's autonomy plan, with a framework and timetable for final-status negotiations.

The Israelis would like to forget the 30 years of occupation, especially the six years of uprising preceding the signing of the Oslo agreement.

Lingering in the rancors of the past can take away from the Palestinians their hope for freedom, dignity and a better future for their children.

Yasser Arafat recently told members of the Council of Foreign Relations, in New York, that a territorial compromise plan drafted two years ago by his deputy, Abu Mazen, and a Labor minister, Yossi Beilin, remained acceptable. This plan is very far from Mr Tarbush's idea of razing the settlements.

Not only does the plan suggest allowing every Jewish settler in the West Bank to keep his house and trees, it presents practical solutions to the tough question of Jerusalem.

Fortunately, the current leadership of the PLO in the territories, as well as many young Israeli leaders, show more responsibility and realism than passing travelers.

It is tragic that the Israeli government and national fanatics on both sides are still busy distorting the past and designing imaginary futures.[7]

To Akiva Eldar's piece, Lord Ian Gilmour gave an eyewitness account in the *IHT*:

Mr Eldar's article is yet another depressing example of Israelis trying to silence their victims. He complains that Mr Tarbush selected 'a very romantic description' of the pre-Israeli West Bank. In fact, Mr Tarbush correctly pointed out that the West Bank used to be a beautiful, cultivated countryside that has now been ruined by Israel's hideous settlements.

Mr Eldar omits the crucial and undoubted fact that the Israeli settlements are illegal. They are also glaringly unjust. Israel's 1967 borders gave it some 77% of the land area of Palestine. To most people, to allow the Palestinians, the indigenous inhabitants, to keep 23% of their country would not

> seem excessively generous. Yet if the settlements remain the Palestinians will end up with very much less than that.
>
> Besides, Israel is still creating new settlements. This month I visited a place near Hebron where a Palestinian Israeli family that had owned the land for centuries had had it stolen from them the day before. This was done with armored cars and settlers but with no shadow of legal justification – not even a scrap of paper. Does Mr Eldar condone such thefts?
>
> If, as they do, settlements 'obstruct any option of territorial compromise,' how can a plan that allows all of them to remain produce a peace without 'rancor'?
>
> Mr Eldar claims that Yasser Arafat recently told members of the Council on Foreign Relations in New York that such a plan remained acceptable. In fact, as the director of the council wrote in Ha'aretz (*May 12*), Mr Arafat merely said that such a plan could serve as the basis of Israeli–Palestinian talks.
>
> If all the Israeli settlements remain, the current system of apartheid on the West Bank and in the Gaza Strip will become permanent, with the Palestinians segregated in a few Bantustans. That would not be a peace or a territorial compromise. It would be an abject and unconditional surrender that would ensure the continuance of deep and fully justified Palestinian rancor.[8]

Fortunately for the truth and the prospects for peace, since the late 1980s Israeli scholars, through rigorous well-documented research, systematically debunked primary Zionist myths. The pioneers were Benny Morris, Ilan Pappé, Avi Shlaim, Simha Flapan and Tom Segev, later followed by Hillel Cohen, Baruch Kimmerling, Idith Zertal, Shlomo Sand and Adam Raz. Their scholarly publications had an initial impact of toning down Zionist propaganda. That's why I was astonished to see a respected columnist, Akiva Eldar, from Israel's oldest and most prestigious daily newspaper, persist in defending as flagrant a myth as the barrenness of Palestine before Zionist ingenuity made it bloom.

Writing 2,000 years ago, Jewish priest, scholar and historian

Flavius Josephus described the areas comprising what is now called the West Bank:

> [They are] made up of hills and valleys, and are moist enough for agriculture, and are very fruitful. They have abundance of trees, and are full of autumnal fruit, both that which grows wild, and that which is the effect of cultivation ... [they] derive their chief moisture from rain-water, of which they have no want; and for those rivers which they have, all their waters are exceeding[ly] sweet: by reason also of the excellent grass they have, their cattle yield more milk than do those in other places ...[9]

The Zionist version of the Palestine narrative is so effective that even knowledgeable Israelis who are actually living on the land – and less-well-informed Westerners, particularly Americans living in the Bible Belt in the southern United States – accepted its veracity uncritically. I could not understand how anyone could reject the fair assumption that the valleys, hills, mountains, rivers, lakes, wildflowers, that now can be seen in Israel and the West Bank did also exist before and did not by some miracle pop up only after Israel's creation in 1948. Was it not logical to assume that traditional Palestinian recipes so rich in wild herbs, fresh vegetables and fruit implied the availability of these products locally? Was it not reasonable to infer that Almighty God, who made thyme, sage, and olives grow on hills in neighbouring Mediterranean countries such as Lebanon, Cyprus, Italy, Spain and Tunisia, did not withhold His blessings from Palestine, the Holy Land? Was it not just plain silly to assume that none of the people who settled in Palestine over the last 20,000 years had ever dabbled in agriculture?

Eldar did not contextualise Mark Twain's writing. Twain had indeed found parts of Palestine arid and inhospitable when he visited in the summer of 1867, but he also wrote about an instance when:

> ... [we] camped in a great grove of olive trees near a torrent of sparkling water whose banks are arrayed in fig-trees,

> pomegranates and oleanders in full leaf ... it is a sort of paradise.[10]

For millennia Palestine was an agricultural country. It formed part of the Fertile Crescent, where agriculture originated more than 10,000 years ago. The landscape of historic Palestine is very diverse, from the Alpine scenery of the slopes of Mount Hermon to the arid landscape of the extreme south of the Negev. In between lie the fertile coastal plains renowned for their citrus groves and bountiful land, the hilly terrain with its legendary olive trees, some of which are thousands of years old, vineyards and fig groves, wheat, barley and cornfields, and the Jordan Valley with its tropical fruit trees like bananas and its cultivated riverbanks.

According to a British survey conducted two years before the creation of Israel, Arabs produced 99 per cent of Palestine's olives, figs, apricots and tobacco, 95 per cent of its melons, 92 per cent of its grain and 86 per cent of its grapes.[11] That is not to underestimate Israelis' later contribution to developing agriculture and augmentation of the land's productivity or their greening of large areas of previously arid land. It is only meant to balance the exaggerated reference to Palestine as being largely desolate – 'a land without a people' – and largely uninhabited by a long-settled population *before* the arrival of Zionism and its immigrants.

It is also important to recall that the Twain expedition in the Fertile Crescent took place in 1867 during a period that saw a steep decline in the Ottoman Empire and its Arab provinces, including Palestine. With the state's coffers empty and the Arab provinces plagued by crude feudalism, heavy taxation drained farmers and peasants while malaria and other infectious diseases were common throughout the Mediterranean basin.

Twain spoke of witnessing people's extreme poverty, which resulted from the exploitation of Palestine and the Arab provinces during the later years of the Ottoman Empire:

> The Syrians are very poor, and yet they are ground down by a system of taxation that would drive any other nation frantic.

> Last year their taxes were heavy enough, in all conscience – but this year they have been increased by the addition of taxes that were forgiven them in times of famine in former years. On top of this the Government has levied a tax of one-tenth of the whole proceeds of the land … These people are naturally good-hearted and intelligent, and with education and liberty, would be a happy and contented race. They often appeal to the stranger to know if the great world will not someday come to their relief and save them. The [Ottoman] Sultan has been lavishing money like water in England and Paris, but his subjects are suffering for it now.[12]

In Jerusalem, Twain found a lively world bursting with cosmopolitanism:

> The population of Jerusalem is composed of Moslems, Jews, Greeks, Latins, Armenians, Syrians, Copts, Abyssinians, Greek Catholics, and a handful of Protestants … The nice shades of nationality comprised in the above list, and the languages spoken by them, are altogether too numerous to mention. It seems to me that all the races and colors and tongues of the earth must be represented among the fourteen thousand souls that dwell in Jerusalem.[13]

Jerusalem's multi-ethnic population was a legacy of war and peace. It is claimed that during its invasion of Palestine and occupation of Jerusalem in 614 CE, the Persian Sassanid army massacred 90,000 Christian inhabitants. Persian rule lasted fourteen years before Palestine was liberated and reintegrated back into the Byzantine Empire. Rivalry in the region continued, and in 634 CE the rising Muslim Empire under the reign of the Khalif Omar invaded parts of the Byzantine Empire and two years later won a decisive victory against it at the Battle of Yarmouk.

The army's commanders, Abu Ubayda and Khalid ibn al-Walid, then continued their advance on Palestine. On reaching Jericho, instead of repeating the Sassanid army's atrocities in 614 CE, they just imposed a siege on Jerusalem, the equivalent of today's economic sanctions. After four months Jerusalem's patriarch, Sophronius, agreed to surrender on condition that Khalif Omar came personally to Jerusalem to negotiate terms. When a few weeks later the khalif arrived, the patriarch was impressed by his humility, despite being khalif of the superpower of the day. He declined the patriarch's invitation to pray at the Church of the Holy Sepulchre, fearing that his co-religionists would convert it later into a mosque. As the new custodian of the Holy Places, the patriarch then gave him the keys of the church. Those keys were ultimately passed on to the ancestors of the Muslim Palestinian Arab Nuseibeh and Husseini clans, who keep them still. A tax called *jizya* was imposed on all non-Muslim Jerusalemite communities in return for guaranteed safety and right of worship.

Apart from 200 years of rule under the crusaders, Palestine remained under Muslim dominance, and tolerance of the other Abrahamic faiths was a hallmark of this rule. When Palestine was invaded by the Muslim Ottomans in 1517, the new Ottoman governors preserved and defended Khalif Omar's stance on other religions until the collapse of their empire in 1917. Also, the Jordanian Muslim Arab government that took sovereignty over Jerusalem after the end of the British Mandate in 1948 kept these traditions intact. The trademark of the Jerusalem of my youth was openness, free movement and its multiracial, multireligious, multicultural social mosaic. Thousands of pilgrims would decide to spend the rest of their lives in that holiest of cities. Their origins and those of their descendants were honoured by naming whole residential quarters after them. Thus Jerusalem still has the Armenian Quarter, the Christians' Quarter, the Jewish Quarter, the Copts' Quarter, the Africans' Quarter and, until 1967, it had the Moroccan Quarter.

☀

If the ongoing unconstructive dialogue demonstrates anything, it is that both Israelis and Palestinians need new thinking for real peace. Despite my initial call for demolishing the illegal settlements, I came to the conclusion that a compromise was needed that would allow for peaceful coexistence between the Israelis and the Palestinians. This could involve the PA and the Arab states all recognising existing Israeli settlements and the right of Israeli Jews to live in them in return for Israel giving the Palestinian refugees the right to return to their places of origin. A very generous trade-off asking the Palestinians and Arabs to agree to the existence of settlements which are considered a war crime under international law versus asking the Israelis to uphold international law with regard to the right of return for refugees.

Apart from a few sites that were built over, most of the land where those Palestinian villages and towns depopulated in 1948 once stood has remained empty.[14] With the help of international donors those Palestinian refugees, many of whom have proven to be capable builders of cities and agricultural plantations in the Gulf states and in other parts of the world, could restore these villages to the flourishing environs they once were. With every stone laid to build a home, a school, a mosque, a synagogue or a church, the painful past could be buried and a new beginning could dawn. Nothing can guarantee the security of Palestinian Arabs and Israeli Jews better, I have concluded, than having them build their lives together.

18

After the signing of Oslo II in September 1995 – which, among other things, stipulated Israeli withdrawal from Palestinian population centres – followed a few weeks later by Prime Minister Rabin's assassination by a Jewish extremist, no withdrawal took place and the construction of settlements continued relentlessly. The situation deteriorated further with the return of the right-wing Likud party to government in 1996. Yet, the fanfare of the peace process did not cease. It must have served some cynical politicians to keep the show going: the Hebron Agreement, the Wye River Memorandum and, to crown it all, the failure of the 2000 Camp David II Summit.

To his credit, Arafat resisted going to Camp David. He knew that he would be powerless there facing an Israeli team backed by an Israel-protecting US administration. Also, since Oslo Israel had not implemented any provisions of the agreements reached there and its governments had declined to formulate any written commitments, all with the acquiescence of a cooperative President Clinton, aided by Dennis Ross, his overtly Israel-backing Middle East envoy. But Clinton insisted on proceeding with Camp David, promising, 'If it fails, I will not blame you.'[1] According to Robert Malley, a key member of the US negotiating team, Israel put its ideas verbally, then 'they generally were presented as US concepts, not Israeli ones'.[2] Ron Pundak, a senior member of the Israeli negotiating team, was more explicit:

> The traditional approach of the US State Department ... was to adopt the position of the Israeli Prime Minister. This was demonstrated most extremely during the Netanyahu government, when the American government seemed sometimes

> to be working for the Israeli Prime Minister … as it tried to convince (and pressure) the Palestinian side to accept Israeli offers. This American tendency was also evident during Barak's tenure.[3]

Saeb Erekat, the chief Palestinian negotiator, told me later that he felt they were negotiating with the same team but with two different flags. Other members of the Palestinian delegation denounced the bias of the US administration in more or less the same terms.

US presidents have invariably appointed supporters of Israel as Middle East envoys while repeatedly claiming to be neutral mediators. It has been like a court composing a jury exclusively from the defendant's family and none from the broader community.

As feared, the Israeli team persisted in making only vague verbal propositions while Clinton expected from Arafat written commitments that, in substance, would have left the Palestinians with a semblance of sovereignty over three disjointed and truncated areas on around 82 per cent of the West Bank and Gaza, only a portion of the Haram al-Sharif compound in East Jerusalem, and without so much as a hint of addressing the right of return to approximately half the Palestinian people who were still living in refugee camps or in exile in the diaspora.

According to Robert Malley, while the US had promised the Palestinians that UN Resolutions 242 and 338 would form the basis for the negotiations, it adopted a position far removed from those resolutions, demonstrating 'a clear bias towards the Israeli negotiating position'.[4] In concert with Ehud Barak and his team, the majority of Clinton's advisers turned their backs on these Security Council resolutions, in which it was affirmed that the Gaza Strip and the West Bank were occupied territory, and instead viewed them as 'disputed' territory, thereby giving the Israelis maximum leeway for haggling.

In an op-ed entitled 'Israel's Lawyer', published in *The Washington Post* on 23 May 2005, Aaron David Miller, a veteran of the State Department who participated in the Camp David II negotiations, offered more insight on the detrimental effects American bias had on mediation between Arabs and Israelis. His comments are still relevant today:

> For far too long, many American officials involved in Arab–Israeli peacemaking, myself included, have acted as Israel's attorney, catering and coordinating with the Israelis at the expense of successful peace negotiations. If the United States wants to be an honest and effective broker on the Arab–Israeli issue, then surely it can have only one client: the pursuit of a solution that meets the needs and requirements of both sides … we listened to and followed Israel's lead without critically examining what that would mean for our own interests … The 'no surprises' policy, under which we had to run everything by Israel first, stripped our policy of the independence and flexibility required for serious peacemaking … Far too often, particularly when it came to Israeli–Palestinian diplomacy, our departure point was not what was needed to reach an agreement acceptable to both sides but what would pass with only one – Israel … we should have resisted Barak's pressure to go for a make-or-break summit and then blame the Palestinians when it failed. What we ended up doing was advocating Israel's positions before, during and after the summit.[5]

The Camp David II summit ended in failure, but that did not stop the Israeli team and their American allies from pronouncing gleefully that an unreasonable Arafat had declined their generous offer. Arafat protested to Clinton that:

> They are not being generous – they are not giving from their pockets but from our land. I am only asking that UN Resolution 242 be implemented. I am speaking only about 22 percent of Palestine, Mr. President.[6]

Robert Malley later reiterated the same idea. The Palestinians were not asking for land to be 'given' to them as a generous gift or concession, they were asking to be 'given back' the land that had been theirs for generations.[7]

The idea that all Palestine's land belongs to Israel is deeply rooted in the Israeli psyche. Zionist indoctrination has achieved its goal with flying colours. Respectable Israeli journalists routinely speak of Israel 'granting' land to Palestinians without blinking. The following passage from *The Times of Israel* speaks for itself:

> The flock probably belongs to the el-Azi [*sic*] family, the lone inhabitants who remained in the region of Tel es-Safi after the other villagers fled in the face of the Israeli military during the War of Independence in 1948. The family's grandfather had been of immense help to the pioneers of nearby Kibbutz Menachem when they were setting up their community in 1939. After the war, the family was granted land and grazing rights to the area.[8]

An extraordinary statement when considering that this family (el-Azzeh) – who happen to be my brother's in-laws – was part of the 1,500 Palestinian inhabitants who owned 96 per cent of the land of Tel es-Safi before the creation of Israel.

After the Camp David deadlock, the president of the world's only superpower reneged on his promise not to hold anyone responsible for the botched negotiations and himself engaged in finger pointing, blaming Arafat. Clinton told a news conference that 'Prime Minister Ehud Barak showed particular courage, vision and an understanding of the historical importance of the moment',[9] while arguing that it was Arafat who had refused to compromise.

Real – and overdue – peace between Israel and the Palestinians needed visionary leaders who could rise above narrow political interests.

Energised by crushing Arafat at Camp David, Israeli leaders moved into a higher gear to undo the cosmetic concessions they had ceded to the PLO after Oslo. That started with General Sharon's visit on 28 September 2000 – accompanied by 1,000 soldiers – to the al-Aqsa Mosque compound, known in Judaism as the Temple Mount. This visit violated Israel's obligation to respect the historical status quo arrangement according to which the holy site's administration belongs to the Jerusalem Islamic Waqf, which is under the custodianship of Jordan. Sharon and his advisers had heard the widespread warnings that this provocative visit would ignite popular protests by the Palestinians and that it should be cancelled. Upon hearing of Sharon's planned visit to the holy site, pro-Israel US envoy Dennis Ross commented, 'I can think of a lot of bad ideas, but I can't think of a worse one.'[10] Yet they persisted, knowing full well that Palestinian protests would erupt and be met with violent Israeli suppression. As predicted, a spiral of violence was set in motion. Within a week four Israelis and seventy Palestinians had been killed, including Mohammed al-Durrah, a twelve-year-old boy who was shot, his death caught by French television cameras as he was sheltering behind his anguished father who was screaming at the Israeli soldiers to stop shooting. The Palestinian uprising, known as the Second Intifada, had begun.

According to rabbinical rulings, the Temple Mount is the object, not the site, of Jewish prayer,[11] and until 1996 there was a rabbinical consensus prohibiting Jews from visiting the Temple Mount[12] out of concern that they might inadvertently enter sacred areas in a ritually impure state. After much debate, and the rising influence of the Council of Yesha Rabbis, a fringe rabbinical group, the ruling was revised and Jews were allowed, even encouraged, to make such visits.[13] The aim of that decision was to block the government from restoring sovereignty over East Jerusalem to the PA.

On the other hand, after the Camp David and Oslo failures, the PA was facing mounting criticism at home for having engaged in negotiations that were doomed from the beginning, and blame by the US administration for its intransigence and rejection of Israel's 'generous' offer at Camp David. It was voiceless in the US and suffered, together with the rest of the Arab world, from the absence of a viable Arab pressure group with the necessary outreach, competence and, it has to be said, commitment to rally public opinion and defend its interests there.

Knowing all that, Sharon turned up the heat. All of Israel's mighty military and its arsenal was at his disposal. It was his opportunity to finish the job left unfinished in Beirut in 1982: the destruction of the PLO, of Palestinian nationalism and, as the Israeli sociologist Baruch Kimmerling later expressed it, the politicide of the Palestinian people. The ultimate aim was, in the words of another writer, 'the dissolution of the Palestinian people's existence as a legitimate social, political and economic entity.'[14]

He waged an all-out war, with soldiers firing on average 40,000 bullets daily against a largely unarmed population.[15] These heavily militarised actions increased once Sharon was elected prime minister in February 2001. By that time, according to Terje Rød-Larsen, the UN emissary, 32 per cent of Palestinians lived below the poverty line, set at two US dollars a day, while the unemployment rate reached 50 per cent in Gaza and 30 per cent in the West Bank.[16] Sharon fully embraced the Council of Yesha Rabbis's position, which further emboldened religious fanaticism, such as the widely broadcast declaration by the former chief rabbi of Israel, Ovadia Yosef, concerning Arabs that 'It is forbidden to be merciful to them. You must send missiles to them and annihilate them. They are evil and damnable.'[17] Sharon succeeded in weaponising religion to mobilise the most extreme layers of Israeli society in order, first, to have the backing he needed to become prime minister and, second, to undermine the peace process. He also knew that with the election of George W. Bush as US president in November 2000, for whom the backing of the Christian right was important, there would be no international force to stop him from reinvading the PA-controlled areas and undermining the Palestinian leadership. A month after taking office his troops invaded parts of the Palestinian-controlled Gaza Strip.

Sharon's aggressive actions and continual provocations were met with violent reactions from Palestinians, which included suicide attacks against civilians within Israel. An Arabic proverb says that someone under fire should not be expected to reason like a spectator from a distance. While I understood the proverb,

I found it incomprehensible how any attack directed at civilians could possibly further the Palestinian cause. During the First Intifada, the photo of a Palestinian boy standing in front of an advancing Israeli tank holding a stone in his little hand had brought understanding and worldwide sympathy to the Palestinian cause. That photo haunted me, and I identified completely with that boy. Palestinians were confronting powerful military and propaganda juggernauts – with their bare hands! While, under international law, an occupied people have an undisputed right to resist colonial occupation 'by all available means, including armed struggle',[18] my view was that this right should only ever be implemented within the confines of international law, never targeting civilians or civilian objects.

In mainstream Western media, the actions of a fringe minority of Palestinians led journalists to depict the whole of the Palestinian nation's struggle for independence and liberty as terrorist violence, while simultaneously glossing over the everyday violence, oppression, injustice and terrorism that Palestinian civilians were subjected to by the Israeli state and settlers. Where were the stories of settlers running Palestinians over with their cars, or shooting Palestinian worshippers as they prayed, or setting fire to Palestinian homes or crops as people slept? What of the stories of Palestinian homes being marked with a cross for demolition, or of Palestinian children being dragged out of their beds in the middle of the night without their parents and roughed up, or worse, by Israeli interrogators? And where were the stories of the overwhelming majority of Palestinians who chose to pursue their rights through non-violent means such as popular resistance against Israeli occupation, boycotts, peaceful protests, strikes and civil disobedience?

General Sharon and his troops could get away with their use of F-16s and Apache helicopters to bombard civilian areas, bulldozing homes and arresting and imprisoning protesting civilians *en masse*, because Israel's PR machinery enabled it to shield the realities of its occupation from the eyes of world public opinion and because of the impunity it enjoyed. As the nineteenth-century German philosopher Arthur Schopenhauer demonstrates in *The Art of Being Right*, well-conceived and performed rhetoric can defeat sound and truth-based arguments.

The Mitchell Report – which was commissioned by the United States to investigate the causes of the Second Intifada and prepared by US Special Envoy George Mitchell – recognised Palestinians' loss of faith in the skewed peace process and Israel's continued settlement construction as causes of the outbreak of violence.

For decades the world had counted Palestinian civilian casualties and losses with apathy, indifference and selective outrage as Israel implemented policies and practices that shared the common aim of displacing and replacing the Palestinian people. The Palestinian leadership, through the peace process and efforts at the UN, had embraced negotiations and peaceful means as the method to achieve the Palestinian people's inalienable rights, including to self-determination. There was a real conviction that legality and peaceful means could bring about liberation. They counted on the international community to help demonstrate to the Palestinian people that these means could work. Instead, Israel's unconditional allies reacted with obstacles at every turn: countless UN Security Council vetoes, skewing peace negotiations in Israel's favour, trying to block all attempts at holding Israel legally accountable for its crimes and the labelling of legitimate criticism of the grave breaches and actions of a state – Israel – as anti-Semitic.

By blocking peaceful efforts, Israel and its allies sent the dangerous message to Palestinians that peaceful means do not work. They sent the message to desperate people on the ground that there was no horizon for them, no hope, and that international law, negotiations and the UN system were not effective when it came to violations against them. Warnings that this irresponsible behaviour would only breed animosity and violence were ignored. For decades pleas for the international community to take action to put an end to the status quo of Israeli structural violence, institutionalised racism, land theft and brutality against the Palestinian people fell on deaf ears. This colossal political and moral failure led to where we were now – a situation that was in the interests of no one, neither the Palestinians nor the Israelis, and that made any prospect for peace and stability in the region more distant.

*

While in 2001 the world's attention turned to the war in Afghanistan and the hunt for Osama bin Laden, hardly anyone paid attention, much less criticised, the asymmetric war that was raging between General Sharon's army and the Palestinians living under Israel's military rule. According to Israeli human rights organisation B'Tselem, over the first year of the Intifada (29 September 2000–22 September 2001), 442 Palestinian civilians were killed by Israeli forces and settlers, including 127 children; 117 Israeli civilians were killed by Palestinians, including twenty-eight children.[19]

The violence persisted and on 28 March 2002 an Arab summit was held in Beirut, at which the Arab Peace Initiative was unanimously agreed by all twenty-two member states of the Arab League. It was based on Security Council resolutions 242 and 338 and the land-for-peace principle. It called for full Israeli withdrawal from the Arab territories occupied by Israel in 1967 and the establishment of a Palestinian state in return for normal diplomatic relations between Israel and the Arab states.

The day after that announcement, Sharon ordered Israeli troops to march into the West Bank. They carried out ground incursions into Palestinian towns and cities, including Ramallah, Nablus and Jenin, where they flouted international conventions, undertaking summary executions, mass arrests, destruction and vandalism of Palestinian property – including homes, schools, mosques and churches – and depriving civilians such basic necessities as food, water and medical care. A representative of Amnesty International who witnessed the extensive destruction of refugee homes in Jenin remarked:

> I have been in urban environments where house to house fighting has happened: Rwanda, Nicaragua, El Salvador, Colombia,

> and a city struck by a massive earthquake: Mexico City. The devastation seen in Jenin camp had the worst elements of both situations. Houses not just bulldozed or dynamited but reduced almost to dust by the repeated and deliberate coming and goings of bulldozers and tanks. Houses pierced from wall to wall by tank or helicopter gunships. Houses cut down the middle as if by giant scissors. Inside, an eerie vision of dining or bedrooms almost intact. No signs whatsoever that that bedroom or dining room or indeed the house had been used by fighters. Gratuitous, wanton, unnecessary destruction.[20]

As the asymmetric Israeli–Palestinian fighting intensified, an opinion poll conducted in October 2003 in fifteen European countries by the European Commission indicated that 59 per cent of respondents considered Israel the largest threat to world peace.[21]

☀

For us, the Palestinians, what had befallen the Holy Land and its people was not a natural disaster. It was a manmade catastrophe – the *Nakba*. Palestinians view the responsibility for the *Nakba* to be widely spread. It is worth reflecting on where Palestinians see the responsibility lying for their catastrophe, especially since their adversaries have shown such competence and made such efforts to present the Zionist narrative to the world.

First and foremost, we must look to Britain. Through the sixty-seven-word Balfour Declaration the British encouraged Zionist immigration to an already populated country with a distinct culture and people that traced its roots deep into ancient history, a people who, like others elsewhere at the time, was becoming increasingly conscious of its own national identity. Post-First World War Palestine had burgeoning cities like Jerusalem, Jaffa and Haifa which boasted commerce, shops, offices, sizable resident populations who frequented cinemas, concert halls and tennis courts and benefited from arguably some of the best schools in the Middle East. But even if one were to ignore the sheer presumptuousness of a British official and his colleagues simply bequeathing a functioning country to a group of actual and potential migrants, the Balfour Declaration was in no way an automatic authorisation to march in and create a new country with a new name and a new population replacing the people who already lived there. The wording that Balfour conjured up for his declaration is worth repeating here and examining in its relevant parts:

> His Majesty's Government view with favour the establishment in Palestine of a national home for the Jewish people, and will use their best endeavours to facilitate the achievement of this object, it being clearly understood that nothing shall be done which may prejudice the civil and religious rights of the existing non-Jewish communities in Palestine ...

The declaration was drawn up in November 1917, at the height of the First World War, at a time when Britain was keen to secure stronger economic and financial support for the war effort from elements of the country's Jewish community. It was only one month later, in December 1917, that the British army led by General Edmund Allenby entered Jerusalem during military operations in the region; Palestine was still technically under Ottoman rule at the time, and Britain had no legal or administrative relationship with Palestine. It was six years later, when the League of Nations ratified a mandate for a British administration of Palestine, that Britain acquired any form of authority in the country. In other words, while Balfour was making commitments about Palestine, the British barely had a presence there let alone any authority to pronounce on its future make-up and composition.

There are other aspects of the declaration that also have significance. It refers to 'in Palestine' and 'existing non-Jewish communities in Palestine' – so it was clearly understood that Palestine existed, as it also was in countless Zionist documents of the time. The migrants would be coming to a recognised country. Then there is the reference to 'the establishment ... of a national home' – nothing about the creation of a separate sovereign state formed from the properties of a dispossessed indigenous population. And, finally, the key qualifier: 'it being clearly understood that nothing shall be done ... [to] prejudice the civil and religious rights of the existing non-Jewish communities in Palestine'. If, for all its flaws, the first part of the declaration is read as opening the door to migration, the latter part can surely only be read as a severe limitation on the political actions and behaviour of those migrants. And does the dispossession of a population of their property and the right to live in their country not 'prejudice' their rights?

In brief, the British were high-handed in presuming to reorder the make-up of the Middle East to suit their apparent short-term interests without taking into account the long-term consequences of their actions. They were remiss, not to say incompetent, in not considering that the Balfour Declaration might unleash in Palestine what we know today as ethnic cleansing.

The second responsibility for the Palestine catastrophe falls on Germany. Its grotesque industrial persecution of Jews gave Zionism a powerful *raison d'être* and the widespread support it desperately lacked during the first forty years of its existence. Before the Second World War Zionism was met with, at best, muted enthusiasm and actual disfavour by world Jewry and by leading Jewish intellectuals including Albert Einstein and Hannah Arendt and public figures such as Edwin Montagu, Lord Balfour's colleague in the British cabinet. During and after the Second World War Zionist PR activists went full throttle to rebrand their movement as a response to Nazism and as the saviours of Jews persecuted under Hitler's genocidal policies. To dilute our *Nakba*, they strove to frame their fight with Palestinians as a fight against all Arabs and all Muslims (despite the fact that the Palestinian people encompass not only Muslims but also Christians, Jews and people of other faiths), whom they often did not shy away from comparing with Nazis. Such tropes became steadily ingrained into the public psyche. After the State of Israel was created, Germany eagerly became one of its principal sources of financial and military aid as a way to assuage national shame and guilt for the genocide that Hitler and the Nazis had perpetrated in the name of the German people.

The third responsibility falls on France, which in the 1940s after the end of the Second World War promoted illegal Jewish immigration into Palestine and later provided Israel with a nuclear capability.

Fourth, the key role played by the US in the creation, protection and expansion of Israel has to be recognised. The US was instrumental in getting the 1947 UN Partition Plan through and thereafter granted unconditional military, political and economic support to Israel, enabling it to delete a whole country and confiscate its people's assets, causing most of them to become refugees or to live under military occupation. Many liberal intellectuals in the US confused their sympathy for the plight of the Jews with support for a colonialist project that blighted the lives of another victim population.

As a result, and perhaps inadvertently, much of the responsibility for the Palestinian disaster emanated from the domestic politics of the US. The power of the Israel lobby in the US has never come from the number of voters it could mobilise but from the power of its purse and the passions and genuine dedication that lie behind it. Consequently, donations or financial backing to politicians running for public office inevitably bear the risk of sometimes being against the democratic process. That is why, in his first year in office, President John F. Kennedy criticised such ways of financing election campaigns as 'highly undesirable' and 'not healthy' because it made candidates 'dependent on large financial contributions of those with special interests'.[22]

Fifth, the so-called 'communist threat'. During the Cold War years, when international rivalry between the United States and the Soviet Union was at its height, the perception in the US and the Western alliance of a communist threat and the dangers of Soviet expansionism underpinned much of the international political discourse and diplomatic atmosphere of that time. And because of the Middle East's colonial and quasi-colonial past, the Soviets had succeeded by the 1950s in building bridges with the Arab world – Egypt, Syria, Iraq and Algeria were all evolving as areas of Soviet interest. So it was considered essential for the US to accept and protect Israel as an ally and to support it economically, diplomatically and military. And, fully aware of its importance to America's international political calculations, it was no wonder that Israel's political and military leaders frequently felt emboldened in pursuing their perception of Israel's interests, irrespective of the consequences for America's broader interests.

And finally, what of the Palestinians themselves and the other Arab countries? Quite apart from the influence of outside factors, what – if any – responsibility should they take for the Palestine catastrophe? Many Palestinians and friends of Palestine have criticised and berated their leaderships and leaders of the Arab world for not having been more effective in mounting a successful response to the actions and behaviour of Israel. In my student days I, too, engaged in the privacy of my own mind with such critiques. But I also recognised the profound asymmetry between Israelis (or Zionists) and Palestinians in their relationship as adversaries.

Indeed, the modern misfortunes of Palestine have to be seen in the context of specific historical realities – and this is not to repeat yet again the narrative of ancient history and historical rights. There is one socio-historical aspect of the story of Palestine which is rarely discussed and which gave Palestinians a notable disadvantage in their later encounters in the matter of Jewish immigration. The issue stretches back several centuries, and its significance became clear only in the later twentieth century; it is that there was no real presence of a Palestinian or even an Arab diaspora in the Europe and America of the eighteenth, nineteenth and early twentieth centuries. This meant there was no opportunity for Palestine-sympathetic communities of professionals, academics and business practitioners to have become embedded in and evolve from the politically and economically dominant societies of the West who would, in due course, feel a natural or cultural affinity for the territory and the plight of their fellow Arabs/Palestinians. This was contrary to the experience of European and, later, American Jews, who not only retained a strong Jewish identity but also existed in significant numbers and who were to form the backbone of what emerged as Zionism. At the time when Zionist movements were taking shape in nineteenth-century Europe there was no Palestinian or other Arab population in Europe to provide any counter-narrative. Mostly under a rather sleepy Ottoman rule, the few Arab traders and students resident in Europe got on with their trading and studies far removed from politics and diplomacy. Even in post-First World War Europe, there were few resident Arabs who might speak out against the Balfour Declaration, Sykes–Picot or the decision-making in Versailles.

So there are plausible political, diplomatic and historical reasons why the Palestinians have found it so difficult to make headway in advocating for their interests. And, while it would be wrong not to acknowledge the external factors which came together to significantly disadvantage the Palestinian cause, it would be equally wrong to portray Palestinians as mere victims, totally at the mercy of outside forces – hapless, helpless and hopeless. The fact – for Palestinians, the sad fact – remains that any exploration of the Palestinian problem must also acknowledge that Palestinians themselves do bear some responsibility for the position in which they find themselves.

Palestinian leadership of all hues since the creation of the State of Israel has been generally weak, ineffective, unsophisticated, divided and easily subjected to manipulation and exploitation by its adversaries. It has largely failed to learn from past errors and completely failed to exploit its strongest potential asset – key membership of an Arab world fellowship, which, if handled more strategically, could have provided far more valuable support to its cause than has been the case, with support for Palestine having been limited mostly to useless rhetoric, symbolism and slogans.

The result has been not only to damage the Palestinian cause but also to undermine the Arab image across the world.

*

Arafat died in November 2004 and immediately rumours and suspicions arose surrounding his death, reportedly widely by the international media. Two months later presidential elections were held, and Mahmoud Abbas won 67 per cent of the vote.

As the human and financial cost of protecting the more than 9,000 Israeli settlers in the Gaza Strip shot up, General Sharon in the summer of 2005 unilaterally decided to dismantle the settlements there and withdraw all Israeli troops from inside Gaza. Gaza remained under Israeli military occupation, however, as Israel retained effective control over the Strip and all critical aspects of life there, including the territorial waters and airspace as well as the border crossings and thus the movement in and out of people and goods, which included food, medicine and other humanitarian supplies.

In January 2006 legislative elections were held in the occupied Palestinian territory, and Hamas, the Islamic Resistance Movement, won by a landslide. In my opinion the election results did not appear to signify an ideological shift in Palestinian society but rather a delayed reaction to what so many Palestinians regarded as the PLO's capitulation at Oslo and the undoubted cronyism within the PA that emerged from those Accords. It was largely a protest vote against the stagnation and ineffectiveness of the mainstream leadership, and revealed a popular sentiment that snubbed any cosy compromises that Israel and its Western allies might offer, which time and time again ignored Palestinians' fundamental rights and core demands of freedom, justice and equality. These results were rejected by Israel and its Western allies, particularly the United States and European Union, which had designated Hamas as a terrorist organization.

To the Israelis and their allies, the fact that the Palestinian people expressed their will democratically was only a trifling detail. By comparison, arrest warrants that had been issued by the British government against Menachem Begin, for example, for terrorist acts committed against British and Palestinian civilians during the British Mandate, had swiftly been dropped after he was elected as prime minister in 1977. To obdurate democrats and devoted supporters of Western ideas of democracy, such double standards and hypocrisy seemed incredible.

Following those elections, after much agitation and haggling, a Palestinian unity government was formed in March 2007. It had a difficult birth and was doomed. It was effectively boycotted by Israel and its Western allies. International aid was suspended, as were tax transfers due to the PA from Israel because a Fatah–Hamas coalition was expected to be dominated by Hamas.[23] Three months after its formation, with all the obstacles it faced, it became inevitable that the fragile unity government would disintegrate.

In undermining that unity between the two wings of the Palestinian movement, Israel's Western allies made a severe misjudgement. While it was clearly in Israel's interests for Palestinians to remain politically, economically and geographically fragmented, and therefore disunited and weak, others in the international community should have been perfectly able to see that coalitions of often mutually hostile factions, despite any obvious radical differences, were intrinsically more stabilising than the persistence of factional antagonisms. For example, a look at the Israeli model – how Israel is run – has clearly shown that coalition governments inclusive of all political formations, from the far right to the furthest left, have been key to Israel's stability. So why did they not recognise the potentially positive benefits of a Fatah–Hamas coalition when it came to Palestinian politics? Why could they not see the value of the incorporation of Hamas, whose leaders expressed a willingness to exercise political pragmatism, into the political realm as opposed to relegating them to the role of 'opposition'? Instead, the alternative, following their veto of any collaboration between Fatah and Hamas, was a detrimental fragmentation that has inevitably led to dissension and at times open armed clashes between the Palestinian factions that were at loggerheads, leaving the common good and the 'peace process' as the victims.

When, in June 2007, the government split and Hamas took over Gaza, instantaneously, in an act of collective punishment, Israel imposed a total land, air and sea blockade on the Strip's more than two million inhabitants, reinforced by rationing water, food items, electricity and other necessities.

*

In the occupied territories the inhabitants did not take all of Israel's measures and incursions into their territory on the chin. Peaceful protests erupted everywhere, calling for an end to the prolonged annexationist occupation, apartheid and dispossession, and in the Gaza Strip these grievances, combined with Israel's imposition of an illegal blockade in 2007, led militants to retaliate by firing rockets into Israel. The military responses from Israel were inevitably brutal and overwhelming. During its invasion of Gaza in December 2007 and January 2008, for example, Israel deployed, in one of the most densely populated areas in the world, F-16s, Apache helicopters, drones, tanks and armoured vehicles, miniature robots, GPS-guided munitions, flechette rounds and white-phosphorus shells.[24] According to B'Tselem, the Israeli human-rights organisation, their twenty-two-day onslaught ended with about 5,000 Palestinians wounded and 1,391 killed, including at least 759 civilians, among them 318 children and 108 women. On the Israeli side, sixty-eight were injured and thirteen killed: three of them civilians, among them one woman, and four killed by Israeli forces in friendly-fire incidents.[25]

Israel explained away the heavy death toll by making allegations that Palestinian militant groups had used civilians as human shields. Amnesty International investigated these claims and published its findings in July 2009. Here are its main conclusions:

> The allegation that Hamas was using 'human shields' was repeatedly made by Israeli government and army officials and spokespersons ... Specifically, they accused Hamas of intentionally using the civilian population as 'human shields' for their military activities by being based within towns and villages; storing rockets and other weapons in populated areas;

firing rockets from close proximity to civilian buildings; and taking cover in civilian buildings after firing. Amnesty International asked the Israeli authorities on several occasions to provide information to substantiate its allegations about the use by Hamas of Gaza's civilians, but has yet to receive a response.

Hamas, on the other hand, makes the argument that, as a political party, a social organization and an armed group, it is based among the population throughout Gaza. Militants affiliated to other armed groups do not dispute this and indeed make similar claims for themselves. They point out that any fighting which took place in Gaza was at the behest of Israeli forces which invaded Gaza, moving with tanks and troops into residential areas, occupying civilian homes and launching attacks from these homes. They maintain that the armed confrontations in or near residential areas were aimed at resisting Israeli ground attacks and deny any policy of endangering civilians or using civilians as cover.

The groups openly acknowledge that their fighters and military facilities are present in towns and villages in Gaza, but argue that their role is to defend their communities against Israeli attacks and invasions. They said that they have no choice as to where they operate from and point to frequent Israeli attacks against civilian homes and targets where there was no presence of fighters or weapons as evidence that Israeli forces do not distinguish between military and civilian targets.

Some of the armed groups deny having fired rockets from populated areas or having stored them there, while others argue that they were merely defending their communities and that Israeli forces targeted civilians not involved in military activities and locations from which no attacks had been launched.

Amnesty International, for its part, did not find evidence that Hamas or other Palestinian groups violated the laws of war to the extent repeatedly alleged by Israel. In particular, it found no evidence that Hamas or other fighters directed the movement of civilians to shield military objectives from attacks. By contrast, Amnesty International did find that Israeli forces on several occasions during Operation 'Cast

> Lead' forced Palestinian civilians to serve as 'human shields'. In any event, international humanitarian law makes clear that use of 'human shields' by one party does not release the attacking party from its legal obligations with respect to civilians.[26]

The UN Human Rights Council appointed a fact-finding mission to investigate the Gaza invasion headed by Justice Richard J. Goldstone of South Africa, the former chief prosecutor of the international criminal tribunals for former Yugoslavia and Rwanda, who had long 'taken a deep interest in Israel, in what happens in Israel' and who had 'been associated with organizations that have worked in Israel'.[27] After eight months of investigations, a 575-page report was produced accusing both Israel and Palestinian armed groups of committing actions amounting to war crimes, possibly crimes against humanity. The report also called for accountability for all violations of international law, if necessary through a referral of the matter to the International Criminal Court.

Despite the clear even-handedness of the report, its reliance on international law as the basis for assessment, and Goldstone's credentials as 'a lifelong friend of Israel and a committed Zionist', Israel attacked it as biased and politically motivated, saying that it ignored Israel's 'right to self-defence'. This despite the fact that the International Court of Justice, the highest judicial body of the UN, had confirmed in its 2004 Advisory Opinion on the Wall that Israel cannot invoke the 'right to self-defence'– which allows states to launch wars – against territory that it occupies. A chorus of denunciations that included character assassinations of Justice Goldstone followed that criticism. Shimon Peres, Israel's president, called him a 'small man ... with no real understanding of jurisprudence'; Yuval Steinitz, Israel's minister of finance, accused Goldstone, himself Jewish, of anti-Semitism, commenting that Jews, too, could be 'anti-Semitic and discriminate against our people'; Alan Dershowitz, Professor at Harvard Law School, called him 'an evil, evil man'; while writer and Nobel laureate Elie Wiesel labelled the report 'a crime against the Jewish people'.[28]

Although the Israeli organisation Breaking the Silence and others corroborated the substance of the report, in the face of such a sustained campaign of intimidation and other pressures Justice Goldstone later modified some of his conclusions, saying that Israel should be judged by its intentions, not its actions. Professor Ilan Pappé found that analysis 'bizarre' and wrote that such a conclusion was impossible to accept based on a reading of the facts.[29]

The Goldstone Report then took its place on UN shelves crowded with many decades'-worth of files and documents calling in vain for Israel's compliance with UN resolutions and international law.

*

In July 2014, five years after the 2008–9 war on Gaza, Israel decided once again to 'mow the lawn' in the Strip. 'Mowing the lawn' is the disturbing metaphor coined by Israeli military strategists to denote the act of launching periodic military assaults on Gaza. That was translated into seven weeks of relentless bombardment of the Gaza Strip that resulted in 2,251 Palestinians killed, including 1,462 civilians. Of the Palestinian fatalities, 551 were children and 299 women; 11,231 Palestinians were injured including 3,436 children and 3,540 women, 10 per cent of whom suffered permanent disability. More than 1,500 Palestinian children were orphaned. The Israeli casualties were: six civilians and sixty-seven Israeli soldiers killed. Up to 1,600 Israelis were injured, including 270 children.[30]

International reactions to these events were muted. Because of the US veto, the UN Security Council could not even agree on a resolution condemning Israel's actions let alone any kind of coercive action under Chapter VII of the UN Charter in response to the military aggression. In an ideal world there should have been a thorough investigation not only into Israel's culpability for war crimes but also into the crucial and complicit role played by a number of states in promoting Israel and giving it all the military, financial and political support that has enabled it to become a repeat offender.

Since 1948, apart from a short-lived lull during the Eisenhower administration in the mid-1950s, successive US administrations turned Israel–US relations into a holy alliance. America's total support for Israel went beyond any reasonable promotion of US interests. US vetoes of Security Council resolutions condemning Israeli conduct that violates international law have become standard rituals. When in March 2014 the forty-seven members of the UN Human Rights Council (UNHRC) voted on resolutions primarily affirming the Palestinian people's rights to American home-grown values, such as the right of self-determination, and the US was the only country to vote against such cherished principles, the council broke into spontaneous laughter.

With blank-cheque impunity, Israel has, for more than five decades, imposed an ideologically based occupation on Gaza and the West Bank, including East Jerusalem. Imagine if the June 1940 German occupation of France had lasted that long and that Germany proceeded to annex or settle its citizens in 60 per cent of France's territory. Imagine, further, that it had turned Marseilles into an enclave and deprived its inhabitants of freedom of movement by land, sea or air while it rationed their water, food and electricity supplies.

That under Israeli occupation two generations of Palestinians have known only Israeli generals and colonels as governors and besiegers of their towns and villages, is incomprehensible. A Palestinian Christian or Muslim living in Bethlehem cannot go to pray at their respective church or mosque in Jerusalem ten kilometres away without a hard-to-obtain permit.

Some of the refugees in Gaza live within sight of the land on the Israeli side where their villages once stood and where, for generations, their forebears had been born and grew up, celebrated marriages, raised families, tilled the soil and buried their loved ones. In March 2018, to bring their plight to the world's attention and highlight the right of return that the UN has been affirming annually since 1948, they decided to organise peaceful rallies, dubbed the Great March of Return, every Friday near the fence separating the Strip from Israel. Two years after the demonstrations began, a report by the UNHRC concluded that Israeli snipers applied shoot-to-kill policies and may have committed crimes against humanity. Between 30 March and 31 December 2018, at the demonstration sites, 189 Palestinians were killed, including thirty-five children as well as two members of the press and three health workers. There were no Israeli casualties.[31]

US organisation Jewish Voice for Peace aptly described these deadly events as, on one side, a military that fired lethal bullets, and, on the other, civilians marching for their basic human rights.[32]

☀

During the next round of assaults on Gaza in May 2021 Israel launched more than 1,500 air and artillery strikes in just eleven days.[33] Once again, Israel's omnipresent state-of-the-art PR machinery worked around the clock to whitewash the horrific crimes it committed during that month, including in the West Bank and against Palestinian citizens of Israel. Its experts are always there to ensure that Israel is perceived by Western public opinion as a democratic Western outpost, a shining beacon in a hostile and wild 'Orient'. Undoubtedly, such systematic PR campaigns have succeeded in influencing Western media outlets and continue to stifle the Palestinian narrative.

EPILOGUE

A Call for a One-State Solution

Throughout its history the Holy Land has always been multi-ethnic, multi-religious and multicultural. For centuries, Palestinians had welcomed peaceful pilgrims who regularly came to Palestine, some of whom chose to settle there and became part of the ethnic mosaic of Palestine's population. The Palestinian people are the sum of the land's history and geography, at the convergence of faith and the crossroads of continents.

But in calling for the creation of a Jewish state in historic Palestine, the fundamental tenet of the Zionist doctrine conceived in 1897 was not to coexist with the native inhabitants but instead to establish a new presence at their expense.

The Zionist dream thus necessitated the Palestinian *Nakba*. How could such a diverse land become a home to one group except at the expense of all others? The Zionist movement's ambitions meant altering the very identity of the land. It distorted history to deny the existence and humanity of the Palestinians who have inhabited and cherished the land for generations. It did not do this alone. The Zionist project succeeded because the international community time and time again supported Israel unconditionally, even when Israeli policies stripped the Palestinian people of their most basic human rights and relegated Palestinian lives to generations of occupation and violence.

In essence, for the Zionist movement religion was a useful rallying cry, but Zionism's main contours were those of settler colonialism, 'a form of colonization marked by ongoing efforts to displace local populations and expropriate their land in order to establish or expand a society dominated by settlers'.[1] In addition to settling in Palestine, Zionist Jews wanted to displace, eliminate and replace its native inhabitants in order to create a permanent Jewish majority. This intention was openly expressed by Theodor Herzl, the founder of modern Zionism, who wrote as far back as 1895, 'We shall try to spirit the penniless [Palestinian] population across the border by procuring employment for it in the transit countries, while denying it any employment in our country ... the removal of the poor must be carried out discreetly and circumspectly.'[2] He also wrote: 'If I wish to substitute a new building for an old one, I must demolish before I construct.'[3]

Other early Zionist leaders also advocated for the ethnic cleansing of Palestinians – euphemistically referred to as 'transfer' – as a condition for the creation of a Jewish state. Those included Ben-Gurion who, in June 1938 during a meeting of the Jewish Agency for Palestine,[4] stated that he 'support[s] compulsory transfer'.[5] In July 1948, when asked what was to be done with the Palestinian inhabitants of the cities of Lydda and Ramla, he confirmed this stance and, according to the memoirs of late Israeli prime minister Yitzhak Rabin, waved his hand in a gesture which said 'Drive them out!'[6] In his own diary Ben-Gurion wrote: 'We must do everything to ensure they [the Palestinian refugees] never do return.'[7] Yosef Weitz, director of the Jewish National Fund land settlement committee, wrote in his diary in 1940: 'It must be clear that there is no room in the country for both peoples ... If the Arabs leave it, the country will become wide and spacious for us ... The only solution is a Land of Israel ... without Arabs ...'[8] In 1941, in a meeting with the Soviet ambassador to London, Chaim Weizmann, president of the World Zionist Organization, suggested that if 'half a million Arabs [Palestinians] could be transferred, two million Jews [Jewish immigrants] could be put in their place. That, of course, would be a first instalment.'[9]

Warnings by early visionary Zionists that this logic of elimination was morally reprehensible and would create longstanding instability were ignored. In his address to the Zionist Congress in 1905, the Hebrew linguist and educator Yitzhak Epstein beseeched the delegates to reconsider, asking, 'Will those who are dispossessed remain silent and accept what is being done to them? In the end, they will wake up and return to us in blows what we have looted from them with our gold!'[10] In 1891, the journalist and essayist Ahad Ha'am expressed alarm at the treatment of Palestinians, writing: 'Yet what do our brethren do in Palestine? ... They treat the Arabs with hostility and cruelty, deprive them of their rights, offend them without cause and even boast of these deeds; and nobody among us opposes this despicable and dangerous inclination.'[11] In 1914 he once again warned against the dangers of Zionist objectives, writing:

> ... [the Zionists] wax angry towards those who remind them that there is still another people in Eretz Israel that has been living there and does not intend at all to leave its place. In a future when this illusion will have been torn from their hearts and they will look with open eyes upon the reality as it is, they will certainly understand how important this question is and how great our duty to work for its solution.[12]

Prominent Jewish intellectuals and thinkers – including Hannah Arendt, Albert Einstein, Sigmund Freud and Erich Fromm – saw this moral deficiency at the heart of the Zionist project and opposed efforts to create an exclusively Jewish state in Palestine.

To achieve its goals the Zionist movement had no qualms about working in concert with imperialist powers of the time. For its own imperialist agenda, Britain pledged in the Balfour Declaration to help the Zionist movement establish a 'national home for the Jewish people' in Palestine. The only Jewish member of the British cabinet at the time, Sir Edwin Montagu, strongly opposed the Balfour Declaration, giving fiery speeches critical of it at cabinet meetings. To him, Zionism was a nationalist movement with political objectives that would be harmful to Jews and Palestinians alike, while Judaism was a universal faith distinct from nationality. In 1917, in a secret memorandum, he wrote:

> I deny that Palestine is today associated with the Jews or properly to be regarded as a fit place for them to live in. The Ten Commandments were delivered to the Jews on Sinai. It is quite true that Palestine plays a large part in Jewish history, but so it does in modern Mohammedan history, and, after the time of the Jews, surely it plays a larger part than any other country in Christian history ... When the Jews are told that Palestine is their national home, every country will immediately desire to get rid of its Jewish citizens, and you will find a population in Palestine driving out its present inhabitants.[13]

When the British began to put the Balfour Declaration into action, facilitating the immigration of European Jews to Palestine and equipping them to establish self-rule, this was opposed by the Palestinians, and it led to massive demonstrations. This pushed Winston Churchill, although a staunch Zionist sympathiser, to affirm in a 1922 white paper that a Jewish home was not to be all of Palestine, but *in* Palestine.[14]

On the ground, such words of reassurance were contradicted by acts. Despite the proviso in the declaration that 'nothing shall be done which may prejudice the civil and religious rights of existing non-Jewish communities in Palestine', Britain treated the Zionist movement as the nucleus for a future state and offered its followers all the training, trappings and logistical support needed to build the necessary para-state institutions.[15] It did not see any irony in allowing the incoming Jewish settlers to arm themselves to protect their *settlements*, while prohibiting the indigenous Palestinians from possessing arms to defend their *native land*.

Since then waves of Zionist immigration into Palestine radically changed the demographic structure of the country and brought an abrupt end to the racial and religious harmony that had hitherto largely prevailed. Constructing Israel inevitably entailed deconstructing Palestine. Progressively, Zionists' dreams turned into Palestinians' nightmares. That turn of events ultimately propelled the Palestinian people into a deeply asymmetric tug of war with Zionist forces that still rages today.

When in 1947 the violence intensified, in line with its colonial doctrine, Britain tossed the Palestine problem over to the newly created UN: divide and rule when the going is good, but divide and quit when things get nasty.

The Palestinian leadership at the time may well have assumed that the referral to the UN would be met with a similar fate as the British commissions of inquiry that were routinely set up to investigate the recurring crisis in Palestine during the Mandate years: their findings and recommendations rarely changed long-term policies and, more often than not, they ended up being dead letters consigned to oblivion. The UN General Assembly's 1947 recommendation that Palestine be partitioned could easily have followed that pattern. Indeed, that non-binding resolution was adopted without the consent of the inhabitants of Palestine,[16] and it sought to impose a flagrantly unequitable partition against their will.[17] Moreover, the UN did not have sovereignty over Palestine and had no legal authority or competence to break up its territorial integrity.[18] Nevertheless, partition was implemented and offered a basis for the creation of the State of Israel. This was in large part a result of the influence and vigorous lobbying by Zionist groups in the United States that resonated with US designs and with its surging ambition to replace Britain in world dominance, combined with political instrumentalisation of the rightful wave of sympathy and guilt that swept across the Western world for the Jewish plight following the Holocaust.

The Palestinian leadership rejected the decision to partition the country as unjust. But it remained hopeful, embracing fantasies about the power and influence of the seven member states of the Arab League – Egypt, Iraq, Transjordan, Lebanon, Syria, Saudi Arabia and Yemen – to put a halt to Zionist ambitions in Palestine.

On their side, Zionist leaders were taking a different tack. On the face of things, they accepted the 1947 UN General Assembly recommendation that gave them 55.5 per cent of Palestine. In reality, that decision was tactical. Ben-Gurion saw it as 'only the beginning'.[19] In 1937 he had told the Zionist Executive 'after the formation of a large army in the wake of the establishment of the state, we will abolish partition and expand to the whole of Palestine'.[20] Moshe Sharett, who became Ben-Gurion's foreign minister in 1948, added that Israel's territory was to be determined by 'possession', not partition.[21] Not wanting to lose the momentum triggered by the Deir Yassin massacre in April 1948, which facilitated territorial expansion by accelerating the flight of Palestinians, Israel continued its military advance and ethnic cleansing operations relentlessly.[22] In the village of Tantura, for example, in May 1948 more than 200 Palestinians were massacred and buried in a mass grave.[23]

By the time the 1949 Armistice Agreements were signed, Israel had extended its frontiers to cover 78 per cent of Palestine, far beyond what had been allotted in the UN Partition Plan and, according to Ilan Pappé, had destroyed and ethnically cleansed 531 villages, including my home village Beit Nattif.[24] Around 750,000 Palestinians, more than half of the Palestinian inhabitants of historic Palestine, had been duly 'transferred'; in other words, dispossessed and rendered refugees. Most, including myself and my whole family, were expelled or fled to the 22 per cent that remained (currently known as the West Bank and Gaza) that came under Jordanian or Egyptian control.

Sporadic Israeli incursions into Palestinian areas did not cease, however, and on three occasions ended in bloody massacres. In 1953 sixty-nine Palestinian civilians were killed in the village of Qibya as a retaliation for a cross-border raid by Palestinian infiltrators in which one Israeli woman and her two children were killed. In 1956 111 civilians were slaughtered in the Rafah refugee camp, which Israel claimed was in response to Palestinian resistance to its occupation of the camp. In Kafr Qasim, forty-eight Palestinians (who were Israeli citizens) were killed by Israeli forces in 1956 for breaking a curfew of which they had not been informed.[25]

When in 1967 Israel occupied the West Bank and Gaza and the Security Council underlined the inadmissibility of the acquisition of territory by force and called for Israeli withdrawal, this call fell on deaf ears. The Israeli foreign minister of the time, Abba Eban, rose to fame as the tireless and eloquent defender of Israel's expansionist polices, offering 'security' as the one-size-fits-all justification. The occupation was never intended to be temporary but was rather a means towards further appropriation of Palestinian land, and so colonisation of the occupied Palestinian territories started, and the first Israeli settlement, Kiryat Arba, was established in the West Bank in 1968.

In 1977 Menachem Begin, who was notorious for his affiliation with the Zionist paramilitary organisation Haganah and the Irgun terrorist group,[26] was elected as prime minister. Although only cosmetic differences existed between Begin's Likud party and Mapai – the socialist party that had ruled Israel during the first 29 years of its existence – on the crucial issues of settlement construction and entrenchment of occupation, Begin's election emboldened what were until then fringe right-wing parties in Israel. In that fundamentalist environment, the Basic Law: Jerusalem, Capital of Israel was passed, declaring that 'Jerusalem, complete and united, is the capital of Israel' thus *de jure* illegally annexing East Jerusalem, and the Drobles Plan, a Master Plan for the Development of Settlements in Judea and Samaria, 1979–1983, was adopted, which set out clear strategies for the establishment of settlements in the midst of populated Palestinian areas and clarifying that the ultimate aim of the settlement drive was to permanently annex the West Bank to Israel.[27] Fundamentalist voices from the growing settler community increasingly claimed their divinely ordained rights to Palestinian land. Curfews, extrajudicial executions, detention without trial, torture, land confiscation, forcible transfer, movement restrictions, the demolition of homes and the uprooting of olive trees became daily routines of Palestinian suffering that continue to this day.

*

More than half a century after the creation of Israel, the Israeli occupation of the West Bank and Gaza has become the longest belligerent military occupation in modern history. Some of us escaped and became the new Wandering Tribe of the Palestinian diaspora, others perished and others still are now living like subhumans, stripped of their basic human rights, in the occupied territories. Against this backdrop the Palestinians have waited for world powers to recognise the disaster their negligence (at best) or complicity (at worst) has precipitated in Palestine, and to take action to stop this downwards spiral and bring an end to this historical injustice.

The story of a land haunted by violence does not need to be the future of Palestine and Israel. A peaceful future is possible, and the international community must help usher in a new chapter in a story that for too long has been marked by conflict and tragedy. As history has taught us from other situations of injustice, Israel will not end its settler-colonial project voluntarily unless it has an incentive to do so and a disincentive not to – that is, unless the cost of continuing is made to outweigh the benefits of finding a new way forward. So far, the benefits of continuing the occupation of the West Bank and Gaza, have far outweighed the costs. In addition to its ideological value to Israel, the occupation of Palestinian land has also been a highly profitable economic venture, particularly through the exploitation and plunder of Palestinian natural resources, agricultural and industrial production in illegal settlements, the turning of the occupied territories into a captive market for Israeli products, the exploitation by the private sector of low-wage Palestinian labour and the testing of Israeli weapons on occupied Palestinians in order to help market its weaponry as 'battle-tested' and expand its arms industry.[28]

This is where the international community has a crucial role to play, and it has a host of tools at its disposal, which it has successfully used to effect policy change before. When apartheid prevailed in South Africa, for example, economic sanctions and a mandatory military arms embargo were instrumental in bringing the apartheid regime to its knees. Other concrete measures that have been deployed to bring an end to conflicts have included military intervention, suspending bilateral relations, prosecuting perpetrators of crimes in international and domestic courts and deploying protection forces. Ending impunity and ensuring accountability for Israel's persistent violations of international law with regard to the Palestinian people is the key to compelling its compliance with the countless UN resolutions that it has routinely ignored – and to ushering in a new chapter of peace, stability and security in the Holy Land.

Such action based on conscience, responsibility, the rule of law and human rights would not be 'pro-Palestinian'. We are not asking for special treatment by the international community – we are simply asking for Israel to stop receiving special treatment and for an end to be put to the culture of impunity. Israel should not continue to be treated as a country above the law, exempted from the same laws and standards that should apply equally to every state. It should not be rewarded for its illegal behaviour. We are not calling on world powers to reinvent the wheel but simply to put an end to double standards and promote respect for the international rules and principles which they have themselves developed. There are, of course, other regimes that suppress human rights and that have enjoyed impunity, but there is no other case of a Western-affiliated regime that denies self-determination and human rights to a people and that has done so for so long.

It is therefore unfair to perceive calls for international action, including sanctions and countermeasures, by Palestinians and people of conscience worldwide as 'controversial', 'one-sided', 'unbalanced' – or, worse, 'anti-Semitic', something that is repeatedly claimed by Israel. That Israel has been violating international law since its inception, that there has been no accountability for these violations, that this impunity is at the core of the recurrence of violations, is not simply a Palestinian narrative based on some abstraction or subjectivity. It is the reality, affirmed by facts and countless reports by the UN, legal experts and civil-society organisations worldwide.

Instead of taking such an approach, however, world powers have remained deaf to Palestinians' pleas. To borrow a metaphor coined by Prince Karim Aga Khan, the Palestinian people felt 'as though in a nightmare, screaming to be heard but making no sound'.[29]

Ever since the creation of Israel, its allies have been nurturing its power, soft and hard, emboldening its already dogmatic leaders and enabling them to conceitedly defy the whole world, including US presidents. For example, during his speech to the US Congress in May 2011, initially organised without the White House's knowledge and aimed at undermining President Barack Obama's foreign-policy priority to reach a deal with Iran on its nuclear programme, Benjamin Netanyahu received twenty-nine standing ovations, a record. A visitor from another planet might have been forgiven for thinking that Netanyahu was the president of the United States. With such an overdose of power, he and his government paid lip service to the so-called peace process launched in Madrid in 1991 and sustained a sterile environment in which a viable peace agreement could not be reached, while gaslighting the outside world by feeding it with skilfully crafted fictions about the situation being 'too complex' to understand or resolve and peace being intrinsically intractable between Israelis and Palestinians. British–Israeli historian Avi Shlaim later described Netanyahu as 'the procrastinator par excellence, the double-faced prime minister who pretends to negotiate the partition of the pizza while continuing to gobble it up'.[30]

The ultimate point of power-driven arrogance was displayed fully in 2017 during President Donald Trump's so-called 'deal of the century'. At their White House ceremony – performed with such pompous exuberance, messianic zeal and with the mindset of real-estate brokers selling what was not for sale to people with no rightful claim – the self-styled new paladins decreed the annihilation of the legitimate national aspirations of twelve million Palestinians. They looked so self-satisfied and conceited. I saw them as abstractions, intransitive verbs, unhitched avatars. They had no qualms about chopping up the little that remained of historic Palestine and permanently turning it into cheap labour reserves.

In parallel, the United States and other allies of Israel, mainly in Europe – including countries that tout themselves as bastions of free speech – have endorsed Israel's campaign to weaponise anti-Semitism by conflating Judaism and Zionism and thereby tainting any legitimate criticism of its Zionist settler-colonial project and violations against the Palestinian people as anti-Semitic. In 2019, for example, President Emmanuel Macron of France stated that anti-Zionism was 'a modern-day form of anti-Semitism'.[31] Such libellous accusations have targeted people from all walks of life who have dared to denounce or even just hint at Israel's mistreatment of the Palestinians, including members of the US Congress, the prosecutor of the International Criminal Court, Nobel Peace Prize laureate Archbishop Desmond Tutu, former mayor of London Ken Livingstone and US political scientist John Mearsheimer, to name a few. Many Jews who oppose Zionism or the colonisation of Palestinian land have been accused of being 'self-hating Jews'.

Anti-Semitism, a real scourge and disgrace in society, is thus cynically exploited to shield illegal actions from criticism and accountability. Many Jewish scholars, jurists and religious leaders have expressed concern that this political instrumentalisation of anti-Semitism actually weakens or trivialises the fight against it, as it deflects attention away from addressing abhorrent prejudice and attacks against Jews and focuses more on covering up the actions of a state. Moreover, conflating Judaism with Israel or Zionism may well feed into a new anti-Semitism again raising its head – not a good outcome for Israel, Palestine or the outside world.

The victims of the Holocaust, pogroms and centuries of persecution and racial violence are to be honoured by upholding the multilateral rules-based order which was established in response to the horrors of the Second World War, including the Holocaust, not by silencing defenders of international law and human rights; they are to be honoured by ensuring the accountability of nation states and war criminals to these laws and norms, not by stifling calls for accountability. As Jewish intellectual Peter Beinart writes:

> Antisemitism isn't wrong because it is wrong to denigrate and dehumanise Jews. Antisemitism is wrong because it is wrong to denigrate and dehumanise anyone. Which means,

> ultimately, that any effort to fight antisemitism that contributes to the denigration and dehumanisation of Palestinians is no fight against antisemitism at all.[32]

What Israeli policymakers and apologists do not seem to recognise is that no amount of censorship or intimidation can completely conceal the oppressive actions of Israeli soldiers and settlers directed at the Palestinian population. The situation in Israel and Palestine has deteriorated so dramatically, especially during the eighteen years when Ariel Sharon and Benjamin Netanyahu were prime ministers, that in 2021 alone Israeli and US human-rights NGOs, B'Tselem and Human Rights Watch respectively, published extensively researched reports concluding that Israel is committing the crime of apartheid against all Palestinians under its jurisdiction or control, including Palestinian citizens of Israel as well as Palestinians in the West Bank and Gaza.

This forms part of a growing international consensus in the global human-rights community that the systematic oppression and domination of Palestinians by Israel between the Mediterranean and the River Jordan has crossed the apartheid threshold as defined under international law. B'Tselem, for example, highlighted that 'one organising principle lies at the base of a wide array of Israeli policies: advancing and perpetuating the supremacy of one group – Jews – over another – Palestinians',[33] while Human Rights Watch stressed that 'the Israeli government has demonstrated an intent to maintain the domination of Jewish Israelis over Palestinians across Israel and the OPT [occupied Palestinian territories]'.[34] Such findings fly in the face of attempts by Israel to portray itself as a vibrant democracy; it should more accurately be described as an ethnocracy, 'a political regime that facilitates expansion and control by a dominant ethnicity in contested lands'.[35]

A number of politicians and public figures have also raised the alarm and spoken of the reality or threat of apartheid in Israel and/or the occupied Palestinian territories. This has included heroes of the anti-apartheid struggle in South Africa, former

US president Jimmy Carter in his book *Palestine: Peace Not Apartheid* and, significantly, no fewer than four Israeli prime ministers – David Ben-Gurion, Yitzhak Rabin, Ehud Barak and Ehud Olmert – among other prominent Israeli officials, including a former attorney general, a former environment minister, a former education minister and the former Israeli ambassador to South Africa.[36]

There is no doubt that Israel's image and standing in the world arena is changing, despite Israel's desperate efforts to polish its 'brand image' by employing PR firms and using its lobbying capacities to present itself as a progressive, freedom-loving liberal democracy. A growing number of Jews worldwide – including Holocaust survivors and their descendants –as well as, increasingly, Jewish Israelis are seeking to disassociate themselves and the humanistic ethics of Judaism from the regressive policies and practices of what is fast becoming viewed as a pariah state. In the United States a growing movement of American Jews against occupation is gradually changing the conversation about Israel–Palestine among the Jewish community and coming out forcefully in support of Palestinians' human rights. This has included members of organisations Jewish Voice for Peace and IfNotNow, presidential candidate Bernie Sanders, rabbinical students and the Jewish Diaspora in Tech.[37, 38] In the UK the group Na'amod: British Jews Against Occupation has been working to 'end the [British Jewish] community's support for Israel's occupation and apartheid'.[39] According to Israeli historian Evyatar Friesel, approximately thirty books written by Jews critical of Israel were published between 2002 and 2017.[40]

Even some historically right-wing Israelis are having second thoughts about Israeli policies and Zionism. Miko Peled, who was born into a prominent Zionist family – his grandfather was one of Israel's founders, his father was a highly decorated army general and a former military governor of Gaza – and who was once in Israel's Special Forces, has written and lectured extensively about the deep structural inequalities inherent in the Israeli state, the negation of the Palestinian people's rights and the need to bring long-overdue justice to the Palestinian people. Another example is Yaakov Sharett. His father was one of Israel's founders and first foreign minister and second prime minister. During his long career in public service, Sharett held several key positions including in the Shin Bet security service. He later became an anti-Zionist. On 19 September 2021 *Haaretz* published an in-depth interview with him in which he declared that:

> Israel ... was born in sin. ... [I am a] collaborator with a criminal country ... The moment Zionism called for the Jews to immigrate to Israel, in order to establish here one home for the Jewish people, which will be a sovereign state, a conflict was created. ... Have you seen anywhere in the world where the majority would agree to give in to a foreign invader, who says, 'our forefathers were here,' and demands to enter the land and take control? ... Our national agenda is blood, death and violence.

Another glaring example of how people are susceptible to changing their minds once reality on the ground clashes with and invalidates previously held dogmas, is the case of the late Abba Eban. I witnessed his metamorphosis from the once staunch defender of Zionism, who pleaded its cause during the 1947 UN Partition Plan session, then later as foreign minister during the 1967 and 1973 wars. Three months into the First Intifada, together with about fifty other people, I listened in disbelief to him declaring that 'The Palestinians are a nation, they are a people. They have legitimate rights, they ... are part of the Arab world, but they are also something in their own right.'[41] I was happy to hear Abba Eban's words. They left me with the comforting impression that people can have the courage to indulge in self-criticism, and that opinions and judgements are not sacrosanct.

A few years earlier, Moshe Menuhin, father of the violinist Yehudi Menuhin and early immigrant to Palestine at the start of the Zionist project, described how he became opposed to Zionism:

> After having been brought up in my grandfather's home in Jerusalem on universal, ethnical, humane, prophetic Judaism ... I could not stomach the daily preachings of Amaynooh, Artzaynooh, Moladtaynooh (our nation, our country, our birthplace) by our hyper-nationalistic, goyim-hating, Zionist Hebrew teachers. Not one of the students at the Gymnasia Herzlin was born in Arab Palestine; we all came to Palestine from Russia, Poland, Romania, Galicia, etc. as refugees or immigrants. The hatred and contempt for goyim (gentiles) – Arabs, in our case – was irrational and inhuman.[42]

The authenticity of such witnesses, their eloquence and outreach, is becoming a force to be reckoned with in opposing Israel's oppression of the Palestinian people, and they are making remarkable strides in refocusing world public opinion and triggering arm's-length dialectical discussions and interrelations. These are the thinkers, leaders and organisations that the Palestinians need to support and team up with to achieve their ultimate freedom.

In response to the critiques of Zionism and the heinous crimes that have been committed in its name, including by prominent Israeli and Jewish figures and organisations, Western liberal and left-wing outlets that had traditionally embraced and defended the Zionist cause are now revisiting their underlying assumptions and publicly admitting that they are having serious afterthoughts, even regrets, about the uncritical enthusiasm with which they had hailed the Zionist movement and the creation of Israel in 1948. As the *Guardian* frankly declared on 7 May 2021, for example, 'Israel today is not the country [the *Guardian*] foresaw or would have wanted.'[43]

With Israel's illegal and discriminatory policies only worsening, combined with a better-informed public opinion, international solidarity movements in support of the Palestinians have grown across all continents. Inspired by the South African anti-apartheid movement, the Palestinian-led Boycott, Divestment and Sanctions movement, launched in 2005 and aimed at pressurising Israel to uphold international law vis-à-vis the

Palestinians, has now become a global movement with supporters including unions, trade academic associations, churches and civil society organisations worldwide, as well as public figures such as Canadian writer Naomi Klein, civil-rights activist Angela Davis, American philosopher Judith Butler, Nobel Prize-winning French novelist Annie Ernaux, Nobel Peace Prize laureate Mairead Maguire, Irish author Sally Rooney, Indian author Arundhati Roy, American actor Danny Glover, Franco-Swiss film director Jean-Luc Godard, British actor Emma Watson and American musician Lauryn Hill. Natural alliances have also been formed with other movements fighting structural racism and oppression, including Black Lives Matter and The Red Nation in the United States. Indeed, Palestine is seen as emblematic of the struggle for liberation everywhere.

Young people worldwide have embraced the Palestinian cause as the cause of their generation. Governments are often left to wonder why the Palestinian people enjoy so much international solidarity, which stubbornly continues despite attempts to muzzle voices that are critical of Israel. The answer is simple. The Palestinians have a legitimate and compelling case that resonates with people everywhere. As Edward Said so eloquently put it:

> Remember the solidarity [shown to Palestine] here and everywhere in Latin America, Africa, Europe, Asia, and Australia, and remember also that there is a cause to which many people have committed themselves, difficulties and terrible obstacles notwithstanding. Why? Because it is a just cause, a noble ideal, a moral quest for equality and human rights.[44]

This cause, this ideal, this quest is not abstract but based on solid, tangible facts. There are countless living Palestinian witnesses with personal stories to tell, with vivid memories of the unspeakable tragedies they suffered and that shattered all aspects of their lives.

*

The status quo is untenable. The die has been cast, and that the day will come when the Palestinians' call for freedom will finally be answered is inevitable. That will also be the day of liberation for Israeli society from its doomed apartheid system. And Israel's overwhelming military will not be able to fight the turning tide of global public opinion and moral outcry. Sophisticated armament and a nuclear capability did not prevent the apartheid regime in South Africa from tumbling like a house of cards. They were useless in the face of surging moral arguments embraced and fostered in the UK and the US, South Africa's staunchest allies, whose governments had the good, albeit long-overdue, sense to yield to the mounting demands of global public opinion and the courage to make the call for economic sacrifices and finally abandon Pretoria's apartheid regime. Then the rotten apartheid system fell.

Even on a realpolitik level, Israel's Western allies will soon find that it is no longer in their national interests to continue to politically, financially and militarily support a state that is so far removed from their professed values of freedom and democracy. Allowing Israel a free hand to continue its annexationist and apartheid policies would bring further accusations of double standards against the West and risk further discrediting the international system as a whole – especially in the Middle East, where faith in international law and the UN has plummeted – which would only create more extremism and instability, both of which are in the interests of no one.

What the United States and other friends of Israel will also realise is that the appeasement of Israel will not help Israel but instead only increase its international isolation and inevitable self-sabotage. As friends they should instead apply the pressure needed for Israel to reassess its policies and grasp the damage it is doing to the long-term interests of its own people, citizens of what is being increasingly recognised as an apartheid state. They should incentivise Israel to end its oppressive measures and usher in the peaceful coexistence with the Palestinian people that it objectively needs.

As the Palestinian people have clearly demonstrated over the past seven decades, they are here to stay, and no amount of subjugation will lead them to surrender or conveniently disappear. Israel's successive wars have gained it more territory but failed to break the Palestinians' will to be free. So to Israel and its allies, I say that it is no use putting your heads in the sand. The status quo is unsustainable, and the vicious cycle – expansion, ethnic cleansing, subjugation – will eventually be broken. The question is whether the world will wait for that to happen gradually, with all of the additional human suffering that would entail, or whether the political will can be mobilised to bring about a solution now. The most talked about are the two-state solution and the one-democratic-state solution.

The two-state solution, which envisions two states living side by side in peace and security on the basis of the pre-1967 borders after the ending of Israeli occupation, is now obsolete and no longer logistically feasible. Attempts to bring it about through the so-called peace process since 1993 have failed dismally, and the possibility of a sovereign, viable Palestinian state is now defunct.

When in 1988 the Palestinian leadership decided to accept the vision for a two-state solution that had been devised by the international community, it did so reluctantly and for good reason. First, the 'solution' entailed accepting that the Palestinian state would be established on only 22 per cent of historic Palestine (the West Bank and Gaza with East Jerusalem as its capital), one of the boldest compromises ever made for the sake of peace. It also meant that in the 78 per cent that would constitute the Israeli state, the Zionist character of Israel would be maintained, with all of its discriminatory implications for the Palestinian citizens of Israel living therein. Second, it meant accepting that there would be no meaningful return for the Palestinian refugees and their descendants to the villages and towns of their origin, despite their rights under international law. Third, the Palestinian state would be disjointed, since the West Bank and Gaza are physically separate. In return for these highly unpopular and divisive concessions, the Palestinian leadership required that the Palestinian statelet thus created would have full sovereignty and its borders not diminished further.

But even these small concessions within a solution that did not meet basic notions of justice were never accepted by Israel. Successive Israeli governments since 1967 have, in both word and deed, consistently rejected the notion of a viable, truly sovereign and independent Palestinian state with East Jerusalem as its capital. Since the peace process started with the signing of the Oslo I Accord in 1993, Israel aggressively accelerated the construction and expansion of illegal Israeli settlements in the West Bank, causing the number of settlers to almost treble in the space of two decades.[45] Emblematically, in 1998 Ariel Sharon, then foreign minister, said, 'Everybody has to move, run and grab as many [Palestinian] hilltops as they can to enlarge the settlements because everything we take now will stay ours ... Everything we don't grab will go to them.'[46]

In 2002 Israel started the construction of its illegal wall,[47] the majority of which is built not *along* Israel's internationally recognised frontiers but *inside* the occupied West Bank. Its route on Palestinian land had been strategically designed to integrate into its western 'Israeli' side the majority of settlements as well as areas designated for future expansion. Once the wall is completed, it is estimated that about 9.4 per cent of West Bank territory,[48] including seventy-one settlements,[49] and Palestinian underground water resources, one of which is Palestine's largest and most productive, the Western Aquifer, will have been incorporated in this way. The wall consists of a hybrid structure that includes trenches, layered razor wire, sand paths and concrete slabs between eight and nine metres in height, and is fully equipped with state-of-the-art surveillance technology. With a wall of such proportions and intent, could there be any other analogy for its purpose than annexation and apartheid?

This occupation infrastructure in the West Bank, bolstered by other restrictions on movement – including checkpoints, roadblocks and settler-only bypass roads and highways – have led to the fragmentation of the West Bank into Palestinian Bantustan-like enclaves that are completely encircled and have little or no territorial contiguity. And in 2007 the geographical, political and social fragmentation of the Palestinian people reached its peak when Israel imposed an illegal air, sea and land blockade on Gaza, which continues to this day.

It became obvious that Israel was using the peace process as a ploy to publicly appear open to negotiations while simultaneously buying itself the time it needed to expand its control on the ground and thereby annex or fragment land that was supposed to have been allocated to the Palestinian state in the two-state vision, thus leaving open only the possibility of a truncated, unviable 'mini-state'. In parallel, Israel made it clear that it would never accept relinquishing control over this mini-state's borders, airspace or water resources, thus ensuring that it would not only be unviable but also wholly dependent, insecure and at the mercy of its former occupier. A 'peace' concluded on these terms would be neither sustainable nor long-lasting, with the partition never equitable.

Despite taking no action to prevent this gradual burial of the two-state vision, the international community robotically continues to hail it as the only possible solution to the Palestine question. It is high time that world powers admit the failure of this vision and the responsibility they bear for their inaction. Journalists, academics, intellectuals and civil society worldwide have been saying it for years: we must face the facts and think creatively beyond partition. The two-state solution is nothing but a two-state 'delusion'.[50]

With support for the two-state plan receding at speed, support for that of a single democratic state in historic Palestine has gained a lot of momentum. The idea underpinning this solution is simple: coexistence and equality. There are two main reasons why interest in the one-state alternative has grown.

The first is practical, and it flows from the fact that realities on the ground need to be recognised for any solution to work: a one-state arrangement in Israel–Palestine already exists, and both Israelis and Palestinians are here to stay. It is a fact that the whole area of land that extends from the River Jordan to the Mediterranean – which includes Israel proper, the West Bank and Gaza – is under the control of one entity, Israel, whether through civilian or military rule. It is also a fact that twelve million people live in this territory – half of them Jews and the other half Palestinian. More than fifty years of occupation and settlement construction in the West Bank has meant that the lives of Jews and Palestinians have become increasingly intertwined. Illegal Israeli settlers – 700,000 people – are now too embedded to be forced out. Short of extermination, Palestinians will steadfastly hold onto their lands and properties and will not budge.

The second is principled and is based on the notion that peace must be accompanied by justice and the fulfilment of rights and that equality as a noble principle should prevail. Whereas the two-state vision had only the ending of the occupation that had started in 1967 as its goal and did not seek to address the Zionist, settler-colonial nature of the Israeli state that has led to the systematic dispossession of Palestinians and the denial of their rights since 1948, the one-state solution seeks to delve deeper into the roots of the problem by advocating a wider process of decolonisation that would ensure the fulfilment of the Palestinian people's fundamental rights and usher in a just, sustainable and lasting peace. It would reunify the Palestinian nation – those living in the West Bank and Gaza, those living in Israel proper as citizens of Israel and the Palestinian refugees who would finally be able to exercise their right of return. In doing so, bringing justice into the conversation alongside peace, the one-state solution would lead to a lasting and sustainable peace.

Decolonisation means abolishing the structures of domination – political, legal, military, economic and cultural – that have led to a preferential regime for Israeli Jews at the expense of the Palestinian people and replacing them with structures of equality and inclusivity, whereby reconciliation becomes possible. Israeli settlers who would wish to stay where they are would be given the right to do so on the understanding that settlements would become desegregated. This egalitarian vision of Jews and Palestinians living together in a shared democratic space is rooted in the universal principle that human beings are all one, all equal and that beauty exists in diversity – moral values, which are in themselves worth fighting for. As the Jewish–American novelist Isaac Azimov wrote to explain his rejection of Zionism:

> I think it is wrong for anyone to feel that there is anything special about any one heritage of whatever kind. It is delightful to have the human heritage exist in a thousand varieties, for it makes for greater interest, but as soon as one variety is thought to be more important than another, the groundwork is laid for destroying them all.[51]

This solution would avoid the complexity of having to draw borders or partitions – including in Jerusalem – or divide resources. Instead, it would restore the Holy Land to its former character as a land of many coexisting identities. As Palestinian writer Ghada Karmi elegantly puts it, 'the one-state solution is actually just a way of restoring a land deformed by half a century of division and colonization to an approximation of the whole country it once was, a rejection of disunity in favor of unity'.[52] In addition, this vision would finally resolve the plight of Palestinian refugees – the most protracted refugee crisis in modern history – by allowing for the implementation of their right of return to their ancestral lands. Practical solutions as to how to achieve this are already being conceived. Palestinian cartographer Salman Abu Sitta, for example, has developed an action plan for return and demonstrates its spatial and demographic feasibility. He finds that 85 per cent of Palestinian lands seized by Zionist forces during the 1948 *Nakba* now consist mainly of agricultural land or public parks and forests and could be resettled.[53] The Israeli NGO De-Colonizer has also been advocating for the need 'for Jewish Israelis to participate in planning the return of Palestinian refugees'.[54]

Taking into account these realities and principles, the one-state solution calls for changing the current one-state reality from one characterised by apartheid to one characterised by equality – one democratic state for all its citizens in the Holy Land. How it should be modelled in practice – whether it should be binational, unitary or federal – has been the subject of numerous studies and intellectual debates.

In the binational model, Palestinians and Jews would share the country but have separate national identities. This idea was floated as early as the 1920s, when a small but prominent group of early Zionists opposed to partition expressed their support for binationalism through groups like Brit Shalom, The Five and Ihud (Unity). Since the 1990s, when the idea of a binational Palestinian–Jewish State made a gradual reappearance, the number of advocates has grown to include, among others, Palestinian intellectual Edward Said,[55] former member of the Knesset Azmi Bishara, Israeli historian Meron Benvenisti, Israeli journalist Gideon Levy, former Zionist and British–American historian Tony Judt and liberal Zionist and former two-state advocate Peter Beinart.[56] The basic idea is that the state would protect not only individual rights but also national rights, ensuring each nation's autonomy in terms of language and communal affairs, while joint institutions would manage issues of common concern such as the economy, defence and foreign policy. Binational proposals have included cantonal, federal and simpler configurations. A modern example is Belgium, where communities with a long history of conflict live in a federal union.

However, I fear that a binational state would perpetuate and exacerbate present feelings of separation under a different name. Moreover, the asymmetry in terms of economic and social equality between today's Jewish Israelis and non-Jewish Israelis is already hard to bridge within Israel proper, while disparity between the broader Israeli and Palestinian societies is so glaring that it would impair harmonious coexistence between the two communities. Such a state would also suffer from the same structural weakness of confessional states such as Lebanon; inherently unstable and a fertile ground for violence, nepotism and corruption.

In my opinion, as someone who has consistently called for a justice-based coexistence between the two Semitic peoples, what is needed is a complete change of paradigm and the creation of a secular, non-racial, non-sectarian, democratic state with equal civil, political, economic and social rights for all of its citizens, regardless of their religion or ethnicity. Here emphasis would be placed on the individual rather than the community. That would require the introduction of a one-person one-vote universal-suffrage system. Like the binational model, the unitary democratic state model is not new. It was notably espoused by the PLO in 1969 when it called for a 'democratic state of Palestine' that would encompass 'all Palestinians, including Muslims, Christians and Jews'.[57]

The unitary-state vision, once seen as utopian or unworkable, has regained popularity over the years, with supporters among both Palestinians and Israelis as well as in academic and intellectual circles, and is now reflected in mainstream discourse on Israel–Palestine as well as forming the basis for detailed discussions and conceptualisations about how it could be structured in practice.[58] It has been embraced particularly by youth movements, which tend to be highly progressive, universalist and opposed on principle to exclusive forms of nationalism.

The name of the state should be neutral – one possibility might be the Holy Land. The official languages of the state would be Hebrew, Arabic and English. National, ethnic or religious collective identities would be protected through constitutional guarantees, while one joint overarching multicultural identity is fostered. Thus, any concerns of the Jewish community that they would become a minority and face discrimination would be alleviated and any such possibility precluded. Such concerns were also expressed by white Afrikaners, who feared that an end to apartheid in South Africa would usher in retribution from the Black majority. This never happened. On the contrary, history has shown that once relationships are no longer defined by domination but instead by equality, even previously hostile communities can end up living in peace. As the German-American philosopher Herbert Marcuse wrote in 1972, 'lasting protection for the Jewish people cannot be found in the creation of a self-enclosed, isolated, fear-stricken majority, but only in the coexistence of Jews and Arabs as citizens with equal rights and liberties'.[59]

In Jerusalem, 1999

As someone who has lived in Switzerland for more than thirty years, the idea of people from diverse linguistic, cultural and religious backgrounds living harmoniously together with equal rights after centuries of war – as the Swiss actually do – is no armchair theorising. It is feasible. Ordinary Israelis and Palestinians can also see the value of reconfiguring their relationships and can accept to convert a fraction of the energy now expended on fighting each other to override all dogmas and embark on the creation of a single truly democratic state. With the right stewardship they will realise and show the world that not only can Jews and Palestinians live together peacefully as equals, as they have done in the past, but that they can also prosper together and build a model of coexistence for the world. I am aware that achieving this would be a very tall order, but many historical events – from the fall of the Berlin Wall to the end of apartheid in South Africa – seemed impossible before they happened.

As the proverb goes, he who wants to reach the spring must swim against the stream, and, as my own story has shown, where there is a will, there is always a way!

Notes

Introduction

1 *Nakba* is the Arabic word for 'catastrophe'. It is used in reference to the mass dispossession of Palestinians, turning them into refugees, and widespread destruction of Palestinian cities, towns and villages in 1948.

Chapter 1

1 A nearby village where one of its leading families bears the same name as my family.
2 I was born in 1948 during the mayhem, violence and breakdown of law and order that prevailed in Palestine at the time. There was no functioning civil administration and no birth-and-death registrations during this period, especially in rural areas, so the exact date of my birth later became a matter of speculation.
3 Walid Khalidi, *All That Remains: The Palestinian Villages Occupied and Depopulated by Israel in 1948* (Washington, DC, 1992), 211.
4 Taha Hussain, 'Mother'.
5 Walid Khalidi, 'Revisiting the UNGA Partition Resolution', *Journal of Palestine Studies*, 27/1 (Autumn 1997), 5–21.
6 Note that those armistice agreements were not intended to create permanent borders but rather only to demarcate interim lines until the establishment of permanent peace treaties.
7 Ben-Zion Dinur, ed., *Sefer Toldot ha-Haganah* [The History of the Haganah] (Tel Aviv, 1973), 3, 244.

Chapter 3

1 Ofer Aderet, 'Testimonies from the Censored Deir Yassin Massacre: "They Piled Bodies and Burned Them"', *Haaretz* (16 July 2017).
2 Mary Wilson, *King Abdullah, Britain and the Making of Jordan* (Cambridge, 1990).

Chapter 6

1 Film of me with my banner can be seen at youtu.be/RI7wOUZr4Xc, at 1'34".
2 J. L. Ryan, 'The Myth of Annihilation and the Six-Day War', *Worldview*, 16/9 (1973), 38–42.
3 Hanny Hilmy, *Decolonization, Sovereignty, and Peacekeeping: The United Nations Emergency Force (UNEF), 1956–1967* (Cham, 2020), 274.

Chapter 7

1 Nabil Elaraby, 'Some Legal Implications of the 1947 Partition Resolution and the 1949 Armistice Agreements', *Law and Contemporary Problems*, 33/1 (1968), 97–109.

Chapter 8

1 Mohammad Tarbush, 'Foreword' in *Palestine or Israel?* (Durham, 1970).
2 Nur Masalha, 'The Concept of Palestine: The Conception of Palestine from the Late Bronze Age to the Modern Period', *Journal of Holy Land and Palestine Studies*, 15/2 (2016): 143–202, 144.
3 Ilene Beatty, 'The Land of Canaan', in Walid Khalidi, ed., *From Haven to Conquest: Readings in Zionism and the Palestine Problem Until 1948* (Beirut, 1971), 4.
4 Ibid., 15.
5 Ibid., 16–18.
6 Eric Fromm, 'The Problem of Power in Israel', *Jewish Newsletter*, XIV/10 (19 May 1958).
7 Or Kashti, 'In Israeli Textbooks, the Palestinians Are All but Invisible', *Haaretz* (21 June 2020).

8 Folke Bernadotte, 'Progress Report of the UN Mediator on Palestine', for the United Nations General Assembly (16 September 1948), ISA FM 2527/9, unispal.un.org/pdfs/AB14D4AAFC4E1BB985256204004F55FA.pdf, accessed online.
9 Later translated into English: Ghassan Kanafani, *Men in the Sun*, Hilary Kilpatrick, tr. (Boulder, CO, 1999).

Chapter 9

1 Benny Morris, *The Birth of the Palestinian Refugee Problem: 1947–1949* (Cambridge, 1989), 63.
2 Benny Morris, *The Birth of the Palestinian Refugee Problem Revisited* (Cambridge, 2003), 166.
3 Shukry Bishara became minister of finance and planning in the Palestinian Authority in 2013.
4 Bradley Burston, 'The "Exodus" Effect: The Monumentally Fictional Israel That Remade American Jewry', *Haaretz* (9 November 2012).
5 Leon Uris, *Exodus* (New York, NY, 1958), 216.
6 John J. Mearsheimer and Stephen M. Walt, *The Israel Lobby and U.S. Foreign Policy* (New York, NY, 2007), 79.
7 Uris, *Exodus*, 228.
8 Ibid., 213.

Chapter 10

1 Sir Isaiah Berlin, quoted in Michael Zander, 'Dr Walter Zander 8 June 1898–7 April 1993', 7, walterzander.info/acrobat/Memorial.pdf, accessed online.
2 Ahad Ha'am, 'Emet me-erets Yisra'el' [Truth from the Land of Israel], quoted in Walter Zander, *Is This the Way? A Call to Jews* (London, 1948), 8, accessed online.
3 Ibid., 26.
4 Zander, *Is this the Way?*, 15–16.
5 Taylor Owen and Ben Kiernan, 'Making More Enemies than We Kill? Calculating U.S. Bomb Tonnages Dropped on Laos and Cambodia, and Weighing Their Implications', *The Asia-Pacific Journal*, 13/17/3 (2015).

6 I asked the Oxford Union whether transcripts of the speeches still existed, but unfortunately none were kept.
7 Alfred Lilienthal, *The Other Side of the Coin: An American Perspective of the Arab–Israeli Conflict* (New York, NY, 1965), 92.
8 This trend continues today. In recent years examples of people who were fired, suspended from their jobs or made to resign as a result of their stance for justice for Palestinians include Professor David Miller (UK), NBC correspondent Ayman Mohyeldin (USA), Professor Steven Salaita (USA), reporter Emily Wilder (USA), United Nations expert William Schabas and Labour Party member and co-founder of the Jewish Voice for Labour Naomi Wimborne-Idrissi (UK).
9 'Iraq – No Bitterness Before the Provocations of Zionism', *Guardian* (12 September 1975).
10 Sir Francis Humphrys to the UK Foreign Office, December 1934: Eastern, E 7707/6495/93.
11 Peter Mandelson, *The Third Man* (London, 2010), 58.
12 Ehud Avriel, *Open the Gates!* (London, 1975), 27.
13 Tom Segev, *The Seventh Million: The Israelis and the Holocaust* (New York, NY, 2000), 28.
14 Mohammad Tarbush, 'Arab uses of wealth', *The Times* (6 July 1976).
15 James A. Malcolm, *Origins of the Balfour Declaration: Dr. Weizmann's Contribution* (reprint edn., California, 1983).
16 'To Be Fair to Both', *The Times* (1 November 1969).
17 Edward W. Said, *The Question of Palestine* (New York, NY, 1979), 175.

Chapter 11

1 The events that took place at Camp David in September 1978 are often referred to as Camp David I, while the summer 2000 summit between the Palestinian Authority and Israel is known as Camp David II.
2 Connor McCarthy, 'A Palestinian Question, An Israel Case', *Politico*; see also Norman G. Finkelstein, *Image and Reality*

of the Israel–Palestinian Conflict (London and New York, NY, 2001), 135.

3 Jimmy Carter, 'For Israel, Land or Peace', *The Washington Post* (26 November 2000).

4 Ibid.

5 Basic Law: Jerusalem, Capital of Israel, passed by the Israeli Knesset on 30 July 1980.

6 Israel Shahak and Morton Mezvinsky, *Jewish Fundamentalism in Israel* (London, 1999), 72.

Chapter 12

1 Christo and Jeanne-Claude, *The Mastaba* (Knokke-Heist, 2007), 88.

2 The average annual population growth rate in the period 1980–5 in the West Bank and the Gaza Strip was 2.4 per cent and 2.9 per cent, respectively; see Dr Wael R. Ennab, *Population and Demographic Developments in the West Bank and Gaza Strip Until 1990* (United Nations Conference on Trade and Development, 1994), 22.

3 Marc Lee Raphael, *A History of the United Jewish Appeal 1939–1982* (Reprint edn., Providence, RI, 2020), 155.

4 'United Jewish Appeal Raises $640 Million in '84 Campaign', *The New York Times* (24 June 1984).

5 'UPA earns Charity Navigator's highest rating yet again,' United Palestinian Appeal [blog], (15 March 2018), upaconnect.org/upa-earns-charity-navigators-highest-rating-yet-again/, accessed online. See the ratings at charitynavigator.org/ein/112494808.

6 Zakaria al-Shaikh, 'Sabra and Shatila 1982: Resisting the Massacre', *Journal of Palestine Studies*, 14/1 (1984), 57–90, 57.

Chapter 13

1 United Nations Security Council draft resolution S/15185 (8 June 1982), available from documents-dds-ny.un.org/doc/UNDOC/GEN/N82/162/67/PDF/N8216267.pdf, accessed online.

2 United Nations Security Council draft resolution S/15255/Rev. 2 (25 June 1982), available from documents-dds-ny.un.org/doc/UNDOC/GEN/N82/180/61/PDF/N8218061.pdf, accessed online.
3 My response to Henry Kissinger's comments, letter, *International Herald Tribune* (3 July 1982).
4 Mearsheimer and Walt, *The Israel Lobby*, 47.
5 Mohammad Tarbush, 'The warnings that the world would not heed', *The Observer* (26 September 1982); Mohammad Tarbush, 'What Are the Palestinian People Supposed to Feel Now?', *International Herald Tribune* (28 September 1982).
6 Geula Cohen, 'Too Many Attacks on Jews in Palestine', *International Herald Tribune* (14 October 1982).
7 Mohammad Tarbush, 'In Palestine: Room for Debate?', *International Herald Tribune* (25 October 1982).
8 Forwarded to the Chief Secretary of the Palestine government, Sir Henry Gurney, by Richard C. Catling, Assistant Inspector General of the Criminal Investigation Division, on April 13, 14 and 16, 1948, dossier no. 179/110/17/GS, deiryassin.org/survivors.html, accessed online.
9 Erskine B. Childers, 'The Other Exodus', *The Spectator* (12 May 1961).
10 Salwa was the small Tunisian town that became home to the PLO's headquarters after Beirut.
11 Mearsheimer and Walt, *The Israel Lobby*, 33, 34, 51.
12 President John F. Kennedy, State of the Union Address, 11 January 1962.

Chapter 14

1 Cheryl A. Rubenberg, *Israel and the American National Interest: A Critical Examination* (Champaign, IL, 1986), 341.
2 Ibid.
3 Review, *The New York Times* (30 September 1983).
4 Review, *Village Voice* (11 October 1983).

5 David Lamb, 'Veil's Revival Reflects Women's Status in Islam', *International Herald Tribune* (22 December 1983).
6 Quran, 4:124.
7 This documentary was later played on her television show in the USA and at the UN in New York and Geneva. Martha Stuart Papers, 'Are You Listening: "Palestinians."' (Schlesinger Library, Radcliffe Institute, 1981), Vt-43.82, available at mps.lib.harvard.edu/sds/video/448079037, accessed online.
8 Joan Peters, *From Time Immemorial: The Origins of the Arab-Jewish Conflict over Palestine* (New York, NY, 1984).
9 Finkelstein, *Image and Reality of the Israel–Palestine Conflict*, 30.
10 Ibid.
11 Albert Hourani, 'An Ancient War', *Observer* (3 March 1985).
12 Ian Gilmour and David Gilmour, 'Pseudo-Travellers', *London Review of Books*, 7/2 (7 February 1985), accessed online.
13 Finkelstein, *Image and Reality of the Israel–Palestine Conflict*, 67.
14 An abridged version of the proceedings was published as a book entitled *Crossed Wires: Improving Media Relationships Between the Arabs and the West* (London, 1985).
15 Ibid., 161.
16 Ibid., 207.
17 Ibid., 246.
18 Ibid., 102.
19 Ibid., 168.

Chapter 15

1 Avram Seal, 'The First Intifada: How the Arab–Israeli Conflict Was Transformed', *Haaretz* (13 December 2012).
2 'Fatalities in the First Intifada', B'Tselem, btselem.org/statistics/first_intifada_tables, accessed online.
3 Amira Hass, 'Broken Bones and Broken Hips', *Haaretz* (4

November 2005); 'Colonel Says Rabin Ordered Breaking of Palestinians' Bones', *Los Angeles Times* (22 June 1990).

4 Julius Berman, 'Confidential Memorandum, Breakfast Meeting with Dr Henry Kissinger, 425 Park Avenue, NY, 10022', February 1988, published as 'Kissinger Behind Closed Doors', *Harper's Magazine* (June 1988). Also reprinted at oldwebsite.palestine-studies.org/sites/default/files/jps-articles/jps.2002.31.4.99.pdf.

5 Israel Shahak, 'What Are My Opinions?', *SWASIA*, 1/48 (27 November 1974).

6 Shahak and Mezvinsky, *Jewish Fundamentalism in Israel*, 77.

7 Edward W. Said, *The Question of Palestine*, (New York, NY, 1980), 113–114

8 Aimé Césaire, *Discourse on Colonialism*, Joan Pinkham, tr. (New York, NY, 2000), 41.

9 Mohammad Tarbush, 'From Old-Fashioned Pickle to New-Fashioned Semitism', *International Herald Tribune* (23 August 1986).

10 This was not just a fleeting idea. In 1985 I told Uri Avnery that by pooling our talents our two peoples could become a great regional power. See Uri Avnery, *My Friend, the Enemy* (London, 1986), 56.

Chapter 16

1 Costs of War, Watson Institute of International and Public Affairs, Brown University, watson.brown.edu/costsofwar/, accessed online.

2 In 1990 Iraq's GDP was US$179.9 billion with a US$10,000 per capita income. After Kuwait its GDP and per capita income shrank by 96 per cent to US$7 billion and US$384 respectively.

3 Jean-Claude Maurice, *Si Vous le Répétez, Je Démentirai: Chirac, Sarkozy, Villepin* (Paris, 2009), 49.

4 'O'Neill: Bush Planned Iraq Invasion Before 9/11', CNN (14 January 2004), accessed online.

5 Joel Roberts, 'Plans for Iraq Attack Began on 9/11', CBS News (4 September 2002), accessed online.

Chapter 17

1 Edward W. Said, *The Edward Said Reader*, Moustafa Bayoumi, Andrew Rubin, eds. (New York, NY, 2000), 438.
2 'PLO Chairman Arafat's Speech at the Signing of the Declaration of Principles – English (1993)', available at the Economic Cooperation Foundation, ecf.org.il/media_items/1229, accessed online.
3 Yossi Beilin as quoted in Geoffrey Aronson, 'Settlement Monitor: Quarterly Update on Developments', *Journal of Palestine Studies*, 25/3 (1996), 131–139, 138.
4 Edward W. Said, *The End of the Peace Process: Oslo and After* (London, 2001), 170.
5 'Arab Boycott Said to Cost Israel $45 Billion over the Past 40 Years', *Jewish Telegraphic Agency* (7 August 1992).
6 Mohammad Tarbush, 'Peace and Belligerent Settlements Are Not Compatible', *International Herald Tribune* (27 April 1998).
7 Akiva Eldar, 'Peace Awaits Beyond Rancor', *International Herald Tribune* (15 May 1998).
8 Ian Gilmour, 'Israeli Settlements', *International Herald Tribune* (28 May 1998).
9 Flavius Josephus, *The War of the Jews*, William Whiston, tr., n.p., Book III, Chapter 3, Clause 4.
10 Mark Twain, *The Innocents Abroad* (Hartford, CT, 1869), 176.
11 J. V. W. Shaw, 'A Survey of Palestine: Prepared in December 1945 and January 1946 for the Information of the Anglo-American Committee of Inquiry', Volume 1 (Jerusalem, 1946).
12 Twain, *The Innocents Abroad*, 165.
13 Ibid., 208.
14 Salman Abu-Sitta, 'The Implementation of the Right to Return', *The Palestine-Israel Journal of Politics, Economics and Culture*, 15–16/3, 2008.

Chapter 18

1 Stephen Zunes, 'Peace Process', in Robert E. Looney, ed., *Handbook of US–Middle East Relations* (London and New York, NY, 2009), 142.
2 Mearsheimer and Walt, *The Israel Lobby*, 47.
3 Ibid.
4 Zunes, 'Peace Process', in Looney, ed., *Handbook of US–Middle East Relations*, 143.
5 Aaron David Miller, 'Israel's Lawyer', *The Washington Post* (23 May 2005).
6 Kathleen Christison, 'Camp David Redux', *CounterPunch* (15 August, 2005), accessed online.
7 Robert Malley and Hussein Agha, 'Camp David: The Tragedy of Errors', *New York Review of Books* (9 August, 2001).
8 Aviva and Shmuel Bar-Am, 'Stunning Views from Goliath's Hometown Show Its Ancient Strategic Importance', *The Times of Israel* (24 April 2021).
9 The New York Times (26 July 2000), as quoted in Looney, ed., Handbook of US–Middle East Relations, 142.
10 Jane Perlez, 'U.S. Mideast Envoy Recalls the Day Pandora's Box Wouldn't Shut', *The New York Times* (29 January 2001).
11 Benjy Singer, 'Senior Rabbis Rule: It's Forbidden to Go Up to the Temple Mount', *The Jerusalem Post* (10 August 2019); Jeremy Sharon, 'Chief Rabbis Reimpose Ban on Jews Visiting Temple Mount', *The Jerusalem Post* (2 December 2013).
12 Motti Inbari, 'Religious Zionism and the Temple Mount Dilemma – Key Trends', *Israel Studies*, 12/2 (Summer 2007), 30.
13 Ibid., 29.
14 Vijay Prashad, 'Palestine's Intifada: The Process of Liberation is Irresistible', *CounterPunch* (19 October 2015), accessed online.
15 Glossary, Just Vision, accessed online.
16 Charles Enderlin, *Les Années Perdues* (Paris, 2006), 26.

17 'Rabbi Calls for Annihilation of Arabs', BBC News (10 April 2001), accessed online.
18 United Nations General Assembly Resolution 37/43, 'Right of Peoples to Self-Determination', UN Doc A/RES/37/43 (3 December 1982).
19 'One Year of the al-Aqsa Intifada', B'Tselem, btselem.org/press_releases/20010924, accessed online.
20 *Israel and the Occupied Territories: Shielded from Scrutiny: IDF Violations in Jenin and Nablus* (London: Amnesty International, 2002), 1.
21 Thomas Fuller, 'European Poll Calls Israel a Big Threat to World Peace,' *The New York Times* (31 October 2003); Peter Beaumont, 'Israel Outraged as EU Poll Names It a Threat to Peace,' *Guardian* (2 November 2003).
22 Seymour M. Hersh, *The Samson Option: Israel's Nuclear Arsenal and American Foreign Policy* (New York, NY, 1991), 97.
23 According to the Oslo Accords Paris Protocol, among other taxes, those on imports into the Palestinian territories and indirect taxes on Israeli goods exported to the Palestinian territories are collected by Israel on behalf of the Palestinian Authority. Israel then transfers these taxes to the PA, subject to a 3 per cent administration fee. Since 1994 Israel has used those taxes as an invisible, invincible weapon. It has withheld or released them as a function of how it assessed the behaviour of the PA and deployed them openly to pressurise the PA.
24 Michele K. Esposito, 'The Israeli Arsenal Deployed Against Gaza During Operation Cast Lead', *Journal of Palestine Studies*, 38/3 (Spring 2009), 175–91; George E. Bisharat, 'Israel's Invasion of Gaza in International Law', *Denver Journal of International Law & Policy*, 38/1 (2009), 41–114.
25 'Fatalities During Cast Lead', B'Tselem, statistics.btselem.org/en/stats/during-cast-lead/by-date-of-incident, accessed online.

26 *Israel/Gaza: Operation 'Cast Lead': 22 Days of Death and Destruction* (London: Amnesty International, 2009), 75–7.
27 Alexander G. Higgins, 'Mideast war crimes probe has unusual leader', *The San Diego Union-Tribune* (18 April 2009).
28 'The Goldstone Report: Excerpts and Responses', *Institute for Palestine Studies*, 39/2 (2009/10), 60.
29 Ilan Pappé, 'Goldstone's Shameful U-Turn', the Palestinian Initiative for the Promotion of Global Dialogue and Democracy (6 April 2011), accessed online.
30 United Nations Office for the Coordination of Humanitarian Affairs, 'Key Figures on the 2014 Hostilities' (23 June 2015), ochaopt.org/content/key-figures-2014-hostilities, accessed online.
31 Human Rights Council, 'Report of the Independent International Commission of Inquiry on the Protests in the Occupied Palestinian Territory' (25 February 2019), accessed online.
32 Jewish Voice for Peace, 'Killed for Protesting: 6 Things to Know about the #Greatreturnmarch' (5 April 2016), jewishvoiceforpeace.org/wp-content/uploads/2018/04/Killed-for-Protesting_-6-Things-You-Need-to-Know-About-the-GreatReturnMarch.pdf, accessed online.
33 Spencer Robinson and Iain Overton, 'The Targeting of High-Rises in Gaza: An Analysis of Israel's Air Strikes on Tall Buildings in 2021', Action on Armed Violence (30 September 2021), accessed online.

Epilogue

1 Andy Clarno, *Neoliberal Apartheid: Palestine/Israel and South Africa After 1994* (Chicago, 2017), 5.
2 Theodor Herzl, in his diary 1895, quoted in Benny Morris, *Righteous Victims: A History of the Zionist–Arab Conflict, 1881–1998* (New York, NY, 2011), 20–1.
3 Patrick Wolfe, 'Settler Colonialism and the Elimination of the Native', *Journal of Genocide Research*, 8/4 (21 December 2006), 388.

4 Note that the Jewish Agency was described by the Anglo-American Committee of Inquiry, which Britain and the US dispatched to Palestine in 1946, as 'one of the most successful colonizing instruments in history'.
5 Morris, *Righteous Victims*, 144.
6 Yitzhak Rabin, leaked censored version of Rabin's memoirs, quoted in David K. Shipler 'Israel Bars Rabin from Relating '48 Eviction of Arabs', *The New York Times* (23 October 1979).
7 David Ben-Gurion, in his diary entry for 18 July 1948, quoted in Michael Bar Zohar, *Ben-Gurion: The Armed Prophet* (Englewood Cliffs, NJ, 1967), 157.
8 Morris, The Birth of the Palestinian Refugee Problem, 27.
9 Benny Morris, 'A New Exodus for the Middle East?', *Guardian* (3 October 2002).
10 Thomas Suárez, *State of Terror: How Terrorism Created Modern Israel* (Northampton, MA, 2016), 35.
11 Hans Kohn, 'Ahad Ha'am: Nationalist with a Difference', in Gary V. Smith, ed., *Zionism: The Dream and the Reality: A Jewish Critique* (New York, NY, 1974), 31.
12 Ibid., 31–2.
13 'Memorandum of Edwin Montagu on the Anti-Semitism of the Present (British) Government – Submitted to the British Cabinet, 23 August 1917', British Public Record Office, Cabinet No. 24/24 (August 1917).
14 Walter Laqueur and Barry Rubin, eds., *The Israel–Arab Reader: A Documentary History of the Middle East Conflict* (5th edn., London and New York, NY, 1995), 40.
15 For more details, see Rashid Khalidi 'The Palestinians and 1948: The Underlying Causes of Failure', in *The War for Palestine: Rewriting the History of 1948*, Eugene L. Rogan and Avi Shlaim, eds. (Cambridge, 2001), 12–36.
16 Noura Erakat, *Justice for Some: Law and the Question of Palestine* (Stanford, CA, 2019), 46.
17 Ardi Imseis, 'The United Nations Plan of Partition for Palestine Revisited: On the Origins of Palestine's

International Legal Subalternity', *Stanford Journal of International Law*, 57/1 (2021), 19.

18 Henry Cattan, *Palestine and International Law: The Legal Aspects of the Arab–Israeli Conflict* (London, 1973), 75–89; Ian Brownlie, *Principles of Public International Law* (6th edn., Oxford, 2003), 163–4.

19 Suárez, *State of Terror*, 237.

20 Simha Flapan, *The Birth of Israel: Myths and Realities* (London and Sydney, 1987), 22.

21 Suárez, *State of Terror*, 273.

22 For further reading, refer to Ilan Pappé, *The Ethnic Cleansing of Palestine* (London, 2007).

23 This is according to an investigative report by *Haaretz* and the Akevot Institute for Israeli–Palestinian Conflict Research carried out in December 2021. See Adam Raz, 'There's a Mass Palestinian Grave at a Popular Israeli Beach, Veterans Confess', *Haaretz* (20 January 2022).

24 Ilan Pappé', *Ten Myths About Israel* (London and New York, NY, 2017), 64.

25 Adam Shatz, 'Ghosts in the Land', *London Review of Books*, 43/11 (3 June 2021).

26 Begin's association with these groups had led Albert Einstein and more than twenty other Jewish intellectuals to write a letter to *The New York Times*, published on 4 December 1948, stating: 'It is inconceivable that those who oppose fascism throughout the world, if correctly informed as to Mr Begin's political record and perspectives, could add their names and support to the movement he represents.'

27 Virginia Tilley, ed., *Beyond Occupation: Apartheid, Colonialism and International Law in the Occupied Palestinian Territories* (London, 2012), 52.

28 In 2013 Israeli filmmaker Yotam Feldman released an investigative documentary entitled *The Lab*, which shows how large Israeli companies test their weapons on Palestinians.

29 Prince Karim Aga Khan, 'A New Beginning for

International Press Cooperation', keynote address to the International Press Institute's 30th Annual General Assembly, Nairobi, Kenya (2 March 1981), barakah.com/2017/08/04/on-media-advice-from-the-aga-khan-for-a-new-beginning-for-the-worlds-press/, accessed online.

30 Avi Shlaim, 'It's Now Clear: The Oslo Peace Accords Were Wrecked by Netanyahu's Bad Faith', *Guardian* (12 September 2013).

31 'Macron Announces Measures to Combat Anti-Semitism in France', France24 (20 February 2019), accessed online.

32 Peter Beinart, 'Debunking the Myth that Anti-Zionism Is Antisemitic', *Guardian* (7 May 2019).

33 B'Tselem, 'This Is Apartheid: The Israeli Regime Promotes and Perpetuates Jewish Supremacy Between the Mediterranean Sea and the Jordan River' (12 January 2021), accessed online.

34 Human Rights Watch, 'A Threshold Crossed: Israeli Authorities and the Crimes of Apartheid and Persecution' (27 April 2021), accessed online.

35 Oren Yifatchel, *Ethnocracy: Land and Identity Politics in Israel/Palestine* (Philadelphia, PA, 2006), jacket text.

36 These are, respectively, Michael Ben-Yair, Yossi Sarid, Shulamit Aloni and Alon Liel. See Mehdi Hasan, 'Saying Israel Is Guilty of Apartheid Isn't Antisemitic: Just Ask These Israeli Leaders', MSNBC (27 May 2021).

37 Philissa Cramer, 'Dozens of US Rabbinical Students Sign Letter Calling for American Jews to Hold Israel Accountable for Its Human Rights Abuses', Jewish Telegraphic Agency (14 May 2021), accessed online.

38 Asaf Shalev, 'Jewish Employees Urge Google to Support Palestinians, Cancel Contracts', *The Jerusalem Post*, 20 May 2021.

39 Na'amod: naamod.org.uk.

40 Evyatar Friesel, 'Jews Against Zionism/Israel: On the Ambivalences of Contemporary Jewish Identity', in Armin Lange et al., *Comprehending and Confronting*

Antisemitism: A Multi-Faceted Approach (Boston, MA and Berlin, 2019), 417.

41 Give Peace a Chance, Brussels Meeting, General Commission for International Relations, 18 March 1988.

42 Moshe Menuhin, 'Jewish critics of Zionism: a testamentary essay, with the stifling and smearing of a dissenter', Arab Information Center (New York, NY, 1974).

43 'The Guardian View on Israel and Palestine: Escape the Past', *Guardian* (1 November 2017), accessed online.

44 From a speech delivered by Edward W. Said to the American-Arab Anti-Discrimination Committee in Washington, DC, later reprinted as 'Dignity and Solidarity' in Edward W. Said, *The Selected Works of Edward Said, 1966–2006*, Moustafa Bayoumi, Andrew Rubin, eds. (New York, NY, 2019), 518.

45 United Nations General Assembly, Report of the Secretary-General, 'Israeli Settlements in the Occupied Palestinian Territory, Including East Jerusalem, and the Occupied Syrian Golan', UN Doc A/67/375 (2012), para. 7.

46 Comments broadcast on Israeli radio, Agence France-Presse (15 November 1998).

47 International Court of Justice, Advisory Opinion, 'Legal Consequences of the Construction of a Wall in the Occupied Palestinian Territory' (2004).

48 United Nations General Assembly, Report of the Secretary-General, 'Israeli Settlements in the Occupied Palestinian Territory, Including East Jerusalem, and the Occupied Syrian Golan', UN Doc A/68/513 (2013), para. 13.

49 United Nations General Assembly, Report of the Secretary-General, 'Israeli settlements in the Occupied Palestinian Territory, including East Jerusalem, and the occupied Syrian Golan', UN Doc A/67/375 (2012), para. 41.

50 Padraig O'Malley, *The Two-State Delusion: Israel and Palestine – A Tale of Two Narratives* (New York, NY, 2016).

51 Isaac Asimov, *In Joy Still Felt: The Autobiography of Isaac Asimov 1954–1978*, quoted by Edward Corrigan in 'Is It

Anti-Semitism to Defend Palestinian Human Rights? Jewish Opposition to Zionism', *Dissident Voice* (1 September 2009), accessed online.

52 Ghada Karmi, 'The One-State Solution: An Alternative Vision for Israeli–Palestinian Peace', *Journal of Palestine Studies*, 40/2 (January 2011), 67.

53 Jeff Halper, 'The "One Democratic State Campaign" for a Multicultural Democratic State in Palestine/Israel', *Socialist Project* (24 May 2018), accessed online.

54 Eitan Bronstein Aparicio, 'The Role of Israeli Jews in Planning for Palestinian Return', +972 *Magazine* (10 May 2016), accessed online.

55 Edward W. Said, 'The One-State Solution', *The New York Times Magazine* (10 January 1999): 'I see no other way than to begin now to speak about sharing the land that has thrust us together, sharing it in a truly democratic way, with equal rights for each citizen.'

56 Peter Beinart, 'Yavne: A Jewish Case for Equality in Israel-Palestine', *Jewish Currents* (7 July 2020), accessed online: 'It is time for liberal Zionists to abandon the goal of Jewish–Palestinian separation and embrace the goal of Jewish–Palestinian equality.'

57 Karmi, 'The One-State Solution', 69.

58 For example, the One Democratic State Campaign, onestatecampaign.org/en/about-us/, established in Haifa, works to evolve 'into a broad popular movement, guided by a clear political program, a participatory and transparent grassroots organization, and an effective strategy for achieving our goal of a democratic state throughout historic Palestine'.

59 Herbert Marcuse, 'Israel Is Strong Enough to Concede', tr., *The Jerusalem Post* (2 January 1972).

Acknowledgements

Throughout my life, I was fortunate to meet and be surrounded by amazing people who had a substantive impact on my intellectual and personal development. They include members of my family, my teachers, my friends and my professional colleagues. Through our social interactions and frequent dialogues, I sometimes felt like a participant in a perpetual seminar. In a variety of ways, they, together with the other friends cited in the narrative, are the silent contributors to this book – without, of course, any one of them being responsible for its content. To them all, I would like to express my deepest affection and gratitude.

During my student years in Britain, I was lucky to have been taught and guided by caring tutors who showed limitless generosity in opening my mind to critical thinking and in sharing their vast knowledge and experience with me, leaving a lasting impact on my world view. I am eternally grateful to Albert Hourani, Wilfrid Knapp, Roger Owen, Robert Mabro, Derek Hopwood, Leslie Brooks, Henry Tudor, Charles Reynolds, David Manning, William Hale, John Burton, John Groom and Dennis Sandole.

My working life was resolutely pleasant and stimulating thanks to the support, generosity and shared skills of a multitude of colleagues with whom my professional relationship often transitioned into a lasting friendship. Roger Azar, Richard Steinig, Bruno Winkler, René Wagner, Christian Reckmann, Herbert Scheidt, Robert Sursock, Nicholas Bradshaw, Peter Skelton, Yves Lamarche, Jeanine Dhallenne, Dominique Santini, Marie-France Belthé, Martin Boyer, Philippe Jabre, William Wainwright, Bruno Meier, Isabelle Picard, Richard Nottage,

Caroline Rieder, Carolla Timull, Marcel Naef, Burkhart Klein, Hans-Jurgen Koch, Martin Hungerbühler, Peter Caminada, Lars Habenicht, Michel Adjadj, Piers Maynard, Mohamed Sammakia, John Fraser, Charles Poncet, Stephan Burgisser, Hans Roethlisberger, Giorgio Campa, Fabien Rutz, Antoine Flouty, Stéphane Mundwiler, Mona Ghafourianpour, Béatrice Chappuis, Pierre-Alain Lapaire, Pierre Dozio, Nathalie Jaggi, Jean-Marc Audétat, Lila Seirafi, Nicolas Vouilloz, Max Sinclair, Carl Heggli, Charles Burkard, Antonino Mandrà, Sloan Stutz, Aline Kleinfercher, Marianne Desponds, Jogishwar Singh, Urs Schneider and Jacques Daumier.

Last, but far from least, are the family members and friends who, at different stages of my life have, individually or collectively, been an inexhaustible source of inspiration and tenderness and, at one point or another, gave me the motivation to get up and face life with all its fickleness and beauty.

Family: Nada, Bassel, Huda, Abed, Youssef, Rania, Elham, Ghassan, Leila, Bassam, Omar, Sami, Susannah, Faten, Hayat, Fadia, Amal, Nadia, Buthaina, Khader, Zohair, Ma'moun, Bahjat, Khaled, Haya, Hiam, Husam, Rula, Amer, Bilal, Rami, Razan, Ziad, Nawal, Sarah and all the rest of the Tarbush clan in Beit Nattif and Beit Jibrin. Also, from the Abu Musallam family, Hanan, Jawad, Fathi, Zainab, Saif, Imad, Fadia, Iman, Atef, Adnan, Sana, Hamed, Mays, Yasmin, Taha, Hani, Samar, Ali, Karam, Nizar, Marwa, Amal, Hisham, Hiyam, Ziad, Fayez, Ahlam, Mariam, Sa'di, Abdallah, Nour, Ibrahim, Dima, Fuad and all the rest of the family. Finally, very special regards to all the other Beit Nattif clans, in particular Aql, Abu Halawah, Khomayess, Abu Shirra, Srour, al-Sayyed Ahmad, Abu Nahla, al-Dibis, Abu Hamad, Abu Adas, al-Rashed, Shahin and al-Bashir. As someone who has spent the bulk of his life living in exile in the diaspora, I am sure that this list is incomplete. I count on the indulgence of those whose names are not listed.

Friends: Nabil Hijazi, Bassam Arafat, Gilbert Sinoué, Huda Kitmitto, Cameron Ott, Andrew and Martin Knapp, Rana Kabbani, Angelica Milia, Abir and Fadia Bamieh, Betty Palmisano, Rana and Muwafak Bibi, the Trio Joubran – Adnan,

Wissam and Samir – Sirine Hadhili, Leila Chahid, Nabil Sha'ath, Rashed al-Rashed, Monique Chemillier-Gendreau, Ali bin Musallam, his wife Faiza al-Jarba and their children Hanouf, Maha, Anoud and Mansour, Youla Haddadin and Ibrahim Khraishi, Martine and Caroline Lyanaz, Robert Donahue, Nabil Chreif, Lucile Bacha, Labib Kamhawi, Shahnaz and Shahbaz Shahnavaz, Walter Wells, Asa'd Abdul-Rahman, Ahmad Fakhro, Youssef Zaman, Farzaneh Pirouz, Taraneh and Farshid Asgari, Mariam Tamari, Charles Pictet, Barbara Fazzari, Peter Galbraith, Chaker Khazaal, Hail and Feryal Fahoum, Hanna Nasir, Ahmed Taleb Ibrahimi, Khalil Shehadeh, Penny Johnson and Raja Shehadeh, Abbas Amanat, Hassan al-Amri, Randa Jamal and Aissa Deebi, Mustapha Kalaji, Musa Buaidery, David McDowall, Raheek and Thierry Ador, Mariam and Dominique Bianche, Dima Asfour, Lana Matta, Suhail Shuhaibar, Rima Khalaf, Hani Hunaidy, Sahar Hunaidy, Wa'el and Mazen Ojje, Mandana Mosafer, Denis Salomon, Randa Salti, Said Hunaidy, Mohamed Mouilah, Faisal Abu Hassan, Monica Merlitti, Monther and Nadia Mojahed, Mark Inch, Sultan Jan-Mohamed, May Seikaly, Suhail Marar, Raeda Taha, Nabil Ramlawi, Imad Saissi, Johnny Rizq, Ghaith Armanazi, John Gurney, Karim Sherif, Leila and Salma Tibi, Miriame Zihri, Annie Pampanini and Ali Tayyeb.